Fiona Plender

From Monymusk

River Don

From Keig

Black Hill

Oxen Craig

Watch Craig

Hermit Seat

1500

1400

1300

1200

1100

1000

900

800

700

Little Oxen Craig

nnoch Vell

Tillymuick

Gadie Burn

600

500

Back o' Bennachie Car Park

From Premnay

500

600

700

3

4

Miles

THE BOOK OF BENNACHIE

The
Book of Bennachie

Edited by
ARCHIE W. M. WHITELEY
M.B.E., M.A., J.P.

Published by the Bailies of Bennachie
Clerk: Algy Watson, M.A., B.A.
1976

Photograph opposite :   DRIFT OXTER DEEP HAPS BENNACHIE   *Algy Watson*

Printed by
William Culross & Son Limited
Coupar Angus, Perthshire, Scotland

Foreword

By the Late LORD ABERDEEN

What can I say that is unsaid about Bennachie? From the roof of Haddo House one used to be able to see, across the green and pleasant acres of Formartine, this stark, frowning sentinel of the northern flank of the Grampians. Now the trees have grown I have to go to the top of one of our little braes to get the view.

When I was a boy I was convinced Bennachie was a volcano, and always associated it with Vesuvius about which I had read in my Children's Encyclopaedia.

In later days when frozen on the plains of Northern France, or frizzled in the sands of Egypt, the sound of the piper playing my Company March—the Back O' Bennachie—induced the most appalling nostalgia and desire to be back at home again and puff up the Mither Tap. To hell with your Alps, Rockies and Himalaya, Bennachie—the centre stone of the County of Aberdeen—is the hill for me.

Aberdeen and Temair.

Preface

We present to you a miscellany of prose and verse about Bennachie, our local mountain, which has aroused so deep affection in the hearts of all born under its shadow, especially in all exiles.

In the Foreword by the Late Lord Aberdeen, first Guardian of Bennachie, you can sense that affection. Laird, Soldier, Councillor—he was the epitome of all that was best in the North-East character.

Our debt to Dr Daniel G. Gordon, our Senior Bailie, cannot be adequately expressed. Without his untiring energy, his enthusiasm and his ceaseless help and assistance to the editor, we doubt if this publication would ever have seen the light of day.

We acknowledge with gratitude our very great debt to all our contributors and especially to the following for permission to reproduce articles, poems and photographs:

Aberdeen Journals Ltd.; Banffshire Journal Ltd.; The Deeside Field Club; Mrs Nan Campbell, Helensburgh; Dr Alexander Keith; Andrew Galloway Fordyce; A. H. M. Campbell, Fyvie; Mrs A. Mitchell, daughter of the late Dr David Rorie; Constable & Co., London; Ordnance Survey and Forestry Commission.

We are greatly indebted to all the many helpers who assisted with the typing. We regret that owing to the lack of space some of the material had to be omitted.

Our most warm thanks are due to our Printers, Messrs. William Culross & Son Ltd., Coupar Angus for their wise guidance and unfailing courtesy.

The Editor.

Contents

CONTENTS—*continued* *Page*

THE COUNCIL OF THE BAILIES OF BENNACHIE

HONORARY BAILIES

AITKEN, R. G., "Dunreath," Monymusk, Sauchen.
FORBES, The Rt. Hon. Lord, K.B.E., J.P., D.L., Balforbes, Alford.
FORBES, Master of, Finzeauch, Whitehouse, Alford.
FORD, Henry, 27 Hillcrest Avenue, Market Harborough, Leicester.
GODWIN, Gunnar, c/o Forestry Commission, 6 Queensgate, Aberdeen.
GRANT, Lady, House of Monymusk, Monymusk.
GRAY, Alexander L., 131 High Street, Inverurie.
HUTTON, Ernest, 1 Maryfield Place, Inverurie.
KEITH, Dr Alexander, Fetteresso Lodge, Bath Street, Stonehaven.
MEARNS, Robert A., "Clach Dhian," Mortimers Lane, Inverurie.
RICHARDS, E. G., "Midmar," Orchard Way, Esher, Surrey.
SMITH, G. R. T., Pittodrie House, Pitcaple.
WOOD, Rev. Dr. James, 10 Westfield Terrace, Aberdeen.
WOODHAM, Dr A. A., "Clava," Cuninghill Road, Inverurie.

Senior Bailie: Dr D. G. GORDON, Inverurie.
Deputy Senior Bailie: JAMES R. MACKAY, Blairdaff, Inverurie.
Clerk: ALGY WATSON, Springbank, Oyne.
Treasurer: LESLIE G. ANDERSON, Oldmeldrum.
Warden of the East Marches: Dr JAMES GILL, Inverurie.
Warden of the West Marches: Dr DOUGLAS L. STEWART, Insch.
Warden of the North Marches: WILLIAM TAYLOR, Oyne.
Warden of the South Marches: A. W. M. WHITELEY, Monymusk.
Wardens of the High Tops: A. WALKER, JOHN STEPHEN, JOHNSTON HAY, Inverurie.
Lady Bailie: Mrs HELEN FRASER, Aquithie, Kemnay.

Editorial Committee

Mrs Helen Fraser, The Master of Forbes, Dr D. G. Gordon, James R. MacKay, Dr Douglas L. Stewart, A. H. Watson, A. W. M. Whiteley (Convener).

THE BAILIES OF BENNACHIE

By Dr D. G. Gordon

This voluntary conservation group came into being when a half dozen friends of Bennachie called a public meeting in Inverurie Town Hall on 9th May 1973. Distressed by the increasing mass of litter and broken glass left on the mountain by the thoughtless among the increasing thousands of climbers, they felt that a membership of around fifty might be hoped for, enough to provide wardens and helpers. The name of Bailie, suggested by Dr James Gill, caught the public imagination. Its connotation was twofold, the town bailie caring for the law and order of his burgh, the country bailie caring for the comfort of his cattle . . . .

We grew in numbers. We had much favourable publicity. In our third year we have over nine hundred bailies who have paid the modest Life Membership of one pound. We produced a Welcome to Bennachie booklet. The first printing of one thousand copies in May 1974 was paid for by the Inverurie philanthropist, Mr Alexander L. Gray. Each bailie received a free copy and a second impression of over two thousand printed in August 1974, including two hundred gifted by the printer, Mr Robert W. Minto, is sold out.

What are our objectives? They are four-fold:
(1) To preserve amenity and fight litter and vandalism.
(2) To preserve rights of way and footpaths.
(3) To study the geology and biology of the mountain and to preserve the flora and fauna.
(4) To collect and preserve the bibliography of Bennachie.

The three lairds of Bennachie, Lady Grant of Monymusk, Lord Forbes succeeded by his son the Master of Forbes and Mr Theo Smith of Pittodrie, along with the Conservator for East of Scotland of the Forestry Commission were made Honorary Bailies, becoming automatically Members of Council. Seven Wardens were appointed, three for the High Tops and one for each of the four marches. The Council was completed by a Lady Bailie, a Senior Bailie and Deputy, and a Clerk and a Treasurer.

Have our aims been fulfilled? We have been very active. The Council has met many times, sometimes in Inverurie Academy, more often in the homes of Council members, where we have been most hospitably entertained.

The Wardens have been at their vigilant best. Compliments and congratulations to the Bailies on the lessening of litter have been numerous. It is a never-ending task, but by example and precept we think we are gaining the young as supporters. Possibly our most useful labours have been the laying and maintenance of steppingstones across the bog above the Rushmill Burn on the path to the Mither Tap. A second labour of love has been the removal of the loose stones on the paths through the hill fort walks. Neither have been herculean tasks, but numerous willing hands have given their mead of toil and sweat to a continuous service.

Our three summer rallies have been held at the Forestry Commission picnic spot at the Back o' Bennachie. Blessed on each occasion by the best of weather, we attracted an attendance of a hundred and fifty in 1973, three hundred odd in 1974, and around four hundred and fifty in 1975. Our autumn rallies have been held in the Inverurie Academy Hall by courtesy of the Rector, Dr Norman Dixon, an enthusiastic bailie. They start with the Annual General Meeting and Council and Financial Reports, followed by a short concert and tea interval and talks illustrated by colour slides and films. Noteworthy were the contributions of Algy Watson and James MacKay, showing wonderful pictures of Bennachie scenery and wild life and a film on the Golden Eagle taken in the Cairngorms by Dr Gordon Beattie, whose talk on the adventure of its taking gave rare enjoyment. A thought-provoking illustrated talk on erosion, dramatically entitled "Are We Trampling Our Mountains to Death?" was given by Dr N. Bayfield of the Nature Conservancy.

Three of our bailies, Louise Donald, May Thomson and Will Maitland have given notable service in verse-speaking at the recitals of Flo Garry's poems in Aberdeen and Peterhead in 1975. It all started with Will Maitland reciting Mrs Garry's classic "Foo Auld's Bennachie" at our autumn rally in 1974. The publication of her collected poems "Bennygoak and Other Poems in the Buchan Dialect" late in 1974 has run into several editions. It was natural that the Glasgow firm of Scotsoun, makers of many cassettes of the Scottish dialects, should make a cassette of Bennygoak, with readings by Flo Garry herself, Douglas Kynoch of the Aberdeen B.B.C. and Will Maitland. To launch the venture, a company of over a hundred, including Professor and Mrs Garry and Dr Philp, Secretary of Scotsoun, climbed the slopes of Bennachie. Looking across the tapestry of the fields of the Garioch to the hills of Bennygoak and the great plain of Buchan, the voices of our three bailies carried on the still autumn air the richness of our native tongue, the doric once described by Ruskin as the most musical in the land. It was an unique occasion. Flo Garry, visibly moved, thanked them. We came down to earth to the foot of the hill, to the welcome of Theo Smith's Rowan Tree, to hear the cassette, while we savoured the hot tea and home-baked scones.

The botanical expedition to Bennachie on 23rd August 1975, led by Professor C. H. Gimingham assisted by Mrs Somerville and James Mackay, was a sheer delight. Over a hundred different specimens were catalogued.

The Council were invited in July 1975 to the opening of the Forestry Commission Information Centre at Woodend in the Lord's Throat. Lady Grant graciously proclaimed it open and planted a commemorative tree. Another was planted by the Senior Bailie on the Bailies' behalf.

The opening in June 1975 of the Rowan Tree beside Pittodrie car park has been a great boon. We are grateful to Mr Theo Smith, the laird of Pittodrie, one of our most enthusiastic bailies, for this amenity and would congratulate him on its construction, its furnishings and its cuisine, which have earned high praise and merited popularity.

The unveiling of the indicator on the Mither Tap on 15th July 1974 ended a saga of real team effort by the Masters and Pupils of Inverurie Academy, who made the top of copper, cement and bullet-proof glass. It was a triumph of craftsmanship. The building of the cairn involved real hard labour for the pupils in carrying cement, sand, water and rocks up the steepest of slopes, involving innumerable journeys. In overall charge, Mr James MacKay as instigator of the Academy effort, with the help of Algy Watson, did the orienteering, the mapping of bearings, often making vain journeys in poor visibility. Ernest Hutton and Robert Mearns, as Masters of theory and practice, were the invaluable artificers of the indicator and were made Honorary Bailies in token of their labour. A week or two later there was a fairy tale ending. Robert Mearns and Tommy Angus invited Mr Henry Ford, an English business man on holiday for a game of bowls on the Inverurie Green and when told of the project and its cost, Mr Ford wrote a cheque for fifty pounds, an amazing act of generosity for which the Bailies remain grateful.

The local Boy Scouts, under Dr Geoffrey Gill, as their project for their jubilee in autumn 1974, spent a whole day cutting back the heather overlapping the Craigshannoch path and made a grand job of it.

For the past two years, James Mackay and Algy Watson have spent many nights giving talks on Bennachie, illustrated by their wonderful slides of its scenery and wildlife, to Clubs, Guilds and Rural Institutes.

This brief account has naturally missed many personal experiences, the camaraderie, the making of friendships, the affection for Bennachie shared by us all.

That then is our story of the past three years. Achievement, they say, is but a milestone on the road of progress; the end of the journey lies ever beyond.

FOO AUL' 'S BENNACHIE?

By Flora Garry

"Foo aul' 's Bennachie? As aul' 's a man?"
Loon-like I wid speir, an leave my bools
A boorach in the kypie at my feet
An stan' an stare oot ower the darknin lan'
Ower parks and ferms, as far's my een could see
To the muckle hill aneth the settin sun.
"Aul'er, laddie, aye, gin Man himsel.
Naebody kens the age o Bennachie."

The years gid in. The bools were putten by.
Like mony anidder Buchan loon sin syne,
Rivven atween the De'il and the Deep Sea,
I swiddert faar to turn, fit road to try.
Hamewith, De'il o the ferm, wark's weird to dree,
The sizzon's quaet, slow-fittit tyranny?
Awa, Deep Sea o learnin an strange folk,
The oonchancy wardle furth o Bennachie?

Bit a' this time the hill wis company,
Pairt o baith my wardles, lookin doon
Sae freenly-like at ploo an hairst an hyowe.
Though aften, tee, a shape o fantasy.

Ararat, the Banks o Italie,
Soracte faar the drift lay oxter-deep,
Atlas, Athabasca, Helicon,
The mountains o the Moon were Bennachie.

Byeuks an learnin took me i the eyn.
Amid the big toons' fyaacht an dirdumdree
The Buchan parks an skies gid oot o min',
My dreams hid idder shapes gin Bennachie.
Ae simmer day, I clim't yon knowe eence mair
An lookit far ootower my ain country,
Ower dykes an steadins, trees an girss an corn
To the west, to the Mither Tap o Bennachie.

Bit smilin there, she wis nae pairt o me.
I wis a stranger chiel in a strange lan',
An ootlin wannert back by some mischance
To tak a teet at the place faar he eese't to be.
Foo aul' 's Bennachie? As aul' 's a man?
Ageless, timeless she, the fickle jaad.
Lichtsome, hertless she, the bonny quine.
I've been ower lang awa. It's me that's an aul' man.

WHICH BENNACHIE?

By Flora Garry

For most of my life there was only one Bennachie. It was a shape on the horizon away to the south-west, a name, a hill remote and inaccessible. A man, I remember, took over a "neipor toon" and he came from a far country called The Geerie, at the Back o' Bennachie. We bairns wouldn't have been astonished if he had sprouted horns and a tail. For Bennachie belonged to legend. It was a small glittering Himalaya on the rim of a white wintry landscape. We watched the "red skies of gloaming" fade behind the Mither Tap. Sometimes the hill withdrew altogether, hidden by veils of mist and blatters of rain. Constant only in its remoteness, a familiar but not a homely presence, Bennachie kept its distance.

Then at long last came the chance to set foot there. The Bailies of Bennachie had planned a tryst, a foregathering of folk whose roots were in the farm lands of Buchan and beyond, who cared for this countryside and its traditions and for "the bonnie dialect that eence was spoken here."

On a fresh blowy afternoon early in October, the leaves still on the trees but in their autumn colours and the hairst gathered in, we drove from Aberdeen through Kintore and Inverurie. All the time, as we drew nearer, the hill changed character, merging into the countryside. We were on it before we knew. I would have liked to walk the last half mile, to savour the approach, perhaps to come upon a notice saying:

"The Hill begins Here."

But we were in the car park at Pittodrie and had stepped down on to solid ground all too quickly. My first thought was "And is this -Yarrow?" And then there flashed across my mind a remembered glimpse on television of the first astronaut seeking a foothold on the moon's surface. But here was no lunar landscape; birch trees and rowan, heather and blaeberry, stone and boulder and a grassy track winding upwards, all real and solid and re-assuring as the friendly welcome and outstretched hands of those who had kept the tryst.

Here was another Bennachie, a homely place set among corn parks, where bairns could play and lads bring their lasses; where old folk, making their leisurely way to a clearing above the tree-line, could seat themselves in comfort and, on the Mither Tap itself, look down on the far-spreading villages and ferm toons of Buchan, and remember.

Two Bennachies. Which would I choose, the real or the illusory? There could be only one answer, both.

PERSONAL RECOLLECTIONS ON FARMING IN THE NORTH-EAST

By Dr Maitland Mackie, c.b.e.

Fifty years ago I used to recite many of the great poems of the North-East by Charles Murray in which Bennachie figures so prominently. I used to feel in those unsophisticated days, deliciously naughty reciting the bit from "Frae France" where a young soldier, writing home from a hospital in France, wishes nostalgically he were back in Aberdeenshire doing various things, including

"An watch the leevers o' the mull gang roon for oors and oors.

An see the Paps of Bennachie stan up atween the shoo'ers."

The threshing mill may be practically a thing of the past, but the Paps of Bennachie are still there and having looked over on Bennachie for these fifty years, I can well understand the young soldier's feelings. From the top of Bennachie, you can see almost the whole of the Aberdeenshire farmlands and be very proud of the traditions of the past and the condition of the land and livestock of today. Perhaps the passing of the threshing mill typifies the change that has come over agriculture in the last thirty years. In previous days, it took a minimum of fourteen workers to have a good thrash. Two good men to fork off the rick on to the mill; two men or women to "lowse" or cut the twine on the sheaf and hand to the man who fed the mill. He was one of two who alternated between looking after the steam engine and feeding the mill. It took two good men to weigh the grain and carry it away to a suitable spot for loading. Then the chaff and "cuffin's" had to be kept clear of the mill by one man or boy. The building of the straw "soo" was an expert job that took one builder and three assistants. Lastly, the hungry engine had to be kept supplied with water and coal which took another man. To gather a squad of fourteen to sixteen people together for the thrash was beyond the capabilities of any one

farm, so the policy of neighbouring or "neeperin" grew. It became an unwritten
·obligation for several farms to join together on thrashing days and as a result
there was great competition between farms to see which could put through the
greatest number of quarters of corn per day. Herculean feats of labour were
accomplished, specially by the grain men when two hundred quarters of oats
or more were bagged, weighed and stacked during one day. Since they lifted
each bag at least twice, they were lifting and carrying some sixty tons by sheer
brute strength, which today, is of course all done mechanically. No wonder
they were ready for the enormous meal of broth, mince and tatties and milk
pudding which was produced by the farmer's wife and helpers on these days.
The change from the steam engine to the tractor and straw buncher then to the
present day combine and straw baler and bulk grain handling can only be
welcomed as a release from this kind of demand on the human frame.

My father once had a grieve who, thinking he had fallen behind with the work
of driving out the muck on to the stubble fields for the subsequent turnip crop
organised himself into filling all the carts in the muck midden. He filled ninety-
six loads every day for three days. Remember, he had to tear or "rive" each
grapeful from the mass of muck tramped down by cattle in the midden and lift
it perhaps an average of six feet. At 15cwts per load that is 216 tons of muck
in those three days. He would need no sleeping pills at night.

Whether organising the thrashing or just the ordinary day to day farm work
on the bigger farms, required a good grieve and a great many of these grieves
became great "characters." They were men of great intelligence, drive and
ability, who, today I fear, would be lost to agriculture because undoubtedly
they would, with the present educational opportunities go on from school to
University and become leaders in other fields than agricultural ones. One such
character, was Jock Wilson, the grieve at Balquhindachy, Methlick. The
farmer, Mr Brebner, was one of the first to abandon the smelly Guano as the
source of nitrogen and roughly ground bones as phosphate for the finely
ground artificial fertiliser containing the proper proportions of nitrogen,
phosphate and potash all in the one mix. When the first load arrived at
"Baldies," Jock opened a bag, smelt no guano, saw no evidence of bones and
was convinced his boss had been sold the proverbial pup. However, his job was
to apply the stuff which he proceeded to do in the then traditional way, with
one man filling the "happers"—hung round the waists of the other men who
swinging their arms with great skill, spread it evenly over the field. About five
o'clock in the afternoon, the orraman who was filling the "happers" came up
very agitated to Jock who like a good grieve was surveying the operation from
the edge of the field, to inform him that they had finished all the manure and
hadn't yet done the "gushet." Without batting an eyelid, Jock said "Awa ye go
back and tell them tae wag yer airms, it'll mak nae bloody difference." Such
was his disbelief in the new fertilisers. Incidentally, Jock had a son, Ernie, who
at the age of eighteen, just after the end of World War I took cattle to Canada
for which he got free passage and £5. He went from Canada to Detroit to the
Ford Motor Company, then started his own Engineering Business and became
one of the first automation experts and in the process, a millionaire. Asking
his way from Montreal to Detroit, he felt very homesick when his first
enquiries were answered in French by French Canadians. He cheered up when

he saw a tall red haired man whom he thought was sure to be a Scot and putting on his best English which would have been the broadest of Buchan, again asked for help, only to have his hopes dashed by the reply in English "Sorry, old boy, don't speak a word of French."

My father had a grieve who would have been a great leader in any profession. He was a great organiser, even to putting my brothers and sisters to work during any school holiday. One day, as we emerged from the house after dinner at 1 o'clock yoking time, he grabbed my brother John to go and shim turnips with a single horse; me to scare the crows from the potatoes and my sister to take a drill plough sock on her cycle to the smiddy for sharpening. When my brother George, aged six, appeared John sarcastically asked—"have ye nae a job for him?" The immediate reply was "Aye—awa ye go to the gairden and scare the fleas oot amon' the carrots." He had his own brand of logic. For instance, one night he was in the house and after discussing the work on the farm, he queried a jury's verdict of suicide while of unsound mind, resulting from an inquiry into the drowning of a man in the Ythan at Ellon. He had left his jacket and watch on the bank, so Andrew Cheyne the grieve, argued he couldn't have been of unsound mind or he would not have left these on the bank and in fact, if he had been mad—"He'd have tried to sheet himsel wi' the Tattie Chapper or droon himsel in the ess midden."

On another occasion my father with some trepidation had engaged a single shepherd called "Big Bob" who had a reputation as an enormous eater. Since the grieve's wife fed the single men for a fixed fee, he enquired, with some misgivings, of the grieve, how his wife was getting on feeding Big Bob. The reply was—"On nae bother ava—we jist gie him a bowl of brose afore ilka diet and that dauchles the bugger some."

The farm men were great timekeepers; the horses emerging from the stable within seconds of yokin time and returning dead on lowsin' time. The farmer at Drumdelgie once asked his grieve how it was that when ploughing or any other operation with horses the men always managed to finish a complete furrow or drill and yet arrive at the stable on the exact minute. The reply he got was, "If ye kent that ye would be fit to be foreman at Drumdelgie."

Of course if there were great grieves there were great farmers. They had a great love of the land and a great eye for good stock. Following the advice of the great improvers, such as Turnip Townsend, the Sinclairs of Thurso and the Grants of Monymusk, there soon emerged the seven course rotation; usually four years grass, two grain crops with a turnip crop between. Even during the depression of the Thirties, when so much land in England was allowed to go uncultivated, the farmers of Aberdeenshire stuck to this well tried rotation and so the land was left in good heart in spite of all economies.

There is the true story of the celebration of the Golden Wedding of Mr & Mrs Crighton, the parents of Arthur and John, both at the time at the Rowett Institute. After the celebrations, Mr Crighton, the bridegroom of fifty years ago and his best man sat down for a news and the best man asked Mr Crighton why he had waited 51 years for his Golden Wedding. He said "No, here is my wedding certificate and its only 50 years ago today, the 31st of December." The best man then said "I don't care for your certificate, the day you were married we ploughed the stable park out of lea and its in neeps this year, so seven sevens are 49 and two is 51." It transpired that in registering a wedding held on the last day of the year (no time was lost on a honeymoon, since New Year's Day was a holiday anyway) the registrar had put on Mr Crighton's copy, the new year's date, but on sending his registrar slip to Somerset House, had corrected the date, as a duplicate copy subsequently proved. Thus, the Aberdeenshire rotation was more accurate than a piece of paper.

Of the pride in their stock, there is no better story than that of Mr McCombie of Tillyfour, whose Aberdeen Angus herd had attracted the notice of Queen Victoria. She elected to come and see this farmer's cattle and she was esconced on a raised chair at the drawing room window while the cattle were paraded round the front of the house. Mr McCombie thought she was not impressed so he sent word to take all the cattle round again, with the stock Bull—bringing up the rear. Again he thought she was not appreciative enough, so he left her side, and darting outside stopped the bull, turned it round to look in at the window and said to the bull—"That's Queen Victoria you're lookin' at." Whether the bull was impressed or not is anybody's guess.

While it is true that the farmers worked hard, they also played hard, and many are the stories of the solo parties and the pranks that were played as a result of a few drams. Once my Uncle Tom, in the early hours of the morning at Mains of Rhynie, found one guest in a drunken stupor and unable to go home, so with the help of others, he was carried out to the dog's kennel, pushed in from the back with his head out of the pophole at the front with the dog's collar and chain round his neck. Imagine the merriment of the men when they yoked a few hours later and saw a well-known farmer in this rather undignified position, still sound asleep.

On another occasion, the late Frank Duff of Old Noth, returning after 5 a.m. from a party, was annoyed to see no sign of life in the foreman's house when he should have been in the stable giving the horses their first feed. He hammered on the door, shouting "fire, fire." Then the foreman appeared in his shirt, the pyjamas of the day, crying "faur, faur"—to be answered "In abody's hoose but yours, you lazy B . . . . get up."

These are only a few recollections of the great times and great men that the two giants Jock o' Noth and Jock o' Bennachie have seen over the past fifty years. I only wish that someone could collect all the personal stories that so many people have of those days and preserve them. Perhaps the Bailies of Bennachie could do something about it.

* * * *

Bennachie, the landmark's
Noo but a pimple,
Stickin on the nose
Of Sir James Dalrymple.

THE HILL—A PERSONAL REACTION

By Norman Dixon, M.A., PH.D., F.E.I.S., J.P.

The early months of 1976 will take my wife and me far away from the scene that has daily sustained and inspired us for almost three whole decades. Of all the changes that have affected us during our years in Inverurie, perhaps the most personal and deep-reaching was the creation of the Academy Playingfield—a creation that removed within weeks the allotments and "rigs" in which the ten acres of land immediately to the south of the present building had been owned and cultivated for several centuries, possibly as part of the kirklands or glebe commemorated to this day in the placename of Kellands. The acquisition of the Playingfield brought some eight acres of green sward to our very door and gave us a spaciousness of living we certainly shall not know where we are going.

Because schoolhouse, Academy and playingfield are all so much now part of one another, it is inevitable that we shall miss the field, its grass, its trees, its Saturday morning stir of games, its Sunday emptiness, its changing face throughout the seasons. Even its bird-life is very much its own: the waxwings and fieldfares of an early winter, the landgulls using the upper field for early morning assemblage, the crows and rooks of January and early February, the oyster-catchers that by the time they have reached ten in number announce to all who see them either in early morning or as the light is falling that Spring is at last here, the September wagtails, the sparrows that seem to glean a worthwhile living in the various small shrubberies, the blackbirds that now more than ever seem to winter with us, and the odd robins, all with their own special territories.

But the Playingfield means something more: topographically it is the very centre of a wonderful circle of land. To the south lies the rising ground of Crichie crowned until the raging storm of 1953 with a coronet of trees with a remarkable resemblance to a railway engine. The storm of the early 50's removed in a single day, a Saturday, the magnificent woods on both Crichie and the high ground of Keithhall, and neither has as yet recovered. To walk only as far as the cricket square brings into a wonderful panoramic view Crichie, Keithhall, Selbie and the surrogate truncated carapace of Inverurie Town Hall. Immediately behind and north of the schoolhouse is the West Church spire, wonderfully starkly chaste as the light is falling in a summer evening. And beyond the main buildings lies Barra, reputedly known to Robert the Bruce.

But the second deepest impression left upon us is a view of the woods of the Upper Davah that even its owner has never had the chance of viewing. Before we leave, we must give him at least one chance of looking from the gymnasia windows out over the rising Playingfield, across the roofs of the new housing, up over the Golf Course and Davah, and up to the woods he has never seen from this angle. To look out from one of the gymnasia windows to the Davah Hill in the freshness of a summer morning can provide a personal catharsis, a cleansing, to which only the wholesome cleanness of early May can give expression.

But the deepest impression is undoubtedly Bennachie. In daylight it is an inspiration, a reminder of continuing stability, a symbol of unchanging integrity. Generations may indeed platitudinously come and go, but "THE HILL" goes on for ever.

In the years ahead it will remain for us the symbol of a wonderful sense of something finished, something done—and of something about to be reborn.

For many years the climax of our working year was the evening of the last day of the summer term—usually June 30th. On that day a whole year had with some distinction and with a certain dignity come to an end. The young people of the area had had their scholastic efforts fittingly recognised and fittingly encouraged. On such an evening—the evening of the Annual Prizegiving—the playingfield assumed a special significance: a luminosity and a numinosity all its own. To walk from the east gate up over the middle roadway to the cricket square as the midnight light was falling was an experience of unusual import; a year had been completed and a year was about to begin. Sometimes the oyster-catchers were calling. To the North-west was the re-birth: the Hill that for countless generations was the symbol of endeavour was standing, the sign still of things to come. There to the north-west was the Hill that epitomised all for which the past year had striven and for which it perhaps had achieved a meaning. There it was: the HILL. Some eight trees' length from the Schoolhouse door it stood and stands: the one unchanging natural symbol of man's continuing dialogue with life: the seventeen hundred feet of Bennachie.

ANETH BENNACHIE, 1972

By Dr Norman Dixon

In the simmer sun
The fairm lies smilin'—
Green with a gerse that is growin'
Or broon with a yirth newly sown.
A pownie nickers
In the thocht that his maister approaches.
In the bullock-pens
The nowt are millin'
For oats they lang syne hae finished.
Swine, mair than a toonsman thinks coontable
Slotter and slitter in the farryin' pens.

The fairm lies smilin'
In the simmer sun,
For a' life is a-growin'
And the gerse is greener.
The morn, the yirth will be covered
And neeps will sprout
In ane mair cycle o' seasons

That these lan's hae kent sae lang,
Frae winter tae seed-time
And frae seed-time tae simmer,
For a' life is a-growin'
As the fairm lies smilin'
In the simmer sun.

*   *   *   *

BENNACHIE

By Daisy Bruce

On every hill there's melody,
    A song in every stream,
With quiet places beckoning
    To challenge or to dream.
Oh, listen where the Gadie lilts
    Its old, far-flung refrain.
        Hearken again!

Then lift your eyes up to the hill
    Whose rocks in silence hold
More wisdom than the singers
    Or the sages ever told.
        Bennachie!

An' aye it's oor ain hill,
It's my hill an' your hill;
    We see't at oor ain door,
    We see't far awa.
Waitin' an' watchin'
Watchin' an' waitin',
    Waitin' wi' welcome
        For ane an' for a'.

When mists draw close, and the days are dreary,
    When on raging winds the snow drives blind,
We turn to the place where hope shone clearly—
    We look for the hill that we cannot find.
        But it's there,
        We know that it's there.
Within the dark and the tempest firmly stands
        Bennachie!

An' aye it's oor ain hill,
It's your hill an' my hill;
Though darkened, it's oor hill
    In snaw or in rain,
Waitin' an' watchin',
Watchin' an' waitin',
        Waitin' until we can welcome't again.

And when we return from the far-off places
    To where we have longed to be,
To the hills and the howes and the weel-kent faces,
    We can glimpse our hill from the sea.
        And then on the road, the homeward road
        We face it full and plain,
    And there we know as we gaze our fill,
        We know we are home again.
For in every line of that old, dear hill
    Lies all that means home to me.
                Bennachie!

For aye it is oor hill,
It's my hill an' your hill,
    Oor ain an' oor dear hill
        Its sicht an' its name.
        Bennachie!
Waitin' to welcome us hame.

THE SEVEN TAPS OF BENNACHIE

By Dr Alexander Keith

A week or two ago I was standing on a brae-set road in the country when a nostalgia swept over me, an utter craving for the high hills under a spacious firmament. This longing for the open air and the hills comes more frequently nowadays than it used to do. Perhaps the black-out is responsible. Perhaps it is just a growing fondness for my own corner of Scotland, a greater sense of identity with the rock from which I was hewn.

And of course when the desire for the hills overcame me I was looking towards Bennachie. "Ay," said the octogenarian, "it's a richt hillie thon. I min' on't ever sin' I wis a loon." It is one of the observations that can with equal justice be laughed at or accepted as a profound truth.

The upshot was that one morning ten o'clock saw me taking the slopes of Craigshannoch from Oyne at a good pace and in an expectant mood.

I think the first maker of the path up Craigshannoch was a goat. It goes almost straight up, with a directness that must revolt the canons of contouring to which, very properly, the members of the Cairngorm Club subscribe. Being no mountaineer, I followed the path instead of the contours.

I hadn't got my second wind till I pulled a handful of cranberries just below the rocky twin summit of Craigshannoch.

A MATTER OF SUMMITS

There are officially eight named "taps" of Bennachie, with two that the map passes over without mention. One of these is east of Craigshannoch, and not very prominent, the other is 1550 feet and lies between Bruntwood Tap and the Mither Tap. This unnamed summit should be included.

On the other hand, Turf Hill, on the western slopes, is nothing at all. Bruntwood Tap offers a fair climb from the Tillyfoure side, but it also is of little consequence otherwise.

I would give Bennachie seven taps, and seven has the additional merit of being the number of perfection. These are: Black Hill, 1412 feet, looking away over the Brindy and the Gadie to Tap o' Noth; Craigshannoch at the north-west corner, over 1450 feet; the unnamed summit near the Mither Tap that I have mentioned already; Watch Craig, 1619 feet, with its prospect over the Don; and the two main peaks. Of these the Mither Tap, though it is at 1698 feet the lower, is both the most difficult and the most striking. Oxen Craig, 1733 feet, the summit of which is like the head of a nowt-beast whose back throws its huge bulk right across the whole Bennachie area to the slopes above the Glenton, has no great attraction. It looks well from the Garioch as part of the whole tumbled group of tops, and on a sunny day from the Mither Tap it seems to beckon across the moorland plateau that lies between the two summits. But that is all.

It is the Mither Tap that is Bennachie. "Yon's the hill rug's at the hert when you're awa." It can rug at the hert in a different way when you are on it, as I learned that day.

NOT AN EASY HILL

For, commencing with Craigshannoch and working widdershins (which may explain my woes), I did all the taps, ending with the Mither Tap. But it was the long haul from Turf Hill round the foot of Watch Craig and the rump of Oxen Craig to Bruntwood Tap that made me feel my muscles.

With its long heather, its carpet of deep lovely mosses, its numerous hags, and its casual water, Bennachie is not an easy hill to walk over. The Tap o' Noth, nothing like so interesting to climb or to be on, is a paradise to the feet with its firm surface and short crisp heather.

From Turf Hill to Bruntwood Tap is three miles of hard plugging and high stepping. By the time I reached the foot of the rocks on the Mither Tap I must have walked a dozen difficult miles without a pause on a breakfast of porridge and a "buttery rowie."

There was a gale blowing, I was tired and cold and hungry, and it took me some effort of will to postpone my lunch until I reached the summit. I didn't stay more than a few seconds there. If I hadn't walked off I should have been blown off.

The long road home threatened to be depressing when rain came on, but there's aye a something. When the shower was at its heaviest, I met a man on a bicycle. "Ay," he remarked, "It's lookin' a bittie like a shoo'erie." What real rain is like in the Burnhervie area I cannot imagine, never having been in the tropics.

BEAUTY OF MOSSES

It was a good day, not only for the physical exertion and the joy of seeing the glorious display of mosses for which Bennachie deserves to be famous. The cushions were in a score of shades, from a fresh pale green through primrose yellow to old rose, scarlet, crimson and maroon. Lovely and restful to the eyes, but singularly taxing to the locomotive muscles are the mosses of Bennachie.

I raised during the day less than a dozen grouse. It was grey weather and inclement for butterflies. In nearly five hours not a human being did I see. This was indeed the perfection of peace.

Yet, as I looked over the Garioch from Craigshannoch and Oxen Craig, away towards the Cabrach from Hermit Seat and Black Hill, and down by Chapel from the Mither Tap, I could not help contrasting the singular repose of the landscape from the tumult of its history.

The very fine fort on the Mither Tap was the last stronghold, the final line of defence, of the robber Leslies of Balquhain. The laird there is said to have sent six sons to Harlaw and they all returned feet first.

Round by Rayne there was, some centuries later, another Leslie whose not very savoury existence reached its apex of good business (perhaps) when, as he says himself:

> I bocht a wife in Edinburgh
> For a bawbee;
> I got a farthin' in again
> To buy tobacco wi'.

And in that same region for many generations the Leiths of Harthill held sway. Their ways were not of pleasantness. One of them, who had a grudge against a Provost of Aberdeen, a Leslie, attempted to usurp the provost's seat in the West Kirk of St. Nicholas and there was a fracas.

TURMOIL IN TOLBOOTH

Leith was arrested and sentenced to be warded in the Tolbooth, that same afternoon. First he tried to set his prison on fire on the plea that his chimney wouldn't draw. Then he made a hole in his cell wall. Next, some of his friends smuggled weapons in to him and he amused himself by taking potshots from the jail window at the passing lieges.

He threatened to shoot any magistrate who came within range. The most extraordinary precautions had to be taken to keep him under surveillance, all the citizens being ordered to take their turn in watching the Tolbooth and its unruly inmate.

Animation of a different sort is the feature of the country a little north of Harthill, away beyond Leslie to the once famous fair ground of Sleepy Market at Christ's Kirk, where, if all stories are true, a King of Scotland watched the midsummer midnight revelry and set the scene down in a rollicking poem, which avers that here in the Garioch—

Was never in Scotland h'ard nor seen
Sic Dancing nor deray.

Let's hope that the happy spirit and the merry heart will never depart from the
gracious shadow of the Mountain of Light.

IN PRAISE OF DONSIDE

By Dr Alexander Keith

The Dee has been so ably and so consistently extolled by a multitude of
admirers, and so variously illustrated by the activities of the Deeside Field Club,
that it may seem temerarious for a native of the neighbouring river to lift up
even a still small voice in praise of Don. Not only in praise of Don, but to
maintain that whatever largesse of admiration is due to Dee, a greater measure
is deserved by its sister river. Loyalties are funny things, and it would not
become one who was bred and reared under the shadow of Bennachie to admit
superiority to Lochnagar or to do other than assert firmly and flatly that—

One mile o' Don's worth twa o' Dee,
Except it be for fish and tree.

The Don is a river unspoilt by popularity. Its claim to be called "royal" is so
old that it is apt to be forgotten. The anxious tourist, hastening hither and
thither to see the natural beauties that he has read of in the guide-books and the
newspapers, has no suspicion of the delights that await the eye along the narrow
road that turns west from the Great North Turnpike where it crosses the
bridge at Inverurie. He seldom takes that turnpike, for from Aberdeen he
follows the roads of fashion, north and south of the Dee. Paradise and the
Lord's Throat and Boglouster mean nothing to him; Kildrummy he may
remember faintly as a place mentioned in the history books at school; but Brux,
Glenkindie Newe, Lonach, Towie, and Corgarff have no significance for him—
he has never heard of them. He hears so much of the moor of Dinnet, of the
birks of Abergeldie (plagiarised from Aberfeldy), of the Linn o' Dee, and the
Braemar Gathering that they have come to represent in his mind the choice of
the beauties of Aberdeenshire. Besides, they are accessible by easy roads,
whereas the path to Paradise is (as indeed it should be) a steep and thorny way
to heaven, and the other outlet from Corgarff is over a hill which has a reputation
that daunts all but the most adventurous of motorists—who are not interested
in scenery in any case.

The truth is, of course, that from Manar to Allargue—the best part of fifty
miles by road—the Don is richer in scenery and associations than any other
river in Scotland, barring the Tweed; and even then, had the Don possessed a
Walter Scott to make its past live for ever in each ruin and in every knowe, the
Border Country would have met its match. "The Loire of Scotland" John
Buchan recently termed the Don: the river of great castles and stirring deeds,
of marches and battles, of fables and scenic grandeurs. Macbeth may have died
at Lumphanan, on the confines of Deeside and Donside; but Robert the Bruce
fought and hunted on Donside, and of the three battles in Scotland which

decisively determined the course of the nation's destinies one occurred in Angus (Nectansmere), one in Stirling (Bannockburn), and one in Donside (Harlaw). Even the Raising of the Standard on the Braes o' Mar in 1715 was determined upon by a meeting in the castle of Glenbuchat, on Donside; and the battle which is regarded by the experts as the masterpiece of the tactical genius of the great Montrose was fought on the Muir of Alford. The last engagement in Scotland's wars that fell out in Aberdeenshire was that of Inverurie, when Lewis Gordon made mincemeat of the Macleans and Munros sent from Inverness by the Hanoverians to purge Aberdeen of the Jacobites in 1745; and one of Aberdeenshire's first great battles was joined on the haughs below Kinkell at the time of the Danish invasions, when the Danes were defeated at a ford of the Don and their leader was buried on the high ground near the farm that is still called after him, Camistone.

The frequency of battlefields in an area indicates its strategical importance, and its strategical importance will usually be found to have some connection with its natural wealth. Frequency of castles is corroborative evidence. Judging then by its combats and its strongholds or mansions, the Don region was always highly thought of by men. The prehistoric remains in the district—the cairns at Tyrebagger and Clinterty, the stone circles at Crichie, Balquhain, and Loanhead of Daviot, the Maiden Stone of Chapel of Garioch and the Newton Stone, to mention only a few examples—are proof of the existence of very early communities in places where game must have abounded and of which, at a later date, the soil was found to be productive. To this day we speak of the Girnal of the Garioch and the lands about Kildrummy and Newe, well into the hill country though they are, can be reckoned high in the agricultural scale; while the fact that at the beginning of last century the haughs of Kintore rented at £4 an acre, compared with an average of about 10/- for the whole country, is impressive testimony to the fertility of Donside. It has always been esteemed a goodly and a kindly valley, a land flowing with milk and honey, with the river itself as fairy godmother periodically manuring the haughs with rich alluvial deposit borne down in spates from the upper reaches. The river also, with its heavy and powerful current, was the reason for the establishment of so many paper and wool factories on its banks, so that Donside is the only industrial valley in Northern Scotland.

The wars of Donside gave rise to many ballads, of which, "The Battle of Harlaw" is among the most famous in that branch of poetry. "Harlaw" as we have it today is comparatively recent, for it cannot be traced back beyond the middle of the eighteenth century and bears internal evidence of having been composed, or re-written off an older form, about that time. But it has character about it that explains why it is still the most popular of our many north-east ballads, for despite its traditional crudities, it is full of emotion and a curious atmosphere of realism. From the stirring rhythm of the opening stanza, with the skirl of the pipes behind it—

As I cam' in by Dunnideer
An' doon by Netherha,
There was fifty thoosand Hielanmen
A' marchin' to Harlaw,

to the lament at the close—

> An' sic a weary buryin'
> I'm sure ye never saw,
> As was the Sunday after that
> On the muirs aneth Harlaw—

we get all the varying fortunes of battle. In some versions the ballad ends with a typically grim Lowland sentiment,

> Gin ony body spier at ye
> For them ye took awa',
> Ye man tell them plain, an' very plain,
> They're sleepin' at Harlaw. . .

Another feature of Donside was the strength of its men. Nathaniel Forbes of Dalnhandy, about 1715, once putted the stone so far that the garters on his legs burst with the exertion. But this feat was as babe's play to the prowess of Jock o' Bennachie. Jock was a giant whose chief bugbear was the impertinence of his neighbour, Jock o' Noth, who lived on Tap o' Noth and was also a buirdly chiel. Jock o' Noth stole Jock o' Bennachie's sweetheart, and it may have been when the latter gentleman saw the two lovers standing on Noth, that he seized a huge stone on Oxen Craig and hurled it across the valley at the Tap, where it crushed the rival and the lady. At all events, the stone was thrown, for it lies on the Tap o' Noth to this day, with the marks of Jock o' Bennachie's fingers on it. At one time, however, Jock o' Noth and Jock o' Bennachie were on sufficiently good terms to join forces and go down to London to rescue Lang Johnnie More, who had been sentenced to death for courting the King's daughter. The upshot, as related in the ballad, was that they cowed the King into releasing Johnnie and giving him his daughter's hand—

> "O take the lady," said the King,
> "Ye welcome are for me;
> I never thought to see sic men
> Frae the foot o' Bennachie."

The whole district abounds with such tales. The legend of the Maiden Stone is that the monolith is the remains of a girl pursued by the devil on her wedding eve, but I have always felt this to be an aspersion on the hardihood of the Garioch lasses. It is much more likely that the Stone is the Devil. Then the Gudeman of Ballengeich travelled in the district, and at least one freehold property by the Don owes its existence to his fondness for Haroun al Raschid benevolence. Nor are the historical tales of the valley less remarkable and romantic. The wooing of the Countess of Mar in Kildrummy by the Wolf of Badenoch's son (later the hero of Harlaw) may not have been so rough as is related—the story goes that he gave the lady the alternatives of marrying him or having her castle burned round her ears—but the death of six strapping sons of the robber lord of Balquhain is authentic, and so too is the horrible murder of the tenant of Dubston by Gordon of Terpersie.

These things, save for the surviving castles and a few relics still more ancient, are of the past, but Donside can claim eminence for its beauties of the present. There can be no hill quite like Bennachie, the presiding deity of the whole valley: the Fujiyama of Aberdeenshire, as Dr Pittendreigh Macgillivray once called it. Bennachie has a bravery about it, a gay intrepidity that fully makes up for its lack of feet. To Deeside one can grant the stupendous magnificence, in very truth the steep frowning glories, of Lochnagar seen from the summit of the road above Gairnshiel, but Bennachie has a hundred impressive aspects. Seen from the extreme north of Buchan it resembles the prow of a proud Viking longship; looked at across the valley from Tyrebagger it seems to spread its covering wings around the whole landscape; from the Howe of Alford it is a lion resting but vigilant; above the road between Insch and Oyne it towers like a turreted fortress; and in all manner of unexpected places the peak of the Mither Tap comes suddenly into view. Without Bennachie the Don valley would lose half its beauty by day and half its witchery by night, for the sunsets behind the Mither Tap are almost as exquisite as those of the Moray Firth. To circle round the base of the hill is to traverse some of the loveliest and most varied scenery in Scotland. The road runs from Keig by the Brindy Hill to Auchleven and along the Gadie on to Oyne. Then, just where

> Gadie wi' its waters fleet,
> Ury wi' its murmurs sweet,
> They hae trysted aye to meet
> Amang the woods o' Logie.

the road goes up by the Maiden Stone and the end of the Devil's Causeway to Chapel of Garioch, and winds through wild country by Dalfluig and Tilly-hashlach to Paradise, where the arms of centuries-old trees come near to enclosing the Don. Then the road climbs steeply through the Glenton by the Lord's Throat and round the quiet policies of Castle Forbes to Keig again.

But all Donside's delights are not concentrated at the foot of Bennachie. It can claim the bewitching view looking north from the Hill of Marcus towards the Mither Tap and Foudland—a prospect that is enhanced after a spate when the valley is dotted with lochans left by the receding waters; the long golden road in May when the broom is in flower that leads to the little Quaker hamlet of Kinmuck, where Adams the philosopher was born; the great tree-lined gorges at Brux and Kildrummy; and the quiet harbourage of Strathdon contrasting sharply with the wild bare expanses that surround the lonely Castle of Corgarff. Deskryside and Nochtyside, Glen Ernan and Glen Buchet, where the deer bell o' nights round the isolated crofts, have all their peculiar charms, and the farms of the Howe of Cushnie, stretching up to the Soccaugh hill, have names as pretty as the scenery—

> And aye she sighed for Sinnahard
> And for Drummallachie.

With here and there the gaunt ruin of an old stronghold—Corgarff, Balfling, Harthill, Hallforest—to link the present and the past, or with the moon shining in ghostly silence upon the circle at Balquhain at the foot of Bennachie, or with the ripple of Don stealing through the dark over the level haughs of Kintore, or with the mingled cries of oyster-catchers, pyats, and greenshanks singing a farewell to departing day in summer, there is enough of beauty, romance, and peace on Donside to make it a haunt of loyalties above all other country places.

Reproduced by the courtesy of *Aberdeen Journals Ltd.* and *The Deeside Field Club.*

REMINISCENCES OF BENACHIE

By James L. Wisely

Away ye naked prairies, ye forests dark and drear,
Ye sluggish streams and marshes, that spread so widely here;
Ye little hills and valleys, ye lakes that stud the plain;
Ye have beauties for the natives of this wide and rich domain,
And for the Yankee traveller who never saw before
The scenery of any land beyond his native shore;
But with all your boasted grandeur, ye have little charm for me,
For I was born in Albin, at the foot of Benachie.

That bold and rocky mountain soon caught my infant eye;
I scanned its azure mantle, its crags so wild and high,
And every day till manhood it loomed before my gaze,
A monster wall of nature to hide the distant maze.
And oft my idle fancy, when I was all alone,
Would shape it into animals with blood and flesh and bone,
The mammoth and the mastodon that long ago have ceased to be,
Of which I often heard and read in sight of Benachie.

And when by years of training, my limbs were waxing strong,
I mounted to the summit among the labouring throng;
And merrily till evening we trundled out the peat,
Laughing, talking, singing, sweating with the heat.
For the goodly mountain yielded fuel for the fire—
Stone to build the dwelling-house, the barn and the byre,
Heather for the roofing, and all were gotten free,
For no oppressive landlord could swallow Benachie.

And in the balmy summer when the heather was in bloom,
Giving of its odours, its rich and sweet perfume—
When bees were very busy providing winter food,
Buzzing, humming, gathering honey sweet and good.
I often scaled the mountain alone to labour there,
And like the bees around me for the winter to prepare;
And till my work was ended I was busy as a bee,
That I might have a leisure hour to spend on Benachie.

And I was ever happy when my daily work was done,
Roaming o'er the mountain before the setting sun,
Moving round the ledges, softly as a boat—
Creeping through the crevices scrambling like a goat,
Perching like an eagle upon the highest peak,
Musing, talking, singing, though none could hear me speak;
Thus I passed my spare time in healthful mirth and glee,
Upon the rocks and ridges and spurs of Benachie.

And everything seemed beautiful in my happy mood;
Beautiful the mountains, and beautiful the wood,
Beautiful the valley, and beautiful the stream,
Beautiful the white clouds fading like a dream,
Beautiful the mansion, and beautiful the cot,
Beautiful the corn-fields, and every grassy plot,
Beautiful the landscape as far as I could see,
Beautiful the heights and depths and slopes of Benachie.

I've listened to the music of the plover and curlew,
That often in their rambles across my pathway flew,
The cackling of the muirfowl, the bleating of the sheep,
The frisking of the lambkins upon the heathy steep,
The bubbling of the fountains, the rushing of the streams,
The sparkling of the quartz in the sun's refulgent beams,
Those sights and sounds of nature, with *my* nature did agree,
And oft till late I lingered 'mid the scenes of Benachie.

I've traced the mountain torrents in their deep and dark ravines
That flooded by the summer rain afforded stirring scenes;
I've watched them in their windings, their pauses and their swells,
Their curves and foaming cataracts, their pools and rocky wells,
Their gambols and caprices as they sought to reach the plain,
To join the peaceful river that would bear them to the main,
And teach them to be gentle ere they mingled with the sea,
Far distant from their sources—the springs of Benachie.

I've often viewed with rapture when the morning mists were gone,
The fairy Vale of Alford stretching far beyond the Don;
With many a princely residence of beauty and of pride,
Mid forest, groves, and hedges, and fields so green and wide.
Backed by the lofty mountains of Leochel and Cromar,
While far beyond their summits rose Byron's Lochnagar
In all its sombre glory beyond the rapid Dee,
Far higher, steeper, grander, than my own loved Benachie.

And all around were mountains and hills of various fame,
But dwarfish in the distance, seemed scarcely worth a name,
Mormond, Fair, and Foudland, the Buck and Dennydeer,
Tap o' Noth, Benrinnes, and when the sky was clear
The bold majestic Grampians, with their many towering Bens—
Presented their proud summits, their gorges and their glens;
But lowering in the distance to meet the western sea,
Many of the boldest were hid from Benachie.

And southward in the valley that stretches at its feet,
Far far below the "Watch Crag" and the "Hermit's Seat,"
Rolled the bright and sparkling water, the broad majestic Don,
Hasting not nor lingering, but ever gliding on;

Bearing in its bosom the waters of the Strath—
And many rural parishes that skirt its mountain path,
Of a hundred hills and valleys that give their tribute free,
To swell its grateful bosom ere it reaches Benachie.

Then like a silken ribbon when unfolded in the light,
It shone and glanced and sparkled to please the roving sight,
Fringed by the verdant meadow, and forests that combine—
The oak, and ash and hazel, and beech, and elm, and pine—
But soon the river vanished in the woods of Monymusk,
Like the planets in the morning, or the distant hills at dusk,
Leaving scenes behind it as fair as fair could be,
And seen in all their splendour from the top of Benachie.

But often in the morning when the mountain top was clear,
A heavy mist enveloped the plains and valleys near;
And I have bathed in sunshine and in the balmy breeze,
When all the world below me seemed buried by the seas;
And on the level surface stretching far away,
Were foaming waves and breakers, all motionless and grey—
It seemed the human family were all engulfed but me
And I was left a hermit on the top of Benachie.

But oftener still the mountain was shrouded in the gloom
And drizzling fog and vapour soaked the heather bloom;
And then the scene was dreary and bleak and dark and chill,
For nought to me was visible but objects on the hill—
Stone and rock and heather, and moss and clay and sand;
A waste and cheerless wilderness, confined on every hand;
For cornfield, and garden, cottage, grove, and tree,
Were hidden from my vision by the mists of Benachie.

And in the stormy winter, the mountain clad in snow,
Gazed like a giant spectre upon the vale below;
Looking wild and angry, and lonely in its pride,
Abandoned to the elements that warred on every side;
Forsaken by the workmen, and those who fondly roam
In quest of health and pleasure, far away from home;
For birds, and beasts, and bees, and men, were glad to flee
For shelter from the tempests and blasts of Benachie.

But even then the mountain was useful in its way,
For when the sun was shining it told the hour of day;
When clock and watch were absent, or resting from their toil,
Or in the hands of workmen, and under brush and oil—
The gigantic crags were pointers, that pointed ever true,
And told us when 'twas meal time and time to yoke the "pleugh,"
And ever in the morning we fondly rose to see
The prospects of the weather from the looks of Benachie.

O, Benachie! thy beauties still linger in my eye.
I see thy blooming heather and thy rocks that pierce the sky;
But a long and weary distance of many thousand miles,
Divides me from thy glories, thy frowns and welcome smiles;
And I would leave the prairie, the forest, and the stream,
To gaze upon thy features that haunt me like a dream;
And though youth and early manhood are now denied to me,
I still would range with rapture on the heights of Benachie.

BENNACHIE ON SKI

By Rev. Dr. James S. Wood

It's a queer thing how a hill can be so woven into the texture of your life that you cannot visualise the pattern of life without it. You become intimately related with the genius of the hill. That's certainly how I feel about Bennachie. When I picture other heights I have known, Blue Mountain Peak in Jamaica, the castellated Wetterhorn, the majestic Eiger, I set them instinctively alongside Bennachie which, though dwarfed by these giants, is yet more luminous and lovely, and different, different as the girl you love is different from all others. Said Romeo of his love "Ah, she doth teach the torches to burn bright." So do I feel about Bennachie, the mountain of light.

I saw the hill as a boy, for the first time, in the red summer gloaming. It was love at first sight and the relationship has deepened with the years. In war it was for me the emblem of peace, and, exiled abroad, the symbol of home. This is a mountain for all seasons, to be climbed in the green days of spring and the purple days of summer, but best of all when mantled deep in snow. This I discovered on a brilliant wartime February day, a day that still glows in the memory. By then I was padre to a mountain battalion and had learned a new and exciting way to climb and enjoy the heights in winter, namely by ski. I had previously skied in Switzerland and the Cairngorms, but Bennachie was unexplored terrain to me. In fact I fondly imagined I was the first to set ski on those snow-covered slopes. To my surprise however, before I reached the summit ridge that day, I came across solitary ski tracks and learned later that the lone skier who had forestalled me was none other than Prince Bernard of the Netherlands, then staying at Lickley Head. But neither was he a pioneer for sometime later I read in an old magazine that two gentlemen had skied across Bennachie in 1888! And who knows, maybe the Picts who once inhabited the hill, had their own primitive form of skis!

Bennachie is not a hill much frequented by skiers for obvious reasons; there is no ski-lift and the hill does not offer the long well-beaten pistes beloved of the downhill-only addict. No, Bennachie is mainly for the langlaufer or ski-trekker, who is interested in the total terrain with its ups as well as its downs, its beauty as well as its thrills. But for such a one a winter's day on Bennachie will be a day of sheer delight as it was for me on that first occasion and on various occasions since. Poetry we are told, is emotion recollected in tranquillity. Not being a poet I must recollect mine in prose and I do so in the hope that some skier may be lured from the crowded winter slopes to assay Bennachie, and see the blessed sights I saw and feel as deeply as I felt and still feel long years after.

The hill may be approached from various angles. That first day I set out from Oyne following the old peat road, skirting the deep cleft made by the waterspout in 1891. Arrived at the Owsen Craig, the hill's highest point, I stood and looked out on the white magnificence of winter. The one living thing in that still and lovely landscape, as far as I could see, was the winding Don, still unbound by frost, flowing silently through the immaculate Vale of Alford. The granite crag surmounting Clochnaben shone like a jewel in the crown of a king. Mount Keen, graceful as a bride in virgin white, stood smiling in the sun. The great white castle of Lochnagar gleamed splendidly beyond, though a slight haze to the east shimmered the ice-cold blue of the North Sea. To the west Tap o' Noth, the Buck and all the Cabrach hills, dressed in spotless surplices, formed a mountain choir.

I looked toward the Mither Tap. The ruins of the Pictish fort and the round houses and the bede houses lay deep under the snow as the bones of their erstwhile inhabitants lay deeper under the moss. Silent were the hill and the surrounding plain which had once echoed to the thunder of cannonade and the sound of the hunting horn and the clatter of clansmen locked in combat at Harlaw. Bestirring myself from reverie I skied zigzag toward the Mither Tap clambering on foot to the rocky peak. There as I lifted my eyes Charles Murray's line came to mind—

Syne on the Mither Tap sae far
Win-cardit clouds drift by abeen,
An' wast ower Keig stands Callievar
Wi' a' the warl' for me atween.

That warl' seen from this high vantage point on a summer's day is a sight to be remembered, but under the transforming hand of winter it is lovelier still. The beauty of it catches the throat even in remembrance. In the far distance the shining ramparts of the Cairngorms thrust upwards into an infinity of blue; and far to the east a glimmer of silver that was the Loch of Skene. The Spirit of the hills was at work that day weaving a tapestry of light and shade, displaying his artistry to one privileged human being on a lone Scottish hilltop.

I have referred to Bennachie as the mountain of light. Could that name have been given because of the strange thing I saw that afternoon when the snow-ridges slowly turned from white to luminous green as if lit up from below? So sure was I of some concealed lighting that I skied to the nearest ridge to inspect the phenomenon. And still it glowed like phosphorescence in a tropic sea, inexplicably green and mysterious.

I now continued my way along the ridge, ski-ing quietly through history and legend, by Watch Craig and Hermit Craig. My tracks led through a maze of fantastic winter sculpture, carved by the sharp unseen chisels of the wind, grottoes of a blue translucency, frozen-furrowed snowfields, foaming breakers arrested on the crest. But by now the shadows were lengthening along the white hollows and it was time to leave the hill. I got me on to the north face and began the long and delightful traverse taking the final slope in a series of christianas, gliding into the valley with the speed and the joy of a homing bird. The delightful descent, "linked sweetness long drawn out," ended in a winding track through the trees round Lickley Head. By Gadieside in the February twilight I took off my skis, and, exhilarated and happy, began the long tramp home.

There is a prophecy in Isaiah which I hope will never be fulfilled. It says "Every mountain and hill shall be laid low." I would hate to live hereafter in an eternity of flatness in an eternal summer. I do not ask for peaks of celestial splendour. I would be satisfied if rising somewhere above the Elysian fields I were to see a replica of Bennachie, and if in place of wings, for winter in Paradise, Gabriel would allow me a pair of skis.

*　*　*　*

THE HAUGHS OF FINTRAY

O'er Bennachie at eventide
The sun's mild rays are shed
But not on gory battlefields—
The dying and the dead—
But quiet homes of happy hearts
That stud our native plain
And thickening herds and frisking flocks
And yellow wavy grain.

Anon.

"WHAUR GADIE RINS"

An extract from "Ten Scottish Songs, rendered into German"

By W. H. MacDonald of Rammerscales, Lockerbie, published 1854

The Rev. Dr. James Wood, sometime of the South Church, Aberdeen, and now a lecturer at Christ's College, contributed two articles to the "Press and Journal" in the nineteen forties on the glory of ski-ing on Bennachie. In 1961 he devised a radio programme on Bennachie for B.B.C., Aberdeen, and a recording of the broadcast was played at the Bailies' Autumn meeting in October 1973. In June 1964, when Dr Wood was in Germany for the baptism of his first grandson, his daughter Margaret produced a copy of MacDonald's "Ten Scottish Songs, rendered into German" including "Whaur Gadie Rins." A brief preface reveals the purpose of the publication, namely, "to show the close affinity in rhyme, rhythm and music between the Scottish and the German tongue." Dr Wood then copied the German version of "Whaur Gadie Rins" and sent it, along with a note of the original text, to Dr D. G. Gordon, Senior Bailie, from whom this information was obtained.

ORIGINAL TEXT (Whaur Gadie Rins)

GERMAN VERSION (Wo Gadie Rinnt)

O, an I war whaur Gadie rins
Whaur Gadie rins, whaur Gadie rins
O, an I war whaur Gadie rins
At the back o' *Bennochie* (sic).

O wär ich nur wo Gadie rinntst
Wo Gadie rinnt, wo Gadie rinnt
O wär ich nur wo Gadie rinnt
Weit über Bennochie.

O, an I war whaur Gadie rins
'Mang fragrant heath and yellow whins
Or brawlin' doon the boskie linns
At the back o' Bennochie.

O wär ich, Gadie wo du rinnst
Durch Heid' und gelben Stachelginst
Und dich durch Klüfte schäumend windst
Weit über Bennochie.

Aince mair to hear the wild birds' sang
To wander birks an' braes amang
Wi' friends an fav'rites left sae lang
At the back o' Bennochie.

Mocht ich der Vöglein wilde Gesang
Und lang verscholl'nen Freundschaftsklang
Noch hören das Waldthal entlang
Weit über Bennochie.

How mony a day in blithe Springtime
How mony a day in Summer's prime
I've saunterin' wil'd awa' the time
On the heights o' Bennochie.

Oft in der frohen Frühlingszeit
Oft in der Sommer Heiterkeit
Ging ich ganz sorglos und erfreut
Hoch auf dem Bennochie.

Ah fortunes flowers wi' thorns grow rife
An' wealth is won wi' toil an' strife
Ae day gie me o' youthfu' life
At the back o' Bennochie.

An Dornen sind die Rosen reich
Erwirbt man Geld durch Kummer gleich
'Nen Tag gib mir voll Jugendstreich
Weit über Bennochie.

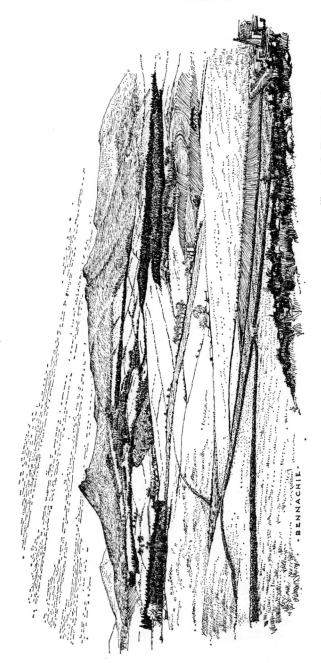

Illustration by HENRY J. L. MANTELL, A.R.I.B.A.

· BENNACHIE ·

SOME PERSONAL MEMORIES OF BENNACHIE

By Professor John Craig

My oldest memory goes back to early childhood when I recall the first time I saw Bennachie. Where I saw it from, I do not remember, but I was with my mother; she told me the meaning of "Ben" and said "There are many other and bigger 'bens' elsewhere in Scotland."

In later childhood with a few other Gordonians we took the railway train to Oyne and climbed to the fort at the eastern end of Bennachie. My memories of the fort then are dim, but I recall the great views we got of the lovely country-side. Since then I have often climbed it with my own family and without them. Once with an older son aged 7 and a younger one not yet 5, my wife and I went up to have a good look at the fort on the Mither Tap, as the mighty eastern summit is called.

With my brother-in-law the late Dr W. Douglas Simpson, I toured the whole district and had visits to many famous castles, and stone circles, and sculptured stones, for the mountain of Bennachie has a fascinating ring of these relics of older days. The district of the Garioch has had cultural and political contacts with the province of Mar since prehistoric times, as Dr Simpson illustrates in his book "The Province of Mar" (1943). This was also shown by the Rev. John Davidson in his long tome "Inverurie and the Earldom of the Garioch" (1878), full as it is of many family connections and other items.

The Mither Tap, the stately part of the ridge of Bennachie, has long had a fascination for me as for others for many generations and has been well described in song and story. At the summit of the granite Tap are the remains of a fort with an amazing tor, 60 feet high with a flat top area of nearly 3000 square feet. About 100 feet below the summit are the remains of the fort wall 15 feet thick and well built. I remember taking photographs of it (plate 37 in "The Province of Mar"), and also I was struck with its contents of the remains of hut circles.

From the Tap summit can be seen many other hill forts in a wonderful view in all directions. The one of these I recall most vividly is the vitrified fort of Dunnideer, which, with my sister, I had the privilege of helping Dr Simpson to survey, and which I photographed extensively (Proceedings of the Society of Antiquaries of Scotland, 1934-1935, Vol. 69, pp.460-470).

Dunnideer is made more conspicuous by the broken wall of an old castle that crowns it. The castle was erected within a vitrified fort some of whose remains are clearly visible today (fig. 6 in the book mentioned). The vitrification in its turn is surrounded by an earthwork fortification that encircled the hill and had inside and outside ditches, which in places can be seen today (fig. 7).

I could describe many trips I had to Bennachie with Dr Douglas Simpson, for he knew every square metre of our lovely mountain with all its stones and castles. He had a great knowledge of its archaeology, but also he had a profound knowledge of its history, and of the families who inhabited the houses and castles.

Two trips I may recall. One was to the stone at Drimmies, then across the fields to the stone circle of Balquhain that you can see from the main road with its lovely stones and then to the ruinous Balquhain Castle.

The other memorable trip was to the ruinous Castle of Harthill with its well-known occupancy by the Leith family in the 16th and 17th centuries. At the end of the 17th century the last Leith of Harthill was deeply in debt and had fallen out with his neighbours. He set fire to the Castle and is said to have watched it burning from a cave (Harthill's Cave, or as it is sometimes called "Leith's Home") on the north side near the summit of Craig Shannoch. Dr Simpson and I climbed to the cave (it holds two people) and had a wonderful view of the surrounding country.

In later years my occupation of physician took me all over the North-East of Scotland, and I saw Bennachie from many places at all times of the year. It was often bluish; sometimes purple in autumn when the heather was out; and in winter it might be white and snow-covered. But I always found it attractive. Most often it was the north side I saw, but occasionally the west side was seen and also the south as one came back from Keig through the "Lord's Throat." Then the south face would show the highest part of the mountain—Oxen Craig, quite a different appearance from the north.

But the best views to me I have had many times in my retirement, when we saw the East side. We would go out from Aberdeen past Monymusk and across the River Don to the Oyne road, and so past the East side, often looking green, with the fort at its top, and we would reach, always stop, at the great Maiden Stone, the best known example, I am sure, of a Christian monument with Pictish symbolism, that strange product found mainly in the Eastern regions of Scotland. It is one of the six stones between the River Dee and the River Spey with Pictish symbols but also with a Cross on one side. Thence our motor would be home by the Chapel of the Garioch and Balquhain Castle and Inverurie; or else we would go on around Bennachie and home by the "Lord's Throat" or by the Keig-Whitehouse road. Home with thoughts in our minds of the Mither Tap that "great bastion of the Highlands thrust boldy forward into the howe of the Garioch."

* * * *

CONTENTMENT

"A pipe, a beuk, a cosy neuk,
A peat fire bleezin' finely;
A frien I ken, the wale o' men
A couthy an' a kindly."

James Milne,
From "The Girnal of the Garioch."

NINETY YEARS ON

By William Cook, F.S.A.SCOT.

This is a big subject, a big mouthful, the Hill of Bennachie. As to when it was formed, I know not. Many things are hidden in the dim and dark ages. Certainly it is one of the most famous landmarks of our county, and I am informed that far out on the North Sea, fishermen and sailors take their bearings from the Mither Tap.

My own personal interest in the hill goes back many years. I was born ninety years ago in December 1884, and as a boy on my father's farm at Counterford of Premnay on the banks of the Gadie, I would guddle for trout, or fish at a grand spot, the intake of the lade to the meal-mill, closed now like many another. Many a good trout we got there. The twin villages of Auchleven and Premany had a natural rivalry. Premnay had the hostelry, Auchleven the wool-mill where you start to climb the Breemie Hill. I well remember my father getting a gig, and sending me down to the woolmill for a gig-rug, for the open gig was a proper starver for the legs. I was tied to a certain sum of money, as like all small farmers, every bawbee was hardily earned. When the old miller heard how much I had he shouted "Laddie, that would hardly buy a bit of shoddy." So home I went, and in spite of my father's shock at the price, he knew we must have it, I was sent back with the extra money, and the rug kept our legs warm for many a year.

I knew many of the crofters of Auchleven. Three acres they rented, half an acre to the shift. As I grew older, and able to drive a pair of horses, I would be sent down to plough the crofts. The kindly crofter wives would bring me tea and jammy pieces. They were in the habit of putting a handful of cloves in the tea-caddy, and the tea tasted very clovy. Naturally there were some great characters, whose rough corners had not been polished off in a day when travel was slow and dear. One I remember was Lang Ross, a great tall streik of a man, who had been grieve at Overton of Premnay, and had the knack of breaking in the vicious young horses. When a lad he was fe'ed at Overhall, where the best barley grew. He used to tell me about setting off with the foreman about four in the morning with two carts loaded with bags of barley. Their destination was the Cabrach, where the Highlanders had gathered from their crofts on their shelts. The barley bags were opened and the grain poured into the panniers a bushel or two to each pony. Premnay barley properly malted and Cabrach water for the still, blended well together. Today in the little glens, from which folk have long vanished, they tell me you can still find the odd ruined stills, where no gauger came.

Now for my memories of Bennachie, the Back o' Bennachie where Gadie Runs. It was always a great place for picnics from far and near. In the 1920's and 1930's when I was farming at Mill of Pittmedden of Oyne, we always had our Sunday School summer picnics from Old Rayne, up by Hordoyne at the foot of Craigshannoch. For the bairns it was a great event. We went by farm cart, fitted with the frames for bringing home the hairst sheaves, to seat a lot of children. The horses were unyoked and tied to a cartwheel, to munch their hay. Soon the kettles were boiling, and the bairns set to their munching with a will, to provide the energy for all the climbing. When lucky for a fine day, it was a delectable spot.

Away up on the top of Bennachie, there is a great moss, where peats were cut. What a labour it must have been to climb up to the 1500 feet level, cast the peats, return to set them and turn them, and then the journey up with the carts to bring the peats home down the rough steep track, parts of which were often washed away by cloud bursts. It must have been a Herculean labour, ended before my time by the coming of the cheap coal.

I remember many characters on the crofts of Premnay, small crofters like Lang Ross, horse-breaker in youth and crofter in his old age. They had a simple life with few bawbees, lived off milk and tatties and meal, with kitchie of rabbit and hare, when they were lucky with their snares. The great boon was their independence; they were their own masters, and could get odd days on the farms at the steam-mill or ditching. If they wanted to be a hairst man, they put a shot corn ear in their bonnets at St. Sairs or Lowrin Fair. As Hamewith said, Lang Ross never spoiled a story by considering "gin 'twas true," and of these characters on the crofts Lang Ross was chief. His talk was a glory, he was a natural teller of tales. When he was grieve at Overton,the old farmer liked full speed ahead at all the work, the threshing mill was driven by water, the flow of which could be regulated by a long handle to make the mill run fast or slow. In the early morning they started at the slow speed as throwing up the sheaves and taking away the straw was hard work. When later the farmer got out of bed, by the time he came across, the mill was birring away at full speed. As a breaker of young horses, which other men had tried to break and failed Lang Ross would tell of a very vicious young mare, which he was able to hold with a special bit. The bit unfortunately cut the tongue, and it took him a lot of honey to get it healed.

Besides the wool-mill, there were all the little shops, each with its own crafts-men, the smiddy with the sweating smith shoeing the Clydesdales, the souter making strong home-made tacket boots which kept out water, as well as the modern wellingtons, and costing one pound only, and the tailor fitting the home-made suits. All of these including the carpenter or vricht's wooden shed with the grand smell of fresh sawdust, were the spots where the country folk gathered of a winter evening, and the news went round while the Bogie Roll tobacco at sixpence for two ounces burned smoothly in the clay pipes, one of which was given free with every purchase of tobacco.

Lowrin Fair was a great annual event. I have seen six hundred horses stanced at Lowrin Fair. It was once a great sheep and cattle market, but that was before my day. John Cooper of Dunnydeer would have two hundred great Clydesdales. There were few holidays, and no half days, but all the countryside made Lowrin a day off work.

I have seen great changes in my ninety years. Much drudgery and much poverty have gone and that is all to the good, but in those pre-1914 days, when we made our own entertainment with the melodeon and the trump and the fiddle with the old tunes like "Gadie Rins," there was a quiet contentment, which lingers in my memory when I take down my old fiddle, and tune her up.

THE BENZIE HOWE

By Frank Benzies, M.B.E.

On his last visit to us in Coupar Angus in the winter of 1931, my father, James Benzies, spoke of the story of his youth and upbringing around Insch. Clearly he loved the district, but his knowledge of the distant past was scant. It was many years later I was able to find spare time to research my forebears' history.

The result was the publication in 1972 of "A Benzies Quest." It involved me in many journeys around the North East, visiting libraries, corresponding with and meeting Benzies from far and near.

On such a journey I learned from Mrs Helen Gordon of Tayloch, Kennethmont, herself a Benzie of Knowehead, of Oyne, that the land at the back of Bennachie was known as "The Benzie Howe." This information intrigued me.

After studying many library sources I now feel assured, as Mrs Helen Gordon always felt "that eleven Benzie sons from their farm in Ardentinnes helped King Robert The Bruce so valiantly at the Battle of Barra in 1308 that he gave them each a grant of land in the Garioch." The record is borne out by the number of Benzie who appear in the following five centuries in Inverurie and district. In Oyne kirkyard I photographed 24 Benzie headstones in 1967. There is no doubt in my mind that here is the heartland of the Benzie who have since spread around the globe.

My own great grandfather William Benzies (1775 to 1848) was born at Coldwells Farm, Insch up by the Foudland Hill. He is buried in Insch Kirkyard and his wonderful daily diary of his work on the farm is in the National Museum of Antiquities in Edinburgh. My own father, James Benzies, was born in Coldwells Farm, Insch, Aberdeenshire, in 1858 and died in Pollokshields, Glasgow in 1931.

Another oral tradition is that the Benzies lived in the forests at the back o' Bennachie, before the battle of Harlaw in 1411 in which they took part. It was therefore a great joy, in these forests, to attend in 1974 the Rally of the Bailies of Bennachie meeting, some of the four hundred people attending, many named Benzie, (introduced by Dr D. Gordon). With me were my wife, son Robert, his wife, my grandson Douglas Benzies, with my grandson Sam Harley from Hudson Heights, Canada, at the Back o' Bennachie.

I had come home to the Benzie Howe.

THE BENZIE HOWE

By J. R. Douglas

Wad ye like to hear o' the Benzie Howe,
Twenty four miles frae the sea,
Whaur Gadie rins 'mang broom and whins,
At the Back o' Bennachie.

Oh, bonnie and green is the Benzie Howe,
When Spring again returns;
The teuchat wheelin' overhead,
And the sough o' the bickerin' burns.

Summer brings the purple bell
In glory on the hills;
While the lingerin' licht o' the gloamin' oors
Sic a holy calm instils.

Autumn comes to the Benzie Howe,
Bedecked wi' ripenin' corn;
The seerin' leaves fae aff the trees
O' their Simmer beauty shorn.

'Tis bleak an' caul' on a winter's day,
When the win's aff Foudland blaw;
The folk o' the glens pluck their fite hens,
And the feathers fa' doon in snaw.

Lat me tell o' the men o' the Benzie Howe,
The men O' the Benzie clan;
Honest, noble, guid and true:
Maist each wis a sax foot man.

There wis Eeseck, oor nearest neighbour,
Braid shouther't—a neighbour true;
He'd crack o' the ferlies he'd seen lang syne,
And the fleg he'd gotten too.

When he saw the phantom funeral
Ae November gloamin' late,
When drivin' hame fae Port Elphinstone
He'd tae stop at the fairm gate.

Twa black horses pu'in a hearse;
A driver o' solemn mien;
When mornin' cam' he speired a' roon,
"Did ye see fat I saw yestreen?"

"Na, na," they said; "there wis naething here:"
But the young man deet that nicht;
The phantom funeral had tauld its tale
O' the strauchtin buird and vricht.

Athol, tee, lat tell o' him,
Precentor in Premnay kirk;
He faun' that gi'en oot the cries
Wis harder than sellin' a stirk.

"So and so's tae be merriet seen,
The hunner and twenty third time"—
"Toots, toots," the Minister said—
"First, second, and third time."

There wis Peter, the flesher—a little man;
He wad kill a sheep or mairt;
Then dirl the goods the kintra roon,
Wi' his little wee horse and cairt.

Parkie o' Parkbrae ne'er miss:
At fairmin' he keepit the van;
A canny, upricht honest chiel,
And a true blue Free-Kirk man.

Goosie, oor elder, o' Gooseknowes,
Cud hannel the ladle fine;
Rakin'in the wee bawbee;
At that he cud fairly shine.

I've watched him as we walked alang
On the weel-worn Auld Kirk road;
He'd a kindly wird for young and auld,
As we hied tae the Hoose o' God.

There wis dyker Jock—he had a faut,
For he liket a wee drap dram:
He nott the breadth o' the turnpike road
While he hame frae Bleezes cam.'

I mind o' watchin' him ae day
When the caul' Mairch win's near froze,
Hanlin' the stanes wi' mittened hauns,
While the drap fell fae his nose.

I maun speak o' Tailor Benzie, too,
Wha liv't up near Parkbrae;
He wad snuff four times in ilka oor,
Then the goose on the claith he'd lay.

He wis wizzent and auld when I a loon
Had tae ca' for my faither's breeks;
Waitin' patiently watchin' him
Finish the last o' the steeks.

There wis Smithy, tee, an auld, auld man;
He'd twa sins, Andy and Sandy;
They were mullerts at Buchanstane,
And lived doon at Bogandie.

> There wis Jackie, tee, a roon-shouthert man,
> Wha livd on the Canel Hill;
> There wis ithers tee wha had worn awa'
> Tae the Hame that is calm and still.
>
> Ye shades o' the men wha lived lang syne,
> While ye pass me in review,
> Wi' the homage o' a namely hert
> I doff my cap to you.

It isn't known when this poem was written—sent to Mr Frank Benzies by Mrs Gordon, Tayloch, by Kennethmont, Aberdeenshire.

THE LORE OF BALLAD AND LEGEND

By Dr D. G. Gordon

One third of the ballads of Scotland belong to the North-East. Handed down from generation to generation by word of mouth, there are many versions or variations of each ballad, sometimes as many as a dozen. Around the turn of the century, Gavin Greig and his assistant the Rev. J. B. Duncan, collected three hundred ballads with a total of over three thousand texts and a similar number of ballad airs. Greig's share was three-quarters of the total. Inkson McConnachie in his classic book on Bennachie published in 1890, includes eight ballads:

(1)   The Rival Giants.

(2)   The Key of Bennachie.

(3)   Lang Johnnie More.

(4)   The Wee, Wee Man of Bennachie.

(5)   The Bonnie Lass of Bennachie.

(6)   Hosie's Well.

(7)   The Devil's Stane o' Kemnay.

(8)   The Battle of Harlaw (parts only).

There is no doubt that ballads have been sung in Aberdeenshire since the Middle Ages. The first mention of ballad singing in literature is found in Barbour's "The Brus." Barbour was Archdeacon of Aberdeen in the fourteenth century. The Edom o' Gordon ballad on the burning of the House of Towie in 1571 during the Gordon-Forbes feuds, appears to be the first ballad to be recorded around the time of the incident and is very much in the same form as the versions handed down by word of mouth and collected in Aberdeenshire.

Allan Ramsay and Bishop Percy started the vogue of ballad-collecting in the middle of the eighteenth century. They have been followed right through the nineteenth century by a spate of collectors. Peter Buchan of Peterhead produced a voluminous collection in 1828, called Ancient Ballads and Songs from his manuscript now in Harvard University. These were collected from 1816 to 1827, many from James Rankin, a professional minstrel of humble origin, to whom the ballads had obviously been handed down by word of mouth over the generations. Buchan's contemporary ballad-collectors were Jameson, Sharpe, Laing, Chambers, Motherwell and last but not least, Sir Walter Scott. Sir Walter Scott was more than a collector. Like Robert Burns, who had spent the last five years of his life in transforming the rude crude folk-songs of Scotland into the greatest of lyric poetry, Scott attempted to do the same with the Border ballads. Although never reaching Burns' heights, Scott by polishing, amending and inventing missing verses, gave to the traditional ancient ballads considerable literary merit. He acknowledged his debt to Peter Buchan. Buchan's ballads collected after 1828 are in manuscript form in the British Museum. Professor Child, greatest of ballad-editors, gave Buchan the place of honour. We all owe him a debt.

Gavin Greig was the country dominie at Whitehill School in New Deer from 1879 till his death in 1914. Born in 1856, he was Fourth Bursar at Aberdeen University in 1872 and graduated M.A. in 1876. He could trace his relationship to Alexander Greig, who emigrated from Buchan to Bergen about 1760 and became the grandfather of Edward Grieg, the Norwegian composer. On his mother's side he could trace his ancestry back to James Burness the great-grandfather of Robert Burns. With such blood in his veins it was little wonder that this quiet, gentle country schoolmaster should be able to rescue for posterity such a wealth of balladry and the ballad airs. Dying at 58 before he was able to publish his completed collection, it was left to Dr James Tocher and the Buchan Club to publish in 1925 "Last Leaves of Aberdeen Ballads and Ballad Airs." Beautifully edited by Dr Alex. Keith, with a memoir on Gavin Greig, it is a real labour of love. His friend and fellow-collector James Bruce Duncan, was minister of Lynturk in Alford for forty years. When Greig died, he took on the task, but lived only a further three years, to die in 1917.

The nineteenth century must indeed have seen the singing of the ballad in full flower. The rural population at its height, the long winter evenings, with the fiddle going by the peat fire in the farm kitchens, and Gavin Greig noting down the words and the tunes learned by the singer from generation to generation. "Hamewith's Packman's Wares," included the chapbooks of ballants.

> "He'd sheafs o' rare auld ballants, an' an antrin swatch he sang
> Fae Mill o' Tifty's Annie, or o' Johnnie More the lang."
> He would lilt you Hielan Harry, till the tears ran doon his nose,
> Syne dicht them wi' a doonward sleeve, an inta "James the Rose."

In Flo Garry's "Figures Receding" the staigman has a similar repertory including Lang Johnnie More.

When we think of the vast canvas of the Scottish scene worthy of ballads, the battles of long ago, the feuds and the frays, the burning of castles, fair ladies dying when crossed in love, it may seem strange that so many ballads arise from Bennachie. If we ponder further and consider how deep an affection the Mither Tap arouses even to-day among our race, it is easier to understand that in more superstitious ages, legends of giants, fairies and even old Satan himself up on the high tops, should live on in ballad form. The great monolith at Craigearn was thrown by the Devil at his arch-enemy, the holy priest of Kemnay. The Maiden Stone was all that was left of the farmer's daughter at Drumdurno when Old Satan tried to catch her. The great rock on the slope of the Tap o' Noth was thrown by Jock o' Bennachie at Jock o' Noth who had stolen his bride, the Lady Anne. You can still see his finger marks on it. Hosie's Well on the path up the Mither Tap commemorates Hosie who was captured by the Highlanders at Harlaw. After many years in prison, he at last got home to Bennachie to find that his promised bride had tired of waiting and married another. He died of a broken heart.

> "The water that rises in Hosie's well
> Is naething but Hosie's tears."

When I was a boy in King Edward VII's time, when the cottages and the country schools were bulging with bairns, when everybody was poor except the Laird and the Auld Kirk minister, there was a robust vigour about country life, at least in the Garioch where I was born. The gramophone and the motor car were new insignificant toys. They were still singing Long Johnnie More, the grandest of ballads, telling of the young giant from the Back o' Bennachie, who was flung into a dungeon in London by the King for daring to lay court to his daughter and had to be rescued by his Uncle Jock o' Bennachie and Jock o' Noth. But 1914 ended an era. Sophistication came. The ballad-singing as entertainment could not stand up to the glamour of cinema, radio and television. Fifty years on, time has gone full cycle and the revival of folk-song in the media's search for material, has brought to the musical young generation of to-day and to the young in heart, a taste of the old magic.

"HAMEWITH" AND BENNACHIE

Commentary by Dr D. G. Gordon

All men worship instinctively the scene of their birth, the home of their childhood. Charles Murray did passionately. He was lucky in the Howe of Alford and Bennachie. So was Kipling in the land of his youth of which he sings:—

> "God gave all men all earth to love
> But since our hearts are small
> Ordained for each one spot should prove
> Beloved over all
> Each to his choice and I rejoice
> The lot has fallen to me."

None better than Kipling can extract the distilled essence of prosaic thought for the delectation and refreshment of the common mind. Similarly, the rural culture of our beloved North-East has been enriched—nay preserved—by Hamewith's uncanny genius in the use of Doric phrase and idiom to reveal in brilliant detail the breadth and depth of character in his native countryside.

Does "Hamewith" mean *Homewards*—or is there something more? Is it expressive of the homing instinct, akin to the compelling inborn urge that hastens back the swallow from the opposite end of the earth to nest again, year after year, under the selfsame bield? David Rorie, then an assistant medico in the industrial north of England, was inspired to write "The Lum Hat wantin' the Croon" at a time when the fleeting memory of "a burn in spate" was "an ice-cold draught in a parched land." The South African veldt, familiar to Charles Murray for so much of his life, likewise was to him *a parched land* under the burning sun:—

> "Here on the Rand we freely grant
> We're blest wi' sunny weather
> Fae cauld an' snaw we're weel awa'
> But, man, we miss the heather."

And there can be no doubt whatever that the heather he missed grew on Bennachie of which he wrote with such deep affection, shared by so many more. James Milne, the tinsmith poet of Inverurie, undertook his accustomed pilgrimage to the summit of the Mither Tap on each successive birthday every year until the age of ninety when he died. It was "Tinny" Milne who conceived the lovely cadence "where Ury gently laves the Bass and Don sings by Ardtannes Mill." His grave lies in the shadow of the Bass and it was here, at the burial, that his friend the Reverend Dr James Wood was moved to say "Here we lay him down to rest within the heather scent of Bennachie, the hill he loved."

With the publication of "Hamewith" at the turn of the century the names of Charles Murray and his work became synonymous. Since then, generations of youngsters have learned to recite "The Whistle," "It wasna' his Wyte" and, later on, "Belcanny." They became known as the poems of "Hamewith." In 1969 the Charles Murray Memorial Trust published "The Last Poems" comprising a selection of previously unpublished works made by the poet's old friend, Dr Alex. Keith who had been appointed to quantify the cream of all the material under review. In her fine foreword to the new volume, Dr Nan Shepherd adjudges "Dockens afore his Peers" and "Fae France" as the two distinctive poems where Hamewith comes nearest to greatness. She also takes considerable pains to illustrate his astonishing faculty for using the mither tongue to crystallise a bulky assortment of hard unyielding facts within the compass of a single gem, e.g. "Drift oxter-deep haps Bennachie." When winter's surly rule comes to an end, the well-shod climber sets out for the hill. Once there, he presses grimly heavenwards towards his distant goal, "despising wind and rain and fire," that he may gaze, victorious, upon the sprawling world below. All the energy, fortitude and enthusiasm being expended in the course of this vigorous exercise are confided to us by Hamewith in one curt, breath-saving remark "Up Bennachie I'm rivin' on." This latter excerpt from his works is culled from a eulogy of the hill itself, simply entitled "Bennachie" in which his adoration of the subject knows no bounds:—

> "There's Tap o' Noth, the Buck, Ben Newe
> Lonach, Benrinnes, Lochnagar
> Mount Keen, an' mony a Cairn I trow
> That's smored in mist ayont Braemar.

Bauld Ben Muich Dhui towers, until
Ben Nevis looms the laird o' a'
But Bennachie—Faith yon's the hill
Rugs at the hairt when ye're awa'.

Schiehallion—ay, I've heard the name
Ben More, the Ochils, Arthur's Seat,
Tak' them an' a' your hills o' fame
Wi' lochans leamin' at their feet;
But set me doon by Gadie side
Or whaur the Glenton lies by Don—
The muir-cock an' the whaup for guide
Up Bennachie I'm rivin' on.

Syne on the Mither Tap sae far
Win'-cairdit clouds drift by abeen,
An' wast ower Keig stands Callievar
Wi' a' the warl to me, atween.
There's braver mountains ower the sea,
An' fairer haughs I've kent, but still
The Vale o' Alford—Bennachie
Yon is the Howe, an' this the Hill.

BENNACHIE FOREST

By A. A. Cuthbert, B.SC. (FORESTRY)

The major part of Bennachie belongs to the Forestry Commission, having been purchased from neighbouring proprietors as five separate lots between the years 1938 and 1956. Two portions on the Mither Tap itself still remain in other hands, an area to the south of the peak, belonging to Monymusk Estate, and the area to the north, north-east and north-west which belongs to Pittodrie Estate. It is over this latter piece of ground that the Maiden Causeway makes its way to the summit.

The area of the hill acquired by the Commission totals just under 4,000 acres or almost exactly six square miles. The Forest itself extends far to the south, covering the greater part of the Millstone Hill, Pitfichie Hill, Cairn William and Corrennie, giving a total area of some 15,000 acres. Despite its widespread nature, the name "Bennachie Forest" was adopted for the whole due to this commanding well-known feature at its northern extremity.

At the time of the acquisition the land was practically treeless. Small remnants of earlier plantings of Scots Pine and European Larch occurred towards the south of the Mither Tap and some of these trees, roughly one hundred years old, may be seen there today. Similar relics occur on the northern face below Craigshannoch. Elsewhere, the predominant vegetation was heather.

A vigorous campaign of planting began in 1939 when the lower southern slopes were tackled. A variety of species was chosen to meet the varying demands of soil and site. On the deeper soils of the lower slopes, Sitka Spruce was used. The native Scots Pine was planted on most of the middle and upper slopes whilst Lodgepole Pine was reserved for the poorest sites where exposure or poor drainage was so severe as to prevent satisfactory growth of these other species. Over a large part of the whole area, European, Japanese and Hybrid Larch was planted either in mixture with these other species or as irregularly shaped blocks. The deciduous Larch serves as a fire break and adds considerably to visual amenity.

The planting programme was interrupted by the war, but by 1947 the programme was again in full swing. It is interesting to note that during this heyday of planting, the labour force on the Forest was 43. Today it totals 12, but this figure is augmented by up to 16 men who are employed by timber merchants in felling the newly productive area.

The northern part of the hill was acquired in the mid 50's and planting was completed there in 1962. The main species used was native Scots Pine usually in mixture with European Larch.

The plantations extend roughly to the 1000 ft contour. Above this height, exposure is generally too severe for successful growth and the thin soils are an inhospitable medium for the tree. Recent ploughing techniques however have enabled cultivation to be undertaken on the better of these high elevation sites and new planting may again be seen at the western end of the hill below Watch Craig.

In 1960, a disastrous fire swept from east to west along the south face of the hill bridging the Birks Burn and finally being brought under control at the Mains of Afforsk on the eastern extremity of the wood. Thus, years of preparation and hard work in establishing the woods were brought to naught in the course of a single day. In all, 584 acres were destroyed. The conflagration was such that the air of Aberdeen was pungent with smoke which could be seen blowing well out to sea.

The burnt area was replanted over the course of the next two years. It was possible to use more advanced techniques in replanting so that the area shows better promise than the original planting.

The older plantations have now reached the stage of timber production. About 8,000 tonnes of products—pulpwood, chipwood and timber is harvested each year from the whole Forest. Production on Bennachie Hill itself is restricted at present to these areas which escaped the fire, but within ten to fifteen years, its slopes should yield upwards of 3,000 tonnes of timber each year.

At about age 25, the plantations are thinned, an operation which is carried out throughout their lives, normally every five years. At Bennachie, this operation is carried out by timber merchants who buy the timber competitively by tender. The forest staff mark and measure the trees to be removed prior to the sale.

The cover afforded by the plantations offers a suitable habitat for many birds and mammals. Capercaillzie and black grouse continue to increase as the trees develop and the Roe Deer finds its haven by the lush clearings on the burnsides. The whole forest area is highly suitable for the Roe Deer and some fine specimens with excellent heads may be seen. The Roe, if uncontrolled, may cause serious damage to young trees and indeed to neighbouring crops so that measures are taken to restrict their numbers to acceptable limits. A census of bucks and does is carried out each year to form the basis of a target cull. Shooting is carried out in the early hours of the morning, either by the Commission's own Ranger or by sportsmen, accompanied by the Ranger, who have purchased a licence from the Forestry Commission for the privilege.

The Red Deer occurs only at Whitehaugh but the occasional wanderer may find its way from time to time on to the Bennachie massif itself.

To meet the ever increasing number of cars and walkers, the Forestry Commission built a car park and picnic site at Puttingstone on the north side of the hill in the Spring of 1973. Accommodation is for 35 cars and the park is normally full to capacity on good days during the Spring and Summer. From the park, a series of hill walks have been prepared and posted to the summits of Oxencraig, Craigshannoch and Mither Tap.

A smaller car park was built in 1972 at Woodend of Braco on the Monymusk/Pitcaple road on the eastern flank of Mither Tap.

In July 1975, a small Information Centre was opened at Donview to illustrate the main features of interest in the Bennachie/Millstone Hill area. This lies on the edge of the River Don and to the south of Millstone Hill. From here, two walks through the woods have been laid out, one short walk through the woods behind, the other to the summit of Millstone Hill itself from which fine views of Bennachie and the surrounding countryside may be obtained.

Plans for the future of the area make provision for extended walking facilities in the woods and for the control and conservation of the varied elements of wild life. Provision is made too for the enhancement of the landscape by judicious planting and felling.

*   *   *   *

"Fin a man gets a smack fae Cupid's little arra,
  It's like hurlin' in a prambulator doon the hill o' Barra;
  But suppose she winna hae ye, it's like lyin' on the rack,
  Wi' a thoosan maggie-mony-feets crawlin' doon yer back.
  Oh, it's aye the very biggest sheep that's smor't amo' the sna';
  Fin ye're fishin' it's the best troot that aye wons awa;
  If there's ae particular lassie that ye think ye'd like tae pet,
  That's jist the very ane ye may be sure ye winna get."

G. Bruce Thomson,
From "Pirn Tae't Jockie."

THE FIRST GARIOCH FARMERS

By Dr A. A. Woodham

"The river Dee for fish and tree
The river Don for horn and corn."

The Garioch district of Donside comprises some of the finest agricultural land in Scotland and its attraction for early settlers is clear from the abundant relics of past ages. Settlement began as early here as anywhere in Scotland, though the attraction for the earliest arrivals was not the quality of the land so much as the well stocked rivers. No indisputable traces of Palaeolithic-Old Stone Age-man have been found in Scotland and this is due to the fact that throughout the period when man was establishing himself on the Continent of Europe and in Southern England, Scotland remained completely covered by ice sheets. Not until these had finally melted and the climate had become considerably less rigorous did the first groups of hunters move northwards. It has long been known that groups of these Mesolithic or Middle Stone Age people established themselves on Dee-side, their typical flint tools having been found at sites near Banchory, notably at Birkwood and Inchmarlo. These tiny beautifully-worked points are called microliths and they are characteristic of peoples originating from the Continent at this time. Their culture is usually referred to as Tardenoisian after the French site where so many of their products have been found. We now know that these same people settled on Donside and some of their worked flints found in the neighbourhood of Inverurie may be seen in the Inverurie Museum. Harpoons and fish gorges have been found associated with contemporary peoples in other parts of Scotland, a famous bone harpoon having been found for instance in Banffshire, and although the Dee and Don have not so far yielded similar unequivocal evidence it may be safely concluded that the rivers were a major attractive feature and that these people were exploiting the fishing here at least as early as 5,000 B.C. No traces of dwellings or burials have been found and we may conclude that these were nomadic peoples living in skin or branch tents or in rock-shelters. It seems certain that a thorough examination of the Don river terraces would provide as much evidence for settlement as has already been found on Dee-side.

Recent discoveries in Scotland suggest that the arrival of peoples who practised systematic agriculture, i.e. crop raising and animal domestication as opposed to mere hunting of wild animals and the gathering of wild berries, may have occurred as early as 4,000 B.C. and it is to these people, the primary neolithic settlers, as well as to their descendants, the secondary neolithic peoples produced by fusion with the indigenous mesolithic hunter-fishers, that we must attribute some of the striking field monuments such as cairns and henges which occur in the North-East of Scotland.

The long barrows and cairns of the north-east are found mainly on the lower ground to the east and north-east of the main Grampian area, but the Cairnborrow cairn near Huntly and the Balnagowan cairns near Tarland indicate that the long cairn tradition is to be associated with the Garioch region. The total number of long cairns and barrows in the north-east is little more than a dozen and it must be concluded that these impressive tombs would have been raised only for selected individuals and families—chieftain's and the like. None of the long cairns, and only one barrow, has been scientifically excavated. This excavation, carried out by Professor Stuart Piggott in 1970/1, was a rescue operation necessitated by the threatened destruction of this newly-recognised long barrow at Dalladies, Edzell. The finds were so similar to those from the many barrows excavated in Southern England that there was no doubt that this structure at least is attributable to the primary neolithic invaders of Scotland. Similarities in size and shape as well as isolated finds in pottery, e.g. in the long cairn at Knapperty Hillock, Maud, strongly suggest that the long cairns were built by the same people.

Henge monuments consisting of flat circular areas surrounded by a ditch and bank and provided with one or two entrances occur at Inverurie and Rhynie. These monuments are analogous to the much more splendid monuments at Stonehenge and Avebury in Southern England and, like them, must be regarded as sacred sites which presumably represented the Churches of the neolithic and early bronze age peoples. Monuments with a single entrance such as the mini-henge in Clashindarroch Forest, Rhynie and the henge discovered on an aerial photograph on the farm of Dubston near Inverurie are attributed to the secondary neolithic peoples while double-entrance henges, represented in this area by the well-known site of Crichie, Port-Elphinstone may well have been constructed around 1500 B.C. by the first metal-using people to come to this area—the Beaker people.

The precise attribution of field remains constructed about this time is still a matter for conjecture. Clearly there was rapid absorption of the new invaders who came by sea from the Netherlands, landing at the mouths of the Dee and Don, and to what extent they were responsible for modifying the architectural ideas of the neolithic builders is unknown. In northern Scotland megalithic structures, i.e. structures involving the use of massive blocks of stone, were erected during neolithic times at least as early as 2500 B.C. to 2000 B.C. Such structures are the chambered tombs of the northern mainland and islands. Megalithic structures in the Garioch include the numerous recumbent stone circles and the Crichie henge—neither definitely attributable to the pre-Beaker neolithic but falling within this shadowy late Neolithic—early Bronze Age period.

The most striking as well as the most numerous class of monument within the Garioch is the recumbent stone circle. Consisting basically of a relatively inconspicuous ring cairn surrounded by a circle of upright stones, the characteristic feature is the recumbent group—a large horizontal stone flanked by two upright pillar stones—the whole forming part of the ring of standing stones. This type of monument is only found in the north-east of Scotland and the greatest density seems to be centred on the Garioch. Well preserved examples are at Loanhead of Daviot and at Aquorthies, Manar. Both are now in the care of the Department of the Environment. The former was excavated in 1933-1934 by Mr Kilbride-Jones, and subsequently, fallen stones were re-erected in their original positions. Much pottery was found during the excavation chiefly of Beaker and Iron Age date, but it was recently noticed that included in the finds, although unrecognised at the time of the excavation, were some pieces of neolithic pottery—the so-called Lyles Hill were named after an Irish site which has yielded much of this pottery. Whether this represents a carrying over into Beaker times of this earlier pottery type or whether the Lyles Hill pottery does in fact pre-date the Beaker pottery, which was found in far greater quantity, it is not possible to say. It may be that the pottery is evidence of a pre-Beaker use of the site, and there is no reason to suppose that the stone circle itself was not erected by the Beaker folk. Although it is clear that the recumbent stone circles had some sacred function, suggestions that they were used for astronomical measurements have not been proved. The use of the recumbent slab as an "artificial horizon" to be used for observing the rising or setting of prominent stars—or the moon—has been suggested but the theory is not borne out very well when applied to particular stones at the time when the monuments were constructed. There are certain similarities between these stone circles and the burial cairns of Clava type found in the Inverness region but the Aberdeenshire circles were not primarily sepulchral and tend to be sited, unlike the Clava cairns, on high ground. Also, of course, the two classes of monument do not over-lap one another geographically.

During the Bronze Age proper various megalithic structures were erected, and one such is the unique stone circle at Cullerlie, Echt. Here a circle of standing stones, without a horizontal recumbent, surrounds eight small cairns, each being contained within a relatively massive boulder kerb. Also excavated by Kilbride-Jones, this monument provided evidence for its use for the deposition of cremated burials and its Bronze Age date was confirmed by a piece of characteristic pottery. Also representative of the Bronze Age are the urn cemeteries such as the one adjacent to the recumbent stone circle at Loanhead of Daviot, and also in the care of the Department of the Environment. Here a number of large cinerary urns were found inverted over cremation deposits and surrounding an extended unburnt burial. Cremations had been carried out within the central area, and the whole cemetery was enclosed by a low circular wall, provided with entrances at opposite sides. A circular burial area provided with two entrances brings to mind the henge at Crichie and there, too, cremations surrounded an unburnt burial. The circles at the Tuach Hill, Kintore and at Fullerton, Inverurie were similar in nature. Recently a cemetery consisting of seven cremations beneath cinerary urns was found at Lowhillside, Bourtie, and in this case there was no sign of any surrounding wall or ditch. The Lowhillside urns are preserved at Marischal College, Aberdeen, and in the Inverurie Museum.

We have now discussed the visible remains of man in this part of Scotland dating from his arrival probably some time earlier than 5000 B.C. and embracing the period up to about 500 B.C. During this time he had made great strides in development and had become skilled in the use of copper and later bronze. It will be noticed that the field remains are exclusively concerned with ritual and burial. We know little of the types of houses built by neolithic and bronze age people in Britain as a whole and we must conclude that, certainly in North-East Scotland, dwellings must have been of a flimsy and ephemeral nature. Doubtless the way of life continued to be nomadic throughout the whole of the period under review here and this would be expected of peoples who were in the slow process of developing agricultural techniques by trial and error.

Index of Sites

Cairnborrow: (NJ543414) 4½m W of Huntly, Neolithic long-horned cairn. Aligned E-W 36m x 15m. Partially excavated. ca 3000 B.C.

Balnagowan: (NJ490005) 2¾m NW of Aboyne. Neolithic long-horned cairn. Aligned ESE-WNW, 54m x 24m. ca 3000 B.C.

Knapperty Hillock: (NJ946503) 2m NE of Maud. Neolithic long-horned cairn. Aligned ESE-WNW, now 66m x 23m, but probably originally 90m long. Cist burials found within cairn in the 19th century, one apparently accompanied by neolithic pottery which is now in the Arbuthnot Museum, Peterhead. One cist still visible. ca 3000 B.C.

Dalladies: (NO627674) 2½m SW of Edzell. Neolithic long barrow. Aligned E-W 65m x 18m. Excavated by Professor Stuart Piggott in 1970-71. Now completely destroyed by gravel pit. Contained wooden mortuary structure and cup-marked stone. ca 4000-3500 B.C.

Clashindarroch: (NJ449307) 4m NW of Rhynie. A mini-henge, with single entrance to the SSE. Circular bank 18m in diameter round a ditch enclosing a flat circular area 6m in diameter. Probably a sacred site of the Neolithic Period. ca 3000-2500 B.C.

Dubston Farm: (NJ744222) 1m W of Inverurie. A single-entrance henge monument practically invisible on the ground but seen on aerial photographs. ca 3000-2500 B.C.

Crichie: (NJ779197) Port Elphinstone, m S of Inverurie. A double-entrance henge monument probably dating from the Beaker Period (1800–1500 B.C.). Excavated in the 19th century and found to enclose a central, unburnt burial surrounded by a number of cremations, some associated with Bronze Age cinerary urns. These were located at the feet of standing stones (two only now remain of an original circle of six). The unburnt burial and a characteristic stone battle-axe date this monument to the Neolithic-Bronze Age transitional period. The central Pictish Class 1 symbol stone was not originally situated in its present position, but was moved there in the mid-19th century.

Loanhead of Daviot: (NJ748288) 4m W of Oldmeldrum. A "recumbent" stone circle dating from the Neolithic-Bronze Age transitional period. Eight upright stones, one cup-marked, in addition to the recumbent group consisting of a large horizontal slab with two flanking pillar stones surround a low ring-cairn. Excavated in 1934 yielding Neolithic, Beaker, Bronze Age and Iron Age pottery. Restored by the excavator and now maintained by the Department of the Environment.

Aquorthies, Manar: (NJ733208) 2½m W of Inverurie. Nine uprights in addition to the "recumbent" group form a circle 20m in diameter but there is no trace of the original ring-cairn of this recumbent stone-circle. ca 2000-1500 B.C.

Cullerlie: (NJ785042) 4m NW of Peterculter. A circle of eight monoliths 10m in diameter encloses eight small cairns each with a massive retaining kerb. The site was excavated in 1935 and the cairns were found to cover cremation pits of the Bronze Age. The site is under the guardianship of the Department of the Environment. ca 1000 B.C.

Tuach Hill: (NJ795155) On the S outskirts of Kintore.

Fullerton Farm: (NJ783182) 1m NW of Kintore.

Lowhillside Farm: (NJ807235) 2½m NE of Inverurie.

These three sites have all on excavation yielded cremations of Bronze Age date, with associated cinerary urns. ca 1200-900 B.C.

THE WEDDED WATERS

By William Thom

Gadie wi' its waters fleet,
Ury wi' its murmur sweet,
They ha'e trysted aye to meet
    Among the woods o' Logie.
Like bride and bridegroom happy they,
Wooing smiles frae bank an' brae,
Their wedded waters wind an' play
    Round leafy bowers at Logie.

O'er brashy linn, o'er meadow fine,
They never sinder, never tyne,
An' oh! I thought sic meetings mine,
    Yon happy hours at Logie.
But Fortune's cauld an' changefu' e'e
Gloomed bitterly on mine an' me,
I looket syne, but cou'dna see
    My sworn love at Logie.

Now lowly, lonely, I may rue
The guilefu' look, the guilefu' vow,
That fled as flees the feckless dew
    Frae withered leaves at Logie.
But Gadie wi' its torrents keen,
An' Ury wi' its braes sae green,
They a' can tell how true I've been
    To my lost love in Logie.

PREHISTORIC COMMUNITIES IN THE GARIOCH

By Dr A. A. Woodham

The introduction of iron working into Great Britain is usually associated with the establishment of relatively organised settlements. Possibly in Scotland settlements may have been established before, but not long before, the introduction of iron smelting. Both bronze and iron were worked at Cullycan, the promontory fort near Pennan in Banff-shire, and the famous bronze hoard found in 1866 at the Braes of Gight near Haddo House and dating from about 500 B.C. was clearly inspired by the same ideas that motivated the earliest ironworkers. It seems that we should be looking for the establishment of village communities at around this period. Confirmation of this has been provided by radio-carbon dates from Cullycan, from the vitrified fort at Craig Phadrig near Inverness, and from the now almost obliterated fort at Burghead of around 400 B.C.

Settlements on hill-tops occur notably in the Garioch region on the Mither Tap itself, on Barra Hill, Tap o' Noth, Barmekin of Echt and Dunnideer, as well as on a number of smaller eminences around the periphery of the Bennachie massif—Maiden Castle, Tillymuick and Bruce's Camp on Crichie Hill. The dated sites listed above are all examples of "vitrified forts"—hilltop and promontory. Vitrified forts are characterised by the fact that part of the massive stone wall rampart has been subjected to intense heat, resulting in the fusing of the individual stones into a coherent mass. This may have been brought about accidentally, for example, by the firing of huts built against the inside of the rampart, itself consisting of alternate layers of timber and stone, or intentionally by attackers lighting fires against the outside of the wall. Examples of such vitrified forts in the Garioch region are Dunnideer and, of course, Tap o' Noth. The remainder of the forts fall into several types.

The very impressive fort surrounding the summit of the Mither Tap of Bennachie consists of an immensely strong stone wall. Parts which remain standing to a considerable height show no signs of having once contained timbers, so we must assume that this fort differed in its construction from that of the forts whose walls are now vitrified. Well chosen stones have been used to build high walls with little batter, and along the North side there remains part of a parapet. Wells can be seen within the *enceinte*. Huts were presumably originally constructed against the inside of the wall for shelter and also because there are few sufficiently flat areas within the centre of the fort. Circular constructions visible at the present day are modern. The limited space suitable for house building as well as the exposed nature of the fort suggest strongly that this fort was primarily intended as a refuge in times of trouble, and lying so close to the path of the Romans between their marching camps of Kintore and Ythan Wells, one is tempted to see here a refuge of the Caledonii during the time that the invaders were in the area. The small fortified enclosures around the base of Bennachie could well be the permanent villages of those who retreated to the high ground in times of danger.

No signs of huts are visible within any of the forts of the area. Excavation at Cullycan indicated that houses were represented only by post-holes in the ground and one must conclude that the type of Iron Age house, the remains of which we refer to as a "hut-circle" and which consisted of a low circular stone wall upon which the roof timbers were bedded, was not necessarily always constructed within the forts. They are certainly to be found in the area on the lower ground, e.g. at the Ratch Hill, Kintore, and on the Moor of Kinellar, and this does lend weight to the idea that the forts were not inhabited for long periods. Equally however one does not find hut circles within the smaller forts situated within easy reach of the agricultural land, and one is left with the impression that permanent homes were undefended and not grouped into villages, and that the people only banded together to build forts when necessary, returning to their isolated homes when the danger was past. Small undefended groups of hut circles may be seen beside Loch Kinnord.

Some forts show signs of having been modified subsequently to the original construction. The impressive hill-fort on the Barmekin at Echt consists of two stone walls surrounded by three predominantly earthern ramparts. This suggests that at some point in the history of the fort it was felt that a greater depth of defence was needed. During the Iron Age weapons were becoming more sophisticated and deadly. An enemy possessing slings and throwing spears would require to be kept at a greater distance than an enemy equipped only with stones, clubs and swords. At Dunnideer also, the inner vitrified wall around the summit is surrounded by an earth bank and ditch some distance away from the wall.

If the forts are considered to be primarily refuges, where were the permanent settlements during the Iron Age? A compact village consisting of a number of large stone walled circular huts with associated cattle-pounds is to be seen beside Loch Kinnord and indeed in this area are many of the typical hut-circles which are generally associated with the Iron Age period. The comparative scarcity of these structures in the Garioch itself may be attributed to the efficiency of land clearance during the late 18th and 19th centuries. The high proportion of arable land must have attracted the early farmers as it did their predecessors, and doubtless their huts were constructed for the most part on land which is now under the plough. They survive only in marginal areas such as the open boggy moorland in the vicinity of Kintore. Other types of dwelling dating from this period include the crannogs or artificial islands constructed in the lochs. A good example is to be found in Loch Kinnord and the general scarcity of suitable sheets of water in north-east Scotland is probably the only reason why more of these structures are not to be found here. None of the dry-stone towers called brochs are situated in the north-east of Scotland. The largest concentration of these defensible farmhouses is to be found of course in the North, notably in Caithness and Sutherland. A thin scatter covers the rest of the Scottish mainland, the north-east excepted. The east coast of Scotland is, however, notable for the concentration of earth-houses or *souterrains*. Known to date from the Iron Age period not only from finds made by excavation but also by their occasional association with hut-circles, these structures remain an enigma. They present differences in various details of construction in different localities. For example the Angus souterrains are large, wide and often appear to have been constructed as a trench which was subsequently roofed with flat slabs. The Aberdeenshire variety is smaller and at least in some cases consist of stone-lined tunnels penetrating a hill-side. It has been suggested that the larger Angus examples were underground cattle-pens associated with surface farm buildings. This explanation is not tenable for the Aberdeenshire examples which are too small and have narrow entrances. Those examples which open into a surface dwelling must be regarded as cellars possibly for the storage of grain. By and large the most acceptable explanation is that they were underground refuges. It has been objected that people in them would be cornered and could be easily "smoked out" by an enemy. This would be true if the attackers were to find them, but it seems at least possible that camouflaging the entrances with vegetation might well prevent discovery by a foe who was unfamiliar with the territory. The Romans would represent such a foe, marching briefly into a strange land, and the contemporaneity of the souterrains with the Roman occupation of Scotland must make this suggestion at least a possibility. Souterrains are to be seen at Kildrummy and in the vicinity of Loch Kinnord. The example at Culsh, near Tarland, is easy of access being situated adjacent to the road.

Mention of the Romans reminds us that although these invaders left no permanent forts in north-east Scotland traces are extant of their marching camps, notable examples being situated at Raedykes near Stonehaven, Normandykes (at Peterculter), Kintore, and at Wells of Ythan. The existence of both large 120 acre, as well as small 30 acre, camps suggest that the Romans visited this part of Scotland on at least two occasions and that the smaller camps at Keith and Wells of Ythan are probably to be attributed to Agricola in the campaign which ended at the Battle of Mons Graupius in 85 A.D. The larger camps may well have been constructed during the Severan campaigns between 209 and 213 A.D.

The so-called Dark Ages and the Pictish period are more or less contemporary in Scotland and perhaps the most characteristic monuments surviving from this time are the symbol stones. The Garioch is particularly rich in stones of the earliest period dating from about 500 to 700 A.D. On these stones the enigmatic symbols, geometric and animal representations, are incised and not accompanied by the Christian Cross. Examples of Class I stones are to be seen in the centre of the henge monument at Crichie and in Inverurie cemetery. Symbols accompanied by the cross are found on the Class II stones and the carvings are usually in relief. A splendid example from the Garioch is, of course, the Maiden Stone and this probably dates from 700-800 A.D. About this time also the earliest Oghams were being carved on stones in the region. This is a form of script consisting of groups of short horizontal and oblique strokes attached to a single vertical line. The Brandsbutt and Newton stones are good examples from the area.

One other prominent feature of the countryside of the north-east Scotland remains to be described. Though not strictly prehistoric the castle-mounds are direct descendants of the hill-forts and crannogs of the Iron Age. They were fortified sites constructed or utilised by Norman overlords during the 13th and 14th centuries A.D. Not all of the mounds were artificial, the Bass of Inverurie being a natural mound which was surrounded by a man-made moat joined at each end to the River Ury. All had castles of stone, or wooden towers, on their summits and all formed the focal point for the community of the time, who sheltered within the sphere of influence of their lord. Examples surviving in this area in addition to the Bass at Inverurie are the Peel at Lumphanan, the Peel of Strathbogie at Huntly, the Peel of Fichlie, the Motte at Midmar and the Doune of Invernochty. The Castle Hill at Kintore, a further example, was destroyed during the construction of the railway.

Index of Sites

Bennachie: (NJ682224) 2m S of Oyne. Hill-top fort surrounding the summit of the Mither Tap o' Bennachie with a massive stone wall and entrance on the NE perimeter. Remains of a parapet exist on the northern side. The fort is probably of Iron Age date and may have been constructed in the 2nd or 3rd centuries B.C.

Tap o' Noth: (NJ484293) 1½m NW of Rhynie. A massive stone wall showing considerable signs of vitrifaction surrounds the somewhat dished summit of this hill. It is roughly oval and measures 100m x 32m. A second wall can be traced lower down the hill on the N and E and there are levelled areas outside the vitrified wall which may have been house sites. ca 400-200 B.C.

Barmekin of Echt: (NJ726072) 1m NW of Echt. Two inner stone walls (un-vitrified) and three outer earthern ramparts crown the summit of the hill. There is an oblique entrance at the E end of the oval fort and there are possibly 2 other original entrances. The structure within the fort is the remnant of a 19th century observatory. ca 400-100 B.C.

Dunnideer: (NJ612281) 1m W of Insch. A single stone wall, much of it vitrified, encloses a rectangular area 70m (E-W) and 24m (N-S). Outside this wall are two ditches separated by a bank which appears to be substantially built of earth, and surrounds the hill roughly one-third of its height below the summit. The gable of a mediaeval castle is a conspicuous land-mark within the fort.

Maiden Castle: (NJ694244) 1½m W of Chapel of Garioch. A bank between two ditches encloses an almost circular area 27-28m in diameter on a spur to the NE of the fort on the Mither Tap itself. The ditches do not continue round the whole fort, being omitted on the steep NE side. The entrance is to the SE.

Tillymuick: (NJ650245) 1½m SW of Oyne. A spur of the Bennachie massif is crowned with an oval fort.

Bruce's Camp: (NJ768190) 1m SW of Port Elphinstone. The summit of a low isolated hill is surrounded by an oval bank and ditch.

Ratch Hill: (NJ774168) 1m W of Kintore. Several Iron Age hut circles are situated on a N-facing slope. Each has a diameter of 30-40 feet, and the entrances can be clearly seen. ca 200 B.C.-200 A.D.

Kinellar Moor: (NJ805140) 2m SE of Kintore. Iron Age hut circles associated with small cairns—probably the results of primitive land clearance. ca 200 B.C.-200 A.D.

New Kinnord: (NJ449001) 1m NW of Dinnet. A group of large Iron Age hut circles and associated animal enclosures, forming a village unit. ca 200 B.C.-200 A.D.

Kinnord Crannog: (NO441997) 1½m NW of Dinnet. An artificial island probably constructed during the Iron Age 200 B.C.-200 A.D. Canoes have been found submerged in the region of the crannog.

Kildrummy Muir: (NJ461197) 2m SW of Lumsden. Two earth houses or souterrains remain of what was once a larger group.

Culsh: (NJ505055) 1½m NE of Tarland. A curving stone-lined passage leads into a hillside for a distance of 14m, widening at its inner end to form a pear-shaped chamber. Cup-marks are visible on stones just inside the entrance. Probably of Iron Age date (200 B.C.-200 A.D.).

Kintore Roman Camp: (NJ786163) This large Roman marching camp enclosing an area of over 100 acres is now invisible from the ground but its straight sides and gateways have been photographed from the air. Much of the present town of Kintore falls within the confines of the Camp which was probably constructed at the time of Severus' punitive expeditions in this area about 210 A.D.

Crichie Stone: (NJ779197) At Port Elphinstone 1m S of Inverurie. This Class I symbol stone was placed in the centre of the Crichie Henge (see Chap. 1) in the mid-19th century, having originally been situated some distance away in the surrounding field. It has two symbols—the so-called "elephant," and an ornamented crescent and V-rod both incised on one face. 500-700 A.D.

Inverurie Cemetery: (NJ781206) Just to the W of the base of the Bass of Inverurie (q.v.) are four symbol stones, all of Class I. Two are fragmentary. One bears a splendid incised carving of a horse—one of the rarer of the Pictish symbols. The other, complete, stone has the double-disc and Z-rod, mirror-case, and ornamented horse-shoe symbols.

Also in this group of stones can be seen the Inverurie mort-safe—a massive granite slab which was placed above newly-buried coffins during the early 19th century to baffle the resurrectionists. The iron tackle used for lowering and lifting the stone was kept in a near-by bakery, and is now in safe-keeping in the Inverurie Museum.

Maiden Stone: (NJ704247) 1m W of Chapel of Garioch. A famous Class II stone having on one face a cross surmounted by a man with arms stretched out, and with fish monsters on either side. On the reverse are various almost indecipherable beasts, the two-legged rectangle and Z-rod, the "elephant" and mirror with comb, all being beautifully executed in relief. ca 8th-9th centuries A.D.

Brandsbutt Stone: (NJ760224) 1m N of Inverurie. Deliberately broken some years ago this stone has been repaired and is now in the care of the Department of the Environment. In addition to the Crescent and V-rod and the serpent and Z-rod symbols incised, there is an Ogham inscription on the same face. ca 9th century A.D.

Newton Stones: (NJ663297) Beside Newton House 3m NE of Insch. Two stones are situated here, both having been moved away from their original positions. One is a Class I symbol stone with the double disc and the serpent and Z-rod symbols. The other stone has a remarkable enigmatic inscription in what may be debased Roman characters. No satisfactory reading has yet been made. In addition this stone has a vertical Ogham inscription down one edge. ca 9th century A.D.

Bass of Inverurie: (NJ782206) In Inverurie cemetery. This natural mound of sand and gravel was the site of a castle—probably a wooden tower—during the 12th and 13th centuries. The Bass and the adjacent Little Bass were surrounded by a moat joined at each end to the river. Considerable quantities of early mediaeval pottery have been found on the site of the moat during grave-digging. 12th-14th centuries A.D.

Peel of Lumphanan: (NJ576037) ¾m SW of Lumphanan. A large artificial mound surrounded by a wide, well-preserved moat. On the mound are visible remains of the foundations of stone buildings and of an encircling stone wall. 12th-14th centuries A.D.

Peel of Fichlie: (NJ459139) 2½m S of Kildrummy. Artificial castle-mound. 12th-14th centuries A.D.

Midmar motte: (NJ701059) 2½m W of Echt. Artificial castle-mound. 12th-14th centuries A.D.

Doune of Invernochty: (NJ352129) At Strathdon. Artificial castle-mound. 12th-14th centuries A.D.

Peel of Strathbogie: (NJ532408) Adjacent to Huntly Castle, Huntly. Artificial castle-mound. 12th-14th centuries A.D.

CASKIEBEN

By Arthur Johnston

The translation of a famous latin lyric by the Renaissance Poet, Arthur Johnston (1587-1641) born at Caskieben, subsequently acquired by the Keith family and re-named Keith Hall.

"Here, traveller, a vale behold,
As fair as Tempe's famed of old,
Beneath the northern sky.
Here Urie with her silver waves
Her banks in verdure smiling laves,
And winding wimples by.

Here Bennachie high towering spreads
Around on all his evening shades,
When twilight grey comes on.
With sparkling gems the river glows;
As precious stones the mountain shows
As in the east are known.

Here nature spreads a bosom sweet,
And native dyes beneath the feet
Bedeck the joyous ground;
Sport in the liquid air the birds,
And fishes in the stream, the herds
In meadows wanton round.

Here ample barnyards still are stored
With relics of last Autumn's hoard,
And firstlings of this year.
There waving fields of yellow corn,
And ruddy apples that adorn
The bending boughs appear.

Beside the streams a castle proud
Rises amid the passing cloud,
And rules a wide domain
(Unequal to its lord's desert).
A village near, with lowlier art,
Is built upon the plain.

Here I was born; o'er all the land
Around the Johnstons bear command,
Of high and ancient line.
Mantua acquired a noted name
As Virgil's birthplace, I my fame
Inherit still from mine."

The quality of the original may be gauged from the last two stanzas:—

"*Propter aquas arx est, ipsi contermina caelo,*
Auctoris menti non tamen aequa sui.
Imperat haec arvis et vectigalibus undis,
Et famula stadiis distat ab urbe tribus.

Haec mihi terra parens: gens has Ionstonia lymphas,
Arvaque per centum missa tuetur avos.
Clara Maroneis evasit Mantua cunis
Me mea natalis nobilitabit humus."

CASTLES

By Jim Buchan, M.A., ED.B.

Possibly the first stone and lime castle in the Garioch was built on the hill of Dunnideer within the remnants of the ancient vitrified fort. Little is known about it although it was for many years one of the most important castles in the area. In 1565, it is named in a charter granted by Mary, Queen of Scots, as the capital messuage for the Lordship and Regality of the Garioch; a century earlier it appeared as the "Castell of Dony Dowre" in Hardynge's map of Scotland; and, according to that map-maker, King Arthur and his Knights of the Round Table held court at "Donydoure," but since the same source would have us believe that the legendary hero also frequented Edinburgh, Stirling, Perth, Dumbarton, Dumfries, and Dunbar, to say nothing of Carlisle, Dover, and Cornwall, we may take his migration from Camelot to the Garioch with the proverbial pinch of salt. And even if the hero-king did grace our area with his presence, it was long before the tower house was built.

A charter of 1260 mentions the "Castle of Dunidor." It was then in the possession of Sir Josceline de Balliol, whose nephew was to become notorious in Scottish history as "Toom Tabard," the king who succumbed to Edward I of England, the Hammer of the Scots. Sir Josceline held the castle in feu from his brother Sir John de Balliol, whose wife, Devorguilla, the founder of Sweetheart Abbey in Kirkcudbrightshire and of Balliol College, Oxford, was the grand-daughter of David, Earl of Huntingdon and Lord of the Garioch, the probable builder of the motte and bailey on the Bass. David had gifted all the parish churches in the Garioch to the Abbey of Lindores in Fife. It was to this abbey that Sir Josceline de Balliol, in the charter of 1260, granted a right of way four and a half feet wide through the land to the east of Dunnideer, from the River Urie to the mill at Insch, in exchange for a pair of white gloves annually! The exact site of the castle mentioned in the charter has not been confirmed but, since the type of masonry still extant in the remnants of the simple, unvaulted rectangular tower on Dunnideer is datable to the thirteenth century and since there is no evidence of any other castle having existed nearby, it seems that the gaunt ruin is all that survives of the building named in 1260. Should this be so, then, here in the Garioch, we have the remains of the second-oldest, authenticated tower house in Scotland. (The oldest is Cubbie Roo's Castle, which seems to have been in existence as early as 1145 on the island of Wyre, in the Orkneys).

The typical tower house was essentially a partial reversion to the Norman keep. It had very thick walls; one room on each floor, with the kitchen in the basement, living accommodation in the hall above, and sleeping accommodation at the top; and, with a minimum of openings in the lower parts of the building, defence was conducted from loopholes in the upper storeys and from the roof parapet. Defensive considerations were obviously predominant in the design and, to give extra security, the door was at first floor level with access by means of a wooden staircase which could be removed if the castle was attacked. The fortification was usually strengthened by the addition of a barmkin or courtyard enclosed by a stone wall. The tower house was the simplest and cheapest way in which a baron or humble bonnet laird could provide himself with a defensible house with "its brow-beating height flaunting his social pride" but it had manifest and manifold shortcomings as a place for comfortable, to say nothing of elegant, living. In time, an L-shaped tower was devised. By adding a wing at right angles to the long side of the main building, the master mason provided extra accommodation with a greater degree of comfort and privacy. It was also possible to have the door on the ground floor in the easily defended, re-entrant angle between the two wings in what was known colloquially as a "tower and a jamb." With the introduction of hand guns, the L-plan was modified and the jamb was replaced by a square or round tower built diagonally, or en echelon, from the main building. Loop-holes were provided on the ground floor and flanking defence of two sides of the main block was possible in such link-plan or two-stepped castles. The obvious, and indeed the logical, development of this plan was to build a castle with towers offset at two diagonally-opposite corners of the main structure. In such three-stepped, or Z-plan, castles, all sides of the main block could be defended from the towers en echelon and they, in turn, could be protected from the central part of the building. Here, with the provision of more residential accommodation and with no part of the castle excluding light from any other part, was the acme of the planning of the Scottish tower house—domestic and military requirements were both satisfied. (Of 64 identified examples of the Z-plan, 19 stand between Aberdeen and Elgin and, since 11 are situated in Mar and the Garioch, it may well be that this type of castle originated in Aberdeenshire, if not in our particular area).

While there is obviously, in castle design in general, a developmental sequence of type-plans this does not mean that, for particular examples, we can deduce a corresponding absolute chronology. We can not infer the building date of a castle from its plan; for instance, L-plan castles continued to be built long after the Z-plan had been devised. Among the castles in the environs of Bennachie, there is ample illustration of the continuity of development, of the persistence of an indigenous tradition of castellated architecture, and of the alterations and additions to existing buildings which were rendered necessary by changing circumstances.

When David, Earl of Huntingdon, was invested with the Lordship of the Garioch, he appointed Malcolm, son of Bartolf, to be Constable of Inverurie. Malcolm's descendant, Sir George Leslie, was granted the barony of Balquhain in 1340, by David II, in recognition of his services to the Bruce family during the Wars of Independence. Presumably, Sir George built a castle at Balquhain but little is known about the oldest structure there except that it was burned by Sir John Forbes of Drumminor around 1420. Its successor was also burned by the Forbeses in 1526 and the ruins which now stand on the steep bank over-hanging the Strathnaterick Burn are all that remain of the building which took its place and was occupied by the Leslies until 1710.

The oldest part of the sixteenth-century castle seems to have been a rectangular tower house, with entry at first floor level, and from the evidence of the few remaining structural features, datable to about 1530. It had the customary vaulted cellars in the basement, the hall on the first floor, and a newel stair to the two floors above. During the next century and a half, or so, this tower became an integral part of an extensive structure with a frontage of some two hundred feet. It is impossible to determine the order in which the additions were made but it seems that, initially, a hall was set at right angles to the north-west corner of the tower house. Then, to the north of the original tower, a central court was created with apartments on either hand. To the west, the buildings included a round tower which seems to date from the early part of the seventeenth century while, on the east side, a symmetrically planned courtyard house was added. Although also attributable to the seventeenth century, this was of more recent date than the other parts of the castle. Could it be that a stone, with the monograms of Jesus and Mary and the date 1677, now built into the gable of a cottage at Mains of Balquhain, gives a clue to the exact date of the last addition to the castle? It is possible that the stone was taken from the ruins of Balquhain Castle where it may have been inserted as a kind of talisman during the alterations to the building.

While it is relatively common to find a stone inscribed with the initials of the owner and his wife, together with the date of construction, in castles in north-east Scotland it is not usual to find the sacred monograms. It is all the more remarkable, therefore, to find a similar stone with the monograms IHS (Jesus Hominum Salvator) and MRA (Maria Regina Angelorum) and the initials PL and MI, with the date 1691, at Fetternear House. The initials are those of Patrick Leslie and his wife, Mary Irvine, who were responsible for an extensive building programme at Fetternear between 1690 and 1693. Patrick Leslie, as well as being the fifteenth baron of Balquhain, was a Count of the Austrian Empire, as were most of the lairds of Balquhain in the seventeenth century. It may be that this long Imperial connection was responsible for the appearance of the sacred monograms at both Balquhain and Fetternear. The cult of the Holy Name had become popular during the counter-Reformation, especially in areas which had been reconverted to Catholicism by the Jesuits. The Counts Leslie would obviously have been well aware of the cult when they participated in the campaigns against the Turks in Bohemia, where Jesuits were active, and Patrick Leslie had recently returned from Austria when he took up residence in Fetternear.

The Leslies had acquired "the palace, tower, and fortalice" of Fetternear at the time of the Reformation when the Barony of Fetternear was granted to William Leslie, ninth baron of Balquhain, as a reward from the Bishop of Aberdeen for his assistance in preventing St. Machar Cathedral being looted by a Reforming mob, which had already plundered St. Nicholas Kirk in Aberdeen. The foundations of a small L-shaped building, known locally as the "Auld Founds," to the south of the House of Fetternear are presumably all that remain of "the palace, tower, and fortalice." Bishop Kyninmund had completed the palace in the 1330's but it was no longer habitable by 1550. William Leslie, or his immediate successor, probably set about building a castle as the focal point of the newly acquired barony, in 1566 or soon afterwards. It is very likely that the small tower house, which is architecturally typical of the second half of the sixteenth century and which was incorporated at the south end of the main block at the House of Fetternear, is the original seat of the Leslies there. From this small beginning, was developed the mansion house which was burned in the disastrous fire in December, 1919, and is now a pathetic ruin. Starting as a laird's tower house in the sixteenth century, it was transformed into a nobleman's palace in the 1690's, and then, when wings were added in 1818 and 1841, it became the seat of a Victorian country gentleman.

When Count Patrick Leslie took up residence in Fetternear in 1690, his son continued to inhabit Balquhain Castle until 1710. For a short time after this, Balquhain was leased to tenants but it was allowed to fall into disrepair and, by 1732, it was described as "an old decayed court." In 1746, when on his way to Culloden, Butcher Cumberland is said to have given orders for the complete destruction of the castle but John Nicol, a tenant on the estate, bribed the redcoats to spare the building; they did so and merely burned bundles of straw at the window to deceive the Duke into believing that it was well ablaze. Three years later, on 2nd May, the "Aberdeen Journal" carried the following item— "By Tradesmen just come from Balquane we hear that on Wednesday the 17th instant, the Roof, Joysts, and Flooring (mostly of Oak) of the Old House of Balquane, with the Iron Stenisons, are to be sold by public roup by Mr John Clerk, Advocate in Aberdeen." And so ended, "not with a bang but a whimper," the ancestral home of the Leslies of Balquhain, a family which included some members notorious for their violence and others famous for their martial prowess.

Perhaps the most violent was the infamous "robber baron," Sir Andrew Leslie, who is said to have left six sons dead on the field of Harlaw in 1411. A scandalous womaniser, he finally abducted the "Fair Maid of Strathavon," daughter of the laird of Inveravon in Banffshire, and was outlawed. He fled to the fort on the Mither Tap of Bennachie but was later hunted down and slain at Braco by the Sheriff of Angus. His descendant, Walter Leslie, son of the laird who probably completed the original Leslie tower house at Fetternear, entered Imperial service; was involved in the murder of Count Von Wallenstein; became a Field Marshal; and founded the line of Counts Leslie in Austria, which lasted until 1802. His nephew, Count James Leslie, also became a Field Marshal and covered himself in glory at the relief of Vienna from the Turks in 1683.

Royalty visited Balquhain on at least one occasion. Mary, Queen of Scots, stayed overnight in the castle during her progress in the north in 1562. Having heard early morning mass in Our Lady's Chapel of the Garioch, she then proceeded to Pitcaple Castle where she breakfasted and then apparently danced under a thorn tree which survived until 1856. (In that year, the site of the thorn tree was marked by the planting of a wych elm and, in 1923, another Queen Mary planted a red maple nearby).

As at Balquhain, precise dating is impossible at Pitcaple Castle. In 1457, James II granted the lands of "Pethapil in the sheriffdom of Abirdene," along with the adjacent lands of Harlaw and Ressivet, to David Leslie, son of the fourth baron of Balquhain. (The charter recording this grant was discovered in Pitcaple Castle in 1947 and is now on display in the museum there). There is no firm evidence of David having built a castle but, in 1956, when the harl on Pitcaple Castle was being renewed, a doorway and gunloops of an early design were discovered at the foot of the smaller of the round towers on the oldest part of the house. If, on the basis of such scanty circumstantial evidence, we may conclude that the rectangular tower house with the round towers at diagonally opposite corners is datable to the late fifteenth or early sixteenth century, then Pitcaple must be one of the oldest examples of a Z-plan castle. (The foundations of the original Z-plan castle at Huntly are datable to about 1452 while the oldest authenticated example of a Z-plan castle was built at Terpersie in 1561). One of the round towers at Pitcaple contains the main stair as far as the third floor while the other, of larger proportions and more massive in construction, is vaulted on the first three floors and is rather reminiscent of the conception of a donjon. The north-west turret is fitted as a dovecot, a reminder of the days when pigeons featured more frequently on the menu. On the ground floor of the main block, the original kitchen fire-place and the well have been discovered by the present laird, both having been covered during alterations by previous occupants.

In 1789, Pitcaple was described as "an old ruinous castle." By then, the last of the Leslie lairds had died and the estate had passed to his half-sister, the wife of John Lumsden, Professor of Divinity in King's College, Aberdeen, whence it descended to Henry Lumsden of Belhelvie and, eventually, to the present owner, Mrs Burges-Lumsden.

About 1830, William Burn, an architect from Haddington, was commissioned to plan extensions and renovations. Wings were added on the south and west; the roof line of the original structure was raised: and fluted roofs were added to the existing towers and turrets. A new lease of life was given to the old Leslie stronghold and the castle continues to be occupied as a family home, as it has been for possibly more than five centuries.

The castle, however, has had its share of violence. It featured frequently in the Covenanting struggles in the middle years of the seventeenth century. In April, 1639, the Royalist Earl of Huntly used it as his headquarters during his negotiations with the Earl of Montrose, then a leading Covenanter. Some five years later, when Montrose was the Royalist champion, the castle was garrisoned by Covenanters but they lost control of it in rather an unusual way. The Covenanters were expecting the arrival of some friends to celebrate a wedding. Their Royalist opponents heard of this and dressed themselves in garments appropriate to wedding guests. Then, led by a piper, they arrived on the green outside the castle and began to dance. The Covenanters, completely deceived by the ruse, came out to join in the celebrations. The Royalists thereupon danced past them and captured the castle without a blow being struck.

In the following year, 1645, Pitcaple was still in Royalist hands. The laird of Newton and the son of the laird of Harthill, while returning home after helping Montrose to win the Battle of Kilsyth, had captured the arch-Covenanter, Andrew Cant, and Baillie Alex. Jaffrey. The prisoners were lodged in Pitcaple Castle where they remained until, managing to gain control, they barricaded themselves inside and withstood a siege until relieved by their Covenanting colleagues. This incident was recalled over three years later when the protagonists requested absolution from the Scottish Parliament for the damage they had caused to Pitcaple Castle. We can almost hear the voice of Andrew Cant as the details unfold—"But the Lord in the verie nick of tyme (quhill the enemies war increasing in power and had so farr prevailled as they had maid ane good progress in undermyning our wallis) furnished us unexpected and wonderfull delyverance by sending to our assistance the Maister of fforbes, Lord

Fraser, the Lairdis of Skene, Monymusk, Echt, Leslie younger who . . . . . used such expedition we war relieved by thame and the enemies put from the sieg." The Covenanters then went their several ways "having set our prison on fire, it not being tenable."

The damage could not have been extensive for in May, 1650, the Marquis of Montrose was lodged for a night in Pitcaple Castle. Having been captured after his defeat at Carbisdale, he was being escorted to Edinburgh, ostensibly to stand trial for treason. Lady Agnes, the wife of the laird of Pitcaple, was Montrose's cousin and she offered him a chance to escape from his room in the big round tower by a secret shaft and tunnel. He refused, saying, "Rather than go down to be smothered in that hole I'll take my chance in Edinburgh." Eight days later, having been denied even the semblance of a fair trial, he was hanged in Edinburgh.

Lady Agnes could barely have recovered from the shock when she was busy entertaining Royalty. Charles II had returned from Holland in an attempt to win back his kingdom from Cromwell. On his way south from Garmouth, he announced his intention of calling at Pitcaple. The laird, John Leslie, was attending St. Sair's Fair when he heard the news. Determined to entertain the king in right royal fashion, he bought all the available claret and hastened home. The royal party, however, mistaking the tents and surrounding bustle at the fair for a Covenanting encampment detoured until they crossed the Urie near Pitcaple Castle. Charles is said to have been so struck with the luxuriance of the crops in the "meal girnal of Aberdeenshire" that he remarked it reminded him of England. (The farm was subsequently known as "England" and remains so today). Next day, Charles left Pitcaple to continue his route south with the Marquis of Argyll, one of the main instigators of the death of Montrose, riding at his left hand. Among the tenantry assembled to witness the departure was a local worthy known as the "Gudewife of Glack" who, patently unabashed by the pomp of the occasion, shouted, "God bless your majesty and send you to your ain; but they are on your left hand that helped tak aff your father's head and if you takna care they will hae yours next!" The king's reaction is not recorded, nor is that of John Leslie, laird of Pitcaple. He accompanied Charles on the invasion of England which ended with the defeat of the Royalists at Worcester, where John Leslie was killed.

Several Garioch families were ardent supporters of the Royalist cause at this time but perhaps none more so than the Leiths of Harthill. Patrick Leith, Younger of Harthill, the captor of Andrew Cant in the incident mentioned above, distinguished himself in the army of the Marquis of Montrose. He was eventually captured and put to death on the scaffold by the Covenanters in 1647. The French ambassador, Jean de Montereal, in a letter to Cardinal Mazarin, gave a moving account of Leith's heroic courage right to the end. He was quick to appreciate the possible effects of such martyrdom and commented, "It would not be to the advantage of this parliament to have many executions of this kind to perform, for such Royalist martyrs cannot but greatly advance the cause of monarchy in this country."

John Leith of Harthill was an equally enthusiastic Royalist, albeit eccentric if not, indeed, mentally unbalanced. At Christmas, 1639, when Aberdeen was firmly in the hands of the Covenanters, vowing "by God's wounds, I'll sit beside the Provost and in no other place o' the kirk," he occupied the Provost's pew in St. Nicholas Kirk and had to be forcibly removed by the town's officers. When he appeared before the magistrates, with the provost presiding, he called the latter "a doited cock and an ass," tore up the charge, and threw the "penner and inkhorn" in the face of the clerk of the court "to the great effusion of his blood." He was ordered to be detained in Aberdeen Tolbooth, where he made himself as much of a nuisance as possible. He tried to set fire to the place because the chimney smoked; had daggers and cudgels smuggled in and attacked the warders; somehow acquired a gun and entertained himself by firing at passers-by on the Castlegate; and, finally, barricaded himself inside. After some nine months of such antics, he was tied in eighteen feet of hempen rope and removed to the Heart of Midlothian, the Tolbooth in Edinburgh. There he remained until liberated by the Marquis of Montrose after the Battle of Kilsyth. Leith returned to Harthill and conducted a vendetta against the minister and kirk session at Oyne, demanding the return of communion cups previously gifted by his brother. Finally, hopelessly in debt, he turned arsonist and, having set fire to Harthill Castle, sat Nero-like in "Harthill's Cave" on Craig Shannoch and watched it burn.

The castle, now roofless but externally almost complete to roof level, is a very good example of the Z-plan with one round and one rectangular tower diagonally offset from the main block. The central and rectangular towers were finished off with crow-stepped gables and tall chimneys while the round tower had a conical cap. The eastern corners of the rectangular tower and the two free corners of the main block have large, corbelled turrets. The doorway, in the re-entrant angle of the offset rectangular tower, was secured in the usual way with a wooden door and an iron yett behind it. In the basement, there are large splayed gunloops ornamented in various ways, while the smaller loops in the turrets are diamond-shaped or circular. The dressed stonework for the doors, windows, corbelling, coping, and gunloops is of pink Bennachie granite, while the rest of the building is of substantial, partly-coursed, rubble work with free use of horizontal pinnings. The barmkin, or courtyard, was enclosed by a wall of which a portion, including the gatehouse, still survives. An angled shot-hole, in the upper part of the latter and orientated to cover part of the barmkin wall, is still extant. A stone, which formerly occupied a position above the gate, was inscribed, "1601 K. J. Most Libera." It may be that this commemorates some action of James VI or it may be somehow associated with the building of the castle which, according to expert opinion, took place about 1600.

Another castle, standing on the south side of the River Don about one mile north of Monymusk village, which featured, albeit fleetingly and indirectly, in Montrose's campaigns was Pitfichie. (It was here that the remnant of a Covenanting army, led by Major-General Urrie, son of a former laird of Pitfichie, came to lick their wounds after being defeated by Montrose). The castle was built on the two-stepped or link plan, possibly soon after 1560. At least the architectural evidence suggests some such date. The masonry is typical of the sixteenth century; the mouldings everywhere are purely gothic; and the gunloops with external splays are an early type. (Designed to provide a good field of fire and to disperse the smoke from the pistols, these gunloops were soon found to be completely unsuitable. The smooth, outer bevel guided shots from attackers to the interior and so the design was soon reversed with the eye of the loop on the outside and the splay on the inside). Moreover, the tentative nature of the plan, deducible from the fact that the doorway was originally intended to be in the main block but was removed to the circular tower during building operations, suggests a date much earlier than 1607, when David Bel, one of the famous family of native, castle-building Master-masons, is known to have been at work at Pitfichie. Internally, the castle was planned in the usual tower house fashion and externally, on the west side, there was the barmkin of which the gate survived as the entrance to the garden of the adjoining farm until 1920, when the arch fell. Sixteen years later, practically all the east wall and the south gable above the basement vault collapsed. Since then, the castle has remained a ghastly ruin.

From the end of the fourteenth century until 1597, the estate of Pitfichie belonged to the Urrie family who then sold it to John Cheyne of Fortrie. His descendants owned it until 1650, when it was acquired by the Forbeses of Monymusk. The last recorded inhabitants were the son of the laird of Monymusk and his family, who are listed in the Poll Book in 1696 as occupants of the Manor House of Pitfichie. A century later, by the time of the Old Statistical Account, the castle was unroofed.

The Forbeses came to Monymusk in the wake of the Scottish Reformation. The Augustinian Priory there had fallen on hard times; in 1549, the conventual buildings were said to be "now in ruins;" in the following year, they were described as "ruinous and almost levelled to the ground;" and, in 1554, they were said to be "alluterlie brint exceptand ane pairt thairof als distroyit with fyre through negligence of the said Priour and his seruandis." In an attempt to raise money to pay for repairs, the Augustinians mortgaged the lands of the monastery within the parish of Monymusk to Duncan Forbes of Corsindae. This mortgage was foreclosed and, in 1584, the last Commendator of Monymusk handed over the ruinous priory to his kinsman, William, son of Duncan Forbes of Corsindae.

In the deed of gift, which states "that the place and monastery of the said Priory of Monymusk is now almost ruined and waste, so that there is no residence or house fit for habitation," William Forbes of Monymusk was enjoined to found and maintain a school "for instructing boys in honourable studies and literature." Forbes ignored this injunction and used the stones from the ruins to build the L-plan tower which is still the nucleus of the present House of Monymusk. There may still be what amounts to visible and tangible evidence of the fact that William Forbes did not fulfil the provisions of the deed of gift. On an aumbry, or wall-cupboard, in the hall of Monymusk House there is a scroll with a hand pointing to "LATYAMSAY" in relief letters of sixteenth century style. It is possible that this was the Forbes way of cocking a snook at criticism of the fact that a school had not been established, in the same way as the Keith who founded Marischal College is said to have given the rejoinder "Thay haif said: Quhat say thay; Lat thame say" to those who passed adverse comments on his acquisition of Church properties.

Another interesting feature within the old hall at Monymusk House is the tempera painting which has been exposed on the wall; there is a shield with the royal arms of Scotland and another shield "Charged with a crescent between three bears' heads, ensigned with a helmet, and flanked by the initials M F, the whole being in a laurel wreath." There is also a decorative pattern on the wall of flower vases and scrolled foliaceous ornament. One of the vases has the date 1618 inscribed on it.

In 1712, Sir Francis Grant, or, to give him his juridical title, Lord Cullen, bought the estate of Monymusk and the Grants have lived there ever since. At various times, the Grants have made additions and alterations at Monymusk and, as is evident from the following account by the son of the new owner in 1712, the Forbeses had also added to the original L-plan castle before then: "The house was an old castle with battlements and six different roofs of various hights and directions, confusedly and inconveniently combined, and all rotten, with two wings more modern, of two stories only, the half of the wondowes of the higher riseing above the roofs, with granaries, stables and houses for all cattle, and of the vermine attending them, close adjoining, and with the heath and muire reaching in angles or goushets to the gate, and much heath near, and what land near was in culture belonging to the farmes, by which their cattle and dung were always at the door . . . . . Much of the land and muire near the house, poor and boggy; the rivulet that runs before the house in pitts and shallow streams, often varying channel with banks, always ragged and broken." It was obviously a rather ramshackle building in unsalubrious surroundings and Sir Archibald Grant, who became one of the leading agricultural reformers of his day, set about its renovation. By 1731, he described it as consisting of a drawing room, dining room, six principal bedrooms, several smaller bedrooms, a kitchen, brewhouse, laundry, cellar, wardrobe, maid's room, cook's room, servants' room, servants' hall, and woman house. This landed gentleman's residence was a far cry from the "two up, one down" accommodation available in the earliest tower houses.

So also were the "hall, four reception rooms, seven bedrooms and four bathrooms with the usual offices and staff accommodation" which were listed in the notice of sale of the Place of Tillyfoure in June, 1966. Tillyfoure (the "e" was added to the name at the end of the nineteenth century) originally belonged to the earldom of Mar. In 1508, Sir John Leslie of Wardhouse, one of the Balquhain family, was created Bailie of the Crown lands in the Garioch and given the estate of Tillyfour. By the time he died in 1546, he may have built the oldest surviving part of the existing house. A modest tower house of two storeys and a garret, designed on a variation of the L-plan, seems to have been erected in the sixteenth century and then altered in the first half of the seventeenth century; a panel above the door with the date 1626 may be associated with the alterations. In 1742, Sir Archibald Grant of Monymusk acquired Tillyfour and it remained in the possession of the Grants until 1884 when it passed to a nephew of the seventh baronet of Monymusk, Francis Gregson. By this time the castle was insufficient for the needs of a country gentleman and Gregson set about creating the Place of Tillyfoure, where he lived until he died in France during the First World War. The restoration and extension were so skilfully handled that it is now barely possible to distinguish the old from the new building. As an article in the "Aberdeen Journal" of 24th June, 1886, when the work was nearing completion, said, "The principal conditions laid down by Mr Gregson were that the character of the old building be preserved unaltered, while the new portion should be in complete harmony with it. The old walls, which in some places were in a very dilapidated state, were restored so as to assume the appearance which they had originally. The crow-stepped gables, so characteristic of the old Scotch Baronial school, were in several places incomplete, but the missing portions were very skilfully replaced by new work . . . . . The roofs were slated with the large stone slates from the Forfarshire quarries, which were extensively used in old Scotch houses of the sixteenth century and which indeed are precisely the same as those with which the old castle itself was roofed. For the masonry only the native granite has been used, the work being chiefly what is known as old-fashioned random rubble, the corners, pediments, and crow-steps being finished with axed work . . . . . A screen wall about eight feet in height, part of which still remains, formed a sort of courtyard to the old building, the entrance being through a circular archway. This feature of the original structure will be reproduced in its complete form."

There is also a contemporaneous account of the building of Castle Forbes which stands on the north side of the River Don to the west of Place of Tilly-foure. The chief seat of the Forbes family had been at Drumminor until, in 1770, the seventeenth Lord Forbes, then in financial difficulties, was forced to sell it. His successor built Castle Forbes on the site of the old house of Putachie.

The laird's son worked on the building and left a brief account of the operations. "I remember," he says, "the foundations of the castle being laid on the 15th June, 1815 . . . . The Architect of the Castle was a Mr Simpson of Aberdeen, but he made some mistakes in the construction of the North Staircase which being communicated to Lord Forbes, led to an architect (whose name I do not remember) being sent from Edinburgh, and Mr Simpson was then discharged and succeeded by Mr Smith of Aberdeen under whose superinten-dance the building was completed in about six years . . . . . My father . . . . being somewhat pinched in circumstances owing to two successive bad seasons, to help him I came to the Castle to work as a Mason and labourer, and remained till it was finished. The greater part of the stone used in building the castle was brought from the wood near the present saw mill (Craigpot), the rest came from Bennachie and being of a better description was used for the mould-ings of the windows, etc. I remember the old house of Putachie, the entrance front of which it was originally intended should form part of the present building, but as there was a difficulty in making the old and the new windows correspond it was finally pulled down. The old house was nothing like so large as the present one. The stones of which the staircase is constructed and also those with which the Hall is paved (in the present building) came from the South . . . . During the building of the Castle only one man was hurt from a fall which broke his leg . . . . I remember when I was occupied in pulling down the former kitchen wall, I came upon a stone set in the wall upside down which I broke with my pick . . . . We sent for the Schoolmaster to decipher the inscription and made out that it came from Drumminor. The kitchen wall appeared to be very old. The mason who contracted for the building of Castle Forbes was Mr Alexander Wallace of Drumnabeg, Cluny, Aberdeenshire . . . . . There is a very old stone, a rude representation of a boar's head, which was taken out of the wall above the back gate of the old house of Putachie. Lord

Forbes wrote from Ireland to beg that it might be preserved. It was found at Logie-Braes of Forbes."

The boar stone, or bear stone as it is sometimes called, is still preserved within Castle Forbes. The stone which was broken during the dismantling of the old kitchen wall was a coat of arms with the motto "Grace me guide;" it was repaired and built into the wall by the side door of the castle. Both stones are reminiscent of the early history of the Forbeses who claimed descent from Ochonchar, son of an Irish nobleman, upon whom the Scottish king conferred "the lands of Logie upon the bank of the river Done." In the words of the old chronicler, " 'Tis storied of this Ochonchar, Knight of Logie how yt he killed a huge Bear and for ys was honoured by the King wt Knighthood and given him to his arms (which the Lords of Forbes bear to this day)—Az. three bears' heads cooped; Ar. muzzled Gules Their motto being Grace me Guide and from thence was surnamed Ochonchar Forbear or Forbass and by contraction Forbes."

Another Forbes stronghold was Lickleyhead Castle, which stands on the right bank of the Gadie in the shadow of Hermit Seat, the western spur of Bennachie. Above the door are the initials of John Forbes and his wife, together with the date 1629, when the present structure is said to have been built. It may be, however, that John Forbes of Leslie renovated an older building at that time for some authorities hold that there is architectural evidence, both internal and external, which points to a building date in the latter part of the sixteenth century. One particularly remarkable feature is the long round tower which is corbelled out only a few feet from the ground. This was a contrivance of Scottish masons in the sixteenth century and was done purely for effect. In common with all other castles in the Bennachie area which are still inhabited, Lickleyhead has been restored on more than one occasion; in 1876, Hugh Lumsden of Auchindoir, then the proprietor, carried out a complete restoration, as did a later owner, Madame de Mier.

North east from Lickleyhead, and about half a mile from Oyne, stands Westhall which, like the former castle, has a stair-turret worthy of note. Instead of being corbelled in the typical Scottish fashion, the turret is supported on a squinch, or arch, above which is a remarkably elaborate label moulding. Although this method of supporting the stair-turret was also used in the old part of Tillyfour, it is not common in north-east Scotland. (The technique is best illustrated in Glenbuchat Castle where two turrets are each supported by arches, or trompes. In this case, it may be that the builder was influenced by the ideas of Philibert de l'Orme, the famous French architect who designed the Tuileries and published a book on architecture in 1567. Could it be that the squinches at Tillyfour and Westhall sprang from the same origin?).

Westhall belonged to the Church and diocese of Aberdeen from the thirteenth century but appears to have passed to the Abercrombies of Pitmathen at the time of the Reformation. The oldest part of the house was apparently a sixteenth century L-plan castle which was altered, probably in the seventeenth century, when a gabled block, with a circular tower at the south-east corner, was added. In 1681, the Rev. James Horne, vicar of Elgin, acquired the estate and added to the castle; a descendant also extended the house about 1838; and so did Lady Leith of Freefield after she became the owner in 1860. The early-tower-house-cum-modern-mansion became a school of farming for a short period after the

Second World War but then it passed to Lord Glentanar and subsequently to its present owner, James Ingleby.

For a time, the neighbouring house of Logie was closely associated with Westhall. In 1754, General Robert Dalrymple-Horne of Westhall married the daughter of Sir James Elphinstone of Logie, thereby acquiring the property and changing his name to Robert Dalrymple-Horne-Elphinstone. He moved from Westhall to Logie at that time and his descendants remained in Logie Elphinstone until 1903. The nucleus of the building was a tall oblong house with a stair-tower at the north-east corner, dating from the seventeenth century. Subsequent additions resulted in the creation of a courtyard with buildings on three sides and a curtain wall with arched gateway on the fourth side. The house became a hotel and conference centre but was extensively damaged by fire in the spring of 1975.

South from Logie, and about one mile west of Chapel of Garioch, Pittodrie House nestles on the north-east shoulder of Bennachie. Still occupied as the family home of the descendants of George Smith who bought it from the Erskines in 1903, Pittodrie is a mixter maxter of the old and the new. Having been severely damaged by the Marquis of Montrose in 1644, the house was extensively reconstructed on at least three separate occasions between then and its acquisition by the Smiths. There is, however, evidence of much older work at Pittodrie: the Erskine coat of arms with the date 1605 is still extant above a doorway and may commemorate the building date of the nucleus of the present house; a detached wing with vaulted cellars is reputed to be the remnant of an earlier structure; and an existing turnpike stair may have been built as early as 1490.

The various buildings described above, part of the priceless heritage of the Garioch, afford ample illustration of almost the whole gamut of castellated architecture. In the grassy mounds of the earliest earthwork and the crenellated and turreted masonry of the fortified houses of generations of lairds the interplay of military and domestic requirements may be seen and, with it, the emergence and persistence of a north-east tradition of castle building which is second to none.

THE BATTLE OF HARLAW

Anon.

As I cam' in by Garioch lands,
    An' doon by Netherha,
I saw sixty thoosand redcoats
    A' marchin' to Harlaw.

Wi' my derry dey, dumpty dow,
A daddle um a dee.

"O did ye fae the Hielans come,
    Or did ye come that wye?
An' did ye see Macdonald's men
    As they cam' fae the Skye?"

"O yes, me fae the Hielans cam',
    An' me their numbers saw,
There was ninety thoosand Hielanmen
    A' marchin' to Harlaw."

So they rode on an' farther on
    Till they cam' to Harlaw,
They baith fell fast on every side,
    Sic fun ye never saw.

Brave Forbes to his brother said,
    "O brother don't you see
How they beat our men on every side
    An' we'll be forced to flee?"

Brave Forbes to his merry men called,
    "Ye'll tak' your breath a while,
Till I do send my servant
    To bring my coat o' mail."

His servant to Drumminor rode,
    His horse he didna fail;
In twa oors an' a quarter
    He brocht his coat o' mail.

Noo back to back these two fierce lords
    They went amangst the throng,
They hewed doon the Hielanmen
    Wi' heavy swords an' long.

Brave Forbes, bein' young an' stoot
  Made the Hielanmen to yield,
As a scythe doth the green grass
  That grows upon the field.

Macdonald bein' young an' strong
  Had on his coat o' mail,
An' he went swiftly through the ranks
  To fecht wi' him himsel'.

The first stroke that Macdonald gave
  It wounded him a dell,
But the next stroke that brave Forbes gave,
  The proud Macdonald fell.

An' sic a lamacheelie, man,
  The like ye never saw,
As there was amang the Hielanmen
  When they saw Macdonald fa'.

An' when they saw their chief was deid,
  Wi' him they ran awa',
An' buried him at Leggat's Den
  A lang mile fae Harlaw.

The battle began on Monday
  Wi' the risin' o' the sun,
An' on Saturday at twal o'clock
  Ye wad scarce kent wha had won.

Out o' sixty thoosand redcoats
  Gaed hame but thirty twa,
An' o' ninety thousand Heilanmen
  Gaed hame but forty three.

O there was sic a burial
  The like ye never saw,
As there was upon the Sabbath day
  On the leas aneth Harlaw.

Gin onybody spier at ye,
  Whaur's the men that gaed awa',
Ye may tell them plain, an' very plain,
  They're sleepin' at Harlaw.

THE FLORA AND FAUNA OF BENNACHIE

By James R. MacKay, B.SC., M.I.BIOL.

Most people who take the time and trouble to climb Bennachie have at least a passing interest in the plants and animals of the hill. My aim in writing this chapter is not to present a scientific treatise for the expert but rather to give enough information to enable the many casually interested people to know *what* to look for, *where* to look for it and to attempt to find out *why* a particular species should be living there. These three questions—"what?," "where?," "why?," deal respectively with identification, the habitat and the ecosystem; the modern science of Ecology is no more than an attempt to answer them.

Bennachie can be divided into two main environmental zones—woodland and moorland. No mention is being made of the low-lying areas such as riverbank and meadow as these, though of great interest, are outwith the scope of this chapter which deals entirely with upland areas.

Possibly woodland is the largest zone. Many hundreds of years ago the slopes of Bennachie would probably have been covered with Scots Pine but none of this remains with the exception of a few of the plants associated with the pine trees like an occasional juniper bush, blaeberry, the little orchid *Goodyera* and even the rare and beautiful Pine associate *Linnaea borealis* (named after Linneaus himself) is believed to grow in two different widely separated areas on Bennachie. The popular name for *Linnaea* is twinflower—as its name suggests it has two beautiful pink bell-like flowers hanging from a single stem, one or two inches high. Anybody finding this plant should admire it and leave it alone. Too many of our uncommon and beautiful plants have become extremely rare at the hands of "collectors" and others who fancy them for their gardens where they rarely thrive. If you are lucky enough to find *Linnaea* or any other rare plant on Bennachie you should inform Mrs Somerville at the Herbarium, Botany Department, University of Aberdeen or myself. Such records are very valuable and will be much appreciated. There are some pine trees on Bennachie today but they were either planted by the Forestry Commission or are the trees or their descendants planted after the division of the Commonty in 1859. Apart from the Scots pine, all the other species of conifer planted by the Commission are not native to this country. The activities of the Forestry Commission are being dealt with in another chapter. It is interesting to identify these different conifers and to compare their rates of growth in different habitats. As an appendix to this chapter there is a key to their identification.

We are fortunate in that, on Bennachie, the Forestry Commission has given us a nice blend of species including a fair amount of Scots Pine in contrast to many other areas where there are large unbroken monotonous stands of Sitka spruce. From my lounge window I can look across to Scare Hill and Millstone Hill and at any time of the year see a glorious mixture of colour and texture.

The amount of shade cast by the different tree species varies considerably and this is reflected in the ground flora. The spruces and Douglas fir allow very little light to penetrate to the forest floor which is consequently more or less devoid of vegetation with the exception of a few mosses and fungi. The pines when not too close, allow enough light through to enable heather to grow and because the larches are deciduous quite a number of early flowering plants such as wood anemone, chickweed wintergreen and wood sorrel can survive. In this area Scots pine is the climax vegetation type so that if heather moor is left untreated there is a succession from heather to birch to pine but the heather often remains. Burning and grazing prevent this succession from taking place. Spruce on the other hand is involved in a succession which does not include heather so that the growing of spruce on heather is somewhat artificial. In fact it is very difficult to get spruce to grow well amongst heather—there are some areas on Bennachie where there are stands of pines and spruces of the same age close to each other. The comparison is remarkable—the spruces are yellow and stunted while the pines are more than twice as tall and thriving. The dead heather often seen beside young spruce trees has not been killed by the spruce but by the Forestry Commission by spraying in an attempt to "get the spruces out of check." Scots pine does not do well in exposed upland areas, e.g. between Mither Tap and Garbet Tap on the South Side of the hill at about 1000 feet there are old pines which are bushes rather than trees. Reference has already been made to the natural birch woods which are slowly (and sadly) disappearing. Birch is of no economic importance—this is unfortunate for those of us who like to wander through a delightful birchwood. There are two local species of birch—most of the Bennachie birches are of the smaller scrubby *Betula pubescens* type (leaves and young twigs hairy) as opposed to the more graceful and taller *pendula* species (more common on Deeside) with hairless leaves and warty rather than hairy twigs. There is not much oak on Bennachie with the exception of the fine oakwood above the Place of Tilliefour on the slopes of Millstone Hill. It is interesting to note that these oaks were probably planted after the Napoleonic wars (when most oak forests were felled) to provide timber for the wooden battleships of the 20th century!

The roads through the forests are all open to walkers and it is from these that most people get their impression of the woodlands. Even on a cold windy wintry day there is peace, warmth and shelter for the walker on a forest road. Many people say that such roads are monotonous, that one stretch is just the same as another, but to the observer there are always new things to be seen with the changing seasons for example in autumn the colourful fungi such as the beautiful but poisonous fly agaric and the lovely Orange Elf Cups are much in evidence. In winter one can identify the tracks in the snow—rabbit, hare, roe deer (the occasional red deer), fox, stoat, weasel, pheasant, and surprisingly common the delicate print of the red squirrel, whose presence can also be deduced by the remains of cones from which most of the scales have been removed to give the industrious little animal access to the nutritious seeds. In spring and early summer the roe deer are probably most noticeable, leaving the shelter of the woods in the evenings to feed on the young grass in the adjoining fields. It is at this time of year that the bucks are particularly savage towards young trees by removing the bark. This is done with the antlers, partly to remove the 'velvet' (the nutritive skin covering the growing antlers) and partly to mark out a territory (there are scent glands at the base of the antlers). Every spring I plant hundreds of trees on my land and without protection a large percentage is killed in this way. Shooting the offending buck is no solution as another one will then take over his territory and start all over again (on different trees of course!). In summer, in my opinion, dawn and dusk are the best times to be on the forest roads. It is then that you are likely to get the best sightings of wild life of all sorts—an occasional badger returning to its set after a night grubbing for beetles and roots, a fox carrying a rabbit, the liquid sound of the blackcock on the lek—all these are a bonus to the wonderful chorus of woodland birds. The wild cat still inhabits Bennachie but is rarely seen. One was shot in the English quarry about 10 years ago and another was taken in a snare (set for a hare) near Mains of Afforsk in 1973. It was a young female and is now in my possession.

The characteristic birds of the forest are of course the wood pigeon, woodcock, the various thrushes and blackbird, four species of tits, golden-crested wren, cuckoo, warblers, sparrowhawk, great spotted woodpecker, tree creeper, finches, buntings, magpie and other members of the crow family including the beautiful but mischievous jay which first appeared in the Bennachie forests in 1974 and which is now occasionally seen moving noisily through the forest in small flocks. The largest forest bird and incidentally the largest grouse in the world (as big as a turkey) is the capercaillie which is quite commonly found feeding on pine shoots. This bird became extinct last century but was re-introduced from Scandinavia. Among the unusual birds recorded were the great grey shrike, crossbills and even a hoopoe.

Above the treeline which in some cases is being pushed above the 1000 foot contour is the moorland proper dominated by ling heather (*Calluna*) which in mid August is a blaze of purple. There are in fact a number of different species of heath each suited to life in particular conditions on the hill. The wettest parts favour the crossleaved heath (*Erica tetralix*) which has pale pink flowers (occasional white forms occur as in the ling). A closely related species is the bell heather (*Erica cinerea*) which, however, prefers much drier areas. It differs from the cross leaved heath in that its leaves are in bunches rather than in fours at each node and of course it is responsible for the rich red colour of the hill in July. If, in my garden, I were only allowed one species of plant, this would be it. In spite of the absence of such a restriction it still features prominently in my layout. It is also a very important plant in honey production the product being a rich dark colour compared with the pale amber ling heather honey. Locally common, e.g. on the decomposed granite beside the Mither Tap path above the Heather Bridge is the bearberry (*Arctostaphylos*) with long trailing stems and shiny dark leaves often cascading over rocks, looking most attractive in winter or with its little bell-like flowers in early summer or in autumn ablaze with red fruits. Higher up, where the soil has a little more peat, grows the crowberry, its small but fleshy leaves giving it the appearance of an *Erica*. Its jet black fruits are often to be found amongst those of the blaeberry; both are edible. Climbing can be thirsty work and what can be more refreshing than a handful of crowberry and blaeberry fruits?—the former to give the juice, the latter the sweetness. The blaeberry (*Vaccinium myrtillus*) is of course deciduous but its relative, the cowberry (*Vaccinium vitis-idaea*), locally known as cran-berry, is evergreen. It too is common on the hill and the red berries used to be picked (perhaps they still are) to make cranberry sauce and jelly. The only other berried shrub to be found on the moor is the averons or cloudberry (*Rubus chemaemorus).* This plant, not actually a heath but a close relative of the raspberry, inhabits the plateau especially where there is a thick layer of peat. The large white strawberry-like flowers are conspicuous in June while the fruits which look like enormous raspberries are produced in August. They are juicy and orange coloured when ripe and are borne just an inch or two above the general level of the peat bog. According to some people they make a delightful jam. Averons are most common on the little knoll just east of Oxen Craig called Averon Knap or Moss Grieve where the peat cutters of last century used to spend the night in the open when the weather was fine.

The wet peat is the home of a number of interesting plants such as the two species of cotton sedge whose white plumes are so outstanding in the summer (pillowcases used to be filled with the cotton heads), *Sphagnum* moss (used in wound dressing during the wars because of its absorptive and relatively sterile properties), the beautiful Grass of Parnassus and Sundew and Butterwort. The last two are fascinating insectivorous plants which have fantastically complex mechanisms used in attracting, catching and digesting small flies. This is a means of augmenting their supply of nitrogen. There is very little decay of plant or animal protein material in a peat bog due to the conditions being too acid for the necessary bacteria and so such habitats have a deficiency of nitrate. These insectivorous plants augment their nitrogen supply by trapping and digesting insects. In the case of the sundew (*Drosera*) the round leaves are produced in the form of a little rosette just about 1″ to 3″ across. Each leaf has on its upper surface a large number of red-knobbed tentacles each with a drop of glistening liquid on its swollen tip. Small flies are attracted and are unable to escape from the sticky fluid. The more they struggle the more firmly they are held and within a few hours all the tentacles have bent over and the fly is completely enmeshed and digestion commences. Within two or three days very little will be left of the fly. Butterwort (*Pinguicula*) has a rosette of larger leaves, yellow green in colour. Under the microscope they are seen to produce large numbers of glands—some with and others without stalks. The stalked glands secrete the sticky liquid and the other ones produce the protein digesting enzyme. Butterwort has a long stalk from the centre of the rosette bearing an attractive dark blue flower while the long stalk of the sundew has a number of small white flowers. Both can be found just below the stepping stones across the boggy area beside the Rushmill Burn. The peaty bogs at lower altitudes are attractive in summer because of the yellow spikes of the bog asphodel (*Narthecium*).

On the windswept summits where the heather is shorter, the odd clubmosses are present. These plants characteristic of *Tundra* conditions are related to ferns. High up on Bennachie both Alpine Clubmoss (*Lycopodium alpinum*) and Fir Clubmoss (*Lycopodium selago*) are to be found, the latter with peculiar little plantlets growing out from between its leaves and enabling it to reproduce in the fairly severe climatic conditions. Lower down, *L. clavatum* (common clubmoss) and *L. annotinum* (jointed clubmoss) are to be found.

Associated with the moorland are many animals such as blue or mountain hare, rabbit, shrew, mouse, vole, grouse, blackcock (and an occasional ptarmigan), meadow pipit, snipe, curlew, golden plover, hen harrier, kestrel, shorteared owl and buzzard (uncommon). Reptiles (most likely to be found sunning themselves on warm days) are lizard, slowworm and adder (rarely seen).

In the space of one chapter it is very difficult to do justice to the subject, for example one could study and write a book on the fascinating organisms of the Forestry Commission fire dams alone. Some very detailed work on particular groups has been done but on the whole Bennachie has been neglected by the research scientists possibly because the acid nature of the rock suggests a very poor collection of species. However in an excursion led by Professor Gimingham and Mrs Somerville of the Botany Department, Aberdeen University in August, 1975, a total of 153 different species of flowering plants and ferns was found on Pittodrie Estate up to the summit of the Mither Tap. There is great scope for the amateur. Lists, probably incomplete, of all the different species of plants, birds, butterflies and moths found on Bennachie have been compiled by various people. I have copies if anybody wishes to consult them: conversely if new records are available we would be very glad to have notification of them.

Appendix—Identification of Conifers on Bennachie

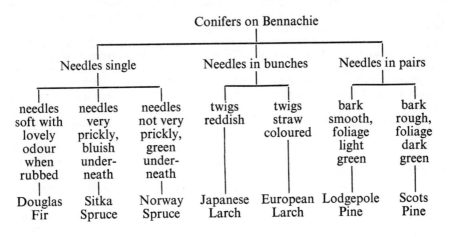

* * * *

The Mither Tap o' Bennachie
The Sailors' Landmark frae the Sea.

JOHN DUNCAN—THE WEAVER BOTANIST

By Mrs Helen P. Fraser

On Bennachie, during the first half of the last century, a short oddly-dressed man, groping his way amongst the heather looking for wild plants, was a familiar sight. To begin with, the local inhabitants of the small hamlets of Blairdaff, Auchleven and Ryehill eyed the little man with suspicion; but soon it was realised that he was a "hairmless craiter" and was accepted as part of the landscape.

John Duncan was born in Stonehaven in 1794. His mother was unmarried and she had to work hard to earn a living for herself and the child. Because of her extreme poverty, she was unable to send the child to school. With other local boys in similar circumstances John played in the surrounding woods and on the seashore. Very often he picked a bunch of wild flowers to take home to his mother and thus, early in life, he was attracted to the plants which were to become the consuming interest of his life. John Duncan was always poor, but he enriched his life with his love of wild flowers.

At the age of ten, John became a herd-boy, working on nearby farms. Life was harsh and he suffered many hardships. When he was fifteen years old, his mother decided that he should learn a trade, and sent him to her native village of Drumlithie, to become apprenticed to a weaver. At this time, he was still unable to read or write, but his love of wild plants—by this time a serious hobby—spurred him on. Fortunately for him, he was helped and encouraged by a kindly landlady and her neighbours. Reading was a slow and laborious business, handicapped as he was with poor eyesight, but he persevered.

An entirely new source of information was now open to him. Shy and retiring by nature, he was diffident about asking questions. Now he was able to read, however slowly, and find out for himself. A neighbour in Drumlithie loaned him a copy of Culpepper's "British Herbal" and from its illustrations, he was able to identify some of his plants. By working harder, he saved enough money to buy his own copy of Culpepper's Herbal. This book formed the basis of an extensive collection of books which, over the years, John Duncan gradually acquired.

After a few years spent working in Aberdeen, in 1824, Duncan came to live and work in Aberdeenshire. The nature of his work did not allow him a long stay in any particular district, but for a number of years he lived and worked in the hamlets around Bennachie—at Longfold, Blairdaff and at Auchleven. Later he lived from time to time at Cornabo and Milldowrie, then back to Auchleven before settling for a number of years at Netherton of Whitehouse. During this time he came to know every inch of Bennachie and the surrounding slopes. It is no exaggeration to say that he crawled all over Bennachie! Because of his short-sightedness, he was often to be seen on his hands and knees, peering at the ground in search of small plants.

When, in 1836, Duncan went to live at Netherton, he carried with him, from Willie Mortimer, shoemaker in Auchleven, an introduction to Charles Black who was head-gardener to the Farquharsons of Whitehouse. Because of their mutual interest in plants, the two men became life-long friends. From Black, John received every encouragement with his hobby. Gradually he was introduced to the scientific classification of plants. At first he refused to believe that this was possible, but Charles Black was a patient teacher. Reading was always for Duncan, the slow process of enunciating each individual letter before he could pronounce the word to his satisfaction. He tackled the Latin names in the same manner, although his pronunciation often brought an amused smile to his teacher's face.

The two friends went on many plant-hunting expeditions together, mainly to Bennachie and the surrounding hills, and along the banks of the Don. In the late evening, and often into the "sma' 'oors," the plants which had been collected were classified, and the best specimens were set aside for pressing. Duncan's lodgings were very humble and there was never much spare room to accommodate his growing collection of plants and books. His plants were carefully pressed between newspapers, but often became mouldy and, from time to time, had to be replaced. This did not inconvenience him much as he knew exactly where he had found each specimen in his collection. If necessary he would walk many miles in an evening just to replace one plant. His knowledge of plants gradually increased his circle of friends and eventually he was able to be of service to serious students of Botany.

In the long summer evenings, when his quota of weaving was finished, he would set off dressed in his 'best' clothes—turned-up trousers, overcoat, a tall hat tilted to the back of his head, tackety boots and a large blue umbrella. There can be no doubt that wherever he made his home Duncan was regarded as being somewhat odd. His interests and his mode of dress assured him his place amongst the "characters" who lived in the shadow of Bennachie last century. At this time the search after knowledge was exciting men and women from all walks of life. Mutual Improvement Societies, Literary and Debating Societies were springing up all over Aberdeenshire. In Auchleven, the Mutual Improvement Society was started in 1850. Duncan, along with Willie Mortimer, the shoemaker and Emslie, the joiner, joined in the discussions and debates. Meetings of the Alford Literary Society were held in the barn of Peter Clerihew, the blacksmith at Muir of Alford.

But progress was to have less happy consequences for some country folk. The results of the Industrial Revolution, and the improvements in agriculture were to end a way of life in Aberdeenshire. People began to leave the hamlets to look for work in the towns and cities; small crofts were incorporated into large farms; the spinning-wheel became idle and so the looms became silent. The tailor and the weaver, if young enough, had to find other employment.

John Duncan spent the last thirty years of his life in a cottage at Drougsburn on the farm of Dorsell near Alford. His friend Charles Black had long since moved South, but they corresponded with each other from time to time. Duncan's energies and interests continued despite his age. He regularly visited his friends at Netherton—Peter Marnoch, the weaver, his former employer, Willie Mitchell at the Post Office who was also Sheriff-officer for the district, and Willie Davidson the innkeeper at Mayfield, Whitehouse. He went further afield to visit his friends at Auchleven, where he was always assured of a warm welcome. Gradually however, Duncan had to face the fact that there was now less demand for "the work of the weaver." Nearing his eightieth year his health began to fail. The prospect of ending his days in the workhouse became a grim reality. But for one of those extraordinary chance meetings, this could well have been his fate.

The life and work of Charles Black had brought him into contact with a journalist and H.M. Inspector of Schools named William Jolly. During conversations with Black, Duncan's story was revealed. Jolly was so intrigued with the story and with the description of John Duncan that he arranged to visit him. He was to spend many hours at Drougsburn listening to the old man recalling his past memories. At the same time he could not avoid seeing that the old weaver was living in extreme poverty. He set about organising a fund— Queen Victoria was one of many who subscribed—to ensure that the old man, at the end of his life, would have some of the comforts which he had not been able to afford during his working years. His neighbours at Drougsburn, Mrs Allenach and her daughter, now attended to his daily needs. With his mind at peace, Duncan set about overhauling his collection of plants for presentation to the Botany Department of Aberdeen University. While he was able, he spent much of his time out of doors tending the patch of wild flowers which he had established at Drougsburn.

But the life of this extraordinary man was drawing to a close. John Duncan, the man born with all the disadvantages of poverty and adversity, died peacefully in 1880, in his 87th year. His biography, written by William Jolly, is not merely the story of John Duncan, it is also a record of the men and women who, a hundred years ago and more, lived and laboured in the shadow of Bennachie.

THE TRYST

By W. Hutcheon

Behind—the mist-clad mountain; ahead—a sunlit track
But vagrant thoughts, uncharted, go drifting, drifting back
To the old home decked in clematis, to visions bitter-sweet
Of the long grey Northern village where Don and Ury meet.

There, watching o'er the valley, stands Benachie on guard
To guide the twining rivers to their tryst by our church-yard,
And the bonnie Bass, awaiting, beckons gentle Ury on
Softly creeping past the sleeping to its meeting with the Don.

The years so swiftly fleeting dim the glow of Memory's rays,
For our lode-star is the living, not dream visions of dead days,
And the cottage with the clematis, the long grey village street
Hold but phantoms flitting trystward where the Don and Ury meet.

Yet—death alone will sever love's link with yonder ground
Where they rest, at peace for ever, in the lythe of Ury's mound
With Benachie still guarding and the river murmuring on
Softly creeping past the sleeping to its meeting with the Don.

THE TOPOGRAPHY OF BENNACHIE

By Algy Watson, M.A., B.A.

"O fondly, O fondly on thee do I gaze,
  Unaltered each feature since life's early days,
  Like twin giant guardians thy lofty bens stand
  A-watching and warding old Buchan's fair land,
  But deeply engraved on my heart's inmost core
  Is each outline and feature, delightful to me
  Are the hills of my childhood, my loved Bennachie."

This opening verse from "The Old Soldier's Song" on Bennachie by an unknown author expresses the feelings of many who have had the good fortune to be brought up within sight of Bennachie. Although not high as mountains go, Bennachie can be seen over a wide area of North-East Scotland, mainly because of its relatively isolated position at the eastern end of the Grampians. The ridge, which runs roughly five miles as the crow flies from east to west, lies between the River Don and the Gadie which flows eastwards on the northern side, better known, of course, as the Back o' Bennachie. The range rises fairly steeply on all sides to a broad, flat top around 1500 feet, and rising above that to a number of crags and taps. There are in fact five main summits over 1500 feet in height; commencing from the east:

Mither Tap	—	1698 feet
Craigshannoch	—	about 1600 feet
Oxen Craig	—	1733 feet
Watch Craig	—	1619 feet
Hermit Seat	—	1564 feet

It can be seen that although the Mither Tap is the best known peak because of its prominent outline, Oxen Craig is actually the highest.

Surrounding most of the Mither Tap are the remains of the mighty Pictish Iron Age fort, a few parts of which are still in an excellent state of preservation. Another feature of historical interest on the top is the rectangle, cut in the bare granite rock, with the date A.D. 1858 and the letters B. P, and L E , standing for Balquhain, Pittodrie, and Logie Elphinstone, reminding us of the Division of the Commonty which the hill had been up to that time. More recently, in 1973, an indicator, designed by the Bailies and built by pupils and staff of Inverurie Academy, has helped visitors to the summit to identify places and peaks seen from the top.

The eastern slopes of the Mither Tap above the farm of Muirton are known as Craignathunder. Almost immediately north of the "Tap" lies a detached mass of rock showing typical tor structure called Nether Maiden. About three-quarters of a mile to the north-north-west of the peak, at a height of 1400 feet, between two small craigs, about 600 feet apart, lies Little John's Length, reputed to be the bed of Jock o' Bennachie who, according to legend, was the giant who guarded the hill. The most popular route to the Mither Tap, the one from the Pittodrie Car Park, crosses the Stay Know, passes Hosie's Well near the head of the Rushmill Burn and on to the route said to have been followed by the Maiden Causeway, a "causey," possibly built at the same time as the fort, but which has long since sunk out of sight under peat and heather.

Craigshannoch ("the hill of the foxes") has a bold appearance from the village of Oyne from which it is approached by a fairly steep path, in places near the top, over large, sloping slabs of granite. Here again on the top can be seen the physical weathering along the lines of weakness in the rock giving rise to the layered structure typical of tors and described in more than one text as "shelving, built-up, masonry-like appearance." Just before the top one such shelving or overhanging rock forms a cave, low at the entrance, but large enough to afford shelter for three or four persons. The cave is known as Harthill's Cave from the tradition that the Laird of Harthill hid here in 1644 while he watched his castle, situated about a mile and half to the north-east, burning.

A little way to the west of Craig Shannoch at a height of about 1300 feet lies the Gill Well, close by which is Jock's Sark, the green spot where Jock o' Bennachie is reputed to have dried his sark. Roughly midway between the slopes of Craigshannoch and Oxen Craig the Gill Burn flows in a fairly steep gully northwards towards Oyne where it is locally known as the Bogie Burn and near which it joins the Gadie Burn. It was near the gully of the Gill Burn that the peat road was destroyed by a great volume of water rushing down it following torrential rain in the early afternoon of 9th August, 1891.

Between Craigshannoch and Oxen Craig lies the insignificant top, Moss Grieve or Averon Knap, a slightly raised area of rock and heather, surrounded by moss. Averons or cloudberries had at one time been very plentiful nearby and a few may still be gathered. It was from the relatively flat area around this peak that inhabitants of surrounding parishes struggled to cut and gather peats up to nearly the end of last century.

Since Oxen Craig is the highest point probably the best and most extensive views can be obtained from this peak—from Aberdeen in the east to the Cairngorms in the west; some say it is possible to see on a clear day, to the north, the hills of Caithness, some 80 miles distant, and of course, to the south Clochnaben is easily identifiable. Descending by the path from Oxen Craig, one passes Little Oxen Craig at about 1400 feet, where granite was once quarried for local buildings, and where a few good lintels are still lying. Just above the tree line lies the Shannoch Well, once used by peat workers, shooters, and hill walkers, especially those who used the former route to the top through "The Beeches." Nearby is a picnic table with seats built of stone and turf but these have fallen into disrepair, but it is hoped to restore them in the near future. The present path, so delightfully chosen and cut by the Forestry Commission, wanders down through the trees and in places passes close to the gurgling, clear water of the Gilree Burn. It is joined by the Ryhill burn and the combined waters flow into the Gadie opposite Bogandy.

Close to the Ryhill Burn, just to the west of Puttingstone lies another well, called the Hill Well, which was often visited by former generations, particularly on the first Sunday of May, for it was believed that the first person who drank from it on that day would be especially lucky. It is reported that during the first half of last century there were several illicit stills on Bennachie and one of these is said to have been in the gully of the Gilree Burn.

About 1000 yards west-south-west of Oxen Craig at a height of 1619 feet lies Watch Craig, best seen from the south side of the hill. This peak is the meeting point of the three parishes—Oyne, Premnay and Keig and may at one time have been used for watching and signalling the approach of enemies. Almost due north of it lies Hummel Craig, a rather indeterminate flat-topped peak, while Hermit Seat at 1564 feet lies a little over half a mile to the north west.

The ridge now descends very gently towards the south-west to Black Hill at 1403 feet, and turning south-south-westwards drops gradually down to the road, near the head of the Lord's Throat.

On the southern slopes are a number of lesser-known peaks such as Turf Hill, Scarfauld Hill, the south-western slopes of which are called Shiel-Know, and Blackwell Head. The March Burn rises near Watch Craig and flows between Scarfauld Hill and Blackwell Head to join the Don near Westhaugh.

Further east lie Bruntwood Tap about 1300 feet and Garbet Tap about 1550 feet in height. A little below the summit of Garbet Tap is Quarry Hill, which is the site of the "English Quarry," so-called because an English Company sent granite blocks from it to help build the docks at Sheerness in the early part of the nineteenth century.

The Ginshie, Garbet and Dalau Burns, all rising on the slopes of Garbet and Bruntwood Taps join to form the Birks Burn which flows westward past the Mill of Tilliefoure, entering the Don near Westhaugh.

Down the eastern side of the col which separates the main ridge from Mill-stone Hill (1340 feet) lying to the south, flows the Clachie (or Clochy) Burn. Situated on this col is the Heather Brig from which a lesser known route makes its way up the southern slopes of the Mither Tap. It was on the left bank of the Clachie Burn that a group of people, later to be known as the "Colonists" settled early last century, and started to "rive in a bit grun'," the evidence of which can still be seen on the area known as "Esson's croft."

Two hills, not forming part of the main range, but worthy of mention are Millstone Hill, situated almost a mile and half south-south-west of the Mither Tap, and Tillymuick roughly the same distance north-north-west of Watch Craig. Millstone Hill is forested up to a height of approximately 1000 feet, but has two flattish heather-covered tops which can easily be reached by either of two paths from the Forestry Information Centre at Donview, and from it a fine view can be had of the Don Valley looking towards the Howe of Alford.

Tillymuick, which means "the sow's hill," is rounded with a flattish top which reaches 834 feet in height. There are the remains of a rampart or earthworks with a diameter of about 200 yards on top.

HAMESICK—IN GLESCA

By Alexander McGregor, M.A.

I'm weariet, sairly weariet; man, I hate the grey steen streets,
　　Though they're thrang's St Sairs, there's deil a nod for me;
Ma lugs is deaved wi' fremit tongues aye kickin' ower the theats,
　　An' I miss the hamely crack o' Benachie.

Ye pey for licht by daytime on this steerin', reekie toun,
　　An' ye've clear een gin the sin ye af'en see;
For the lift itsel's as brookie as the weet it's teemin' doon—
　　O gi'e me the caller rain aff Benachie.

Fae the brigs the 'ily water leuks as gin 'twis sprayed wi' tar,
　　Jist to keep the king o' fishes i' the sea;
But silly fish an' foul he'd be that wan'ert sooth sae far
　　Fan burns as clear's the A'an feeds Don and Dee.

Fae skreich o' day tull lowsin' time their hemmers dird an' clang,
　　An' ma daumert heid's as licht as licht can be;
I wass I'd hear the studdy ring like meesic o' a sang
　　Fan the smith a "chappie" cries—neth Benachie.

Gin the wark aboot the Clyde be fool, the siller's clean, they say;
　　I'm dootfu', for a sicht o't's a' they gi'e;
I'd redder darg for little o't, nor pech for bigger pey
　　Sae far fae Aiberdeen—an' Benachie.

Here they're daft t' see the "picters," but sit coortin' i' the dark,
　　O' a routh o' ferlies little meets their e'e;
A breemie loan's a lyther tryst, like thon by Backie's park,
　　Wi' twa—forbye the meen—an' Benachie.

An' af'en in ma dreams I hear the muircock on the braes
　　Abeen far Don gaes slippin' throu' the lea;
An' faith, afore a week wins oot, I'll cheenge t' Sunday claes,
　　An' rope ma kist for hame—an' Benachie.

＊　＊　＊　＊

When Bennachie pits on its tap
The Garioch lads will get a drap.

GEOLOGY OF BENNACHIE

By Dr James G. Anderson

The Bennachie ridge and its sister ridge, Cairnwilliam, South of the River Don are part of a large roughly-circular red granite mass. To the north lies the Insch Gabbro and to the east and west metamorphic rocks, known as the Ellon Gneisses and Fyvie Schist. The Bennachie ridge rises steeply on all sides to form an east-west trending body with a broad flat top around 1500 feet, capped by a number of Craigs and Taps which exhibit excellent Tor structures.

Strong physical weathering back along major zones of weakness in the mass has left these residual crags which have taken their typical layered appearance, i.e. Tor structure, by weathering along horizontal joints and development of spheroidal (onion-skin) exfoliation.

The granite which forms the ridge is one of a series of Caledonian Granites, approximately 400 million years old, that form the Grampian Highlands. Along the ridge the granite shows a number of interesting variants. The typical granite as seen at Mither Tap is a coarse grained type consisting of two feldspars (red and white), glassy quartz and black mica. The large red feldspar crystals give the granite its distinctive porphyritic texture. A fine grained vuggy type of granite occurs as two irregular masses at Little Oxen Craig and Little John's Length North. The vugs (cavities) in this granite are lined by perfect small crystals of smoky quartz (Cairngorm) and feldspar.

The granite on every Tap and Crag is cut by a series of irregular veins. Usually these are fine grained—aplites—and resemble the fine grained type of granite seen at Little Oxen Crag and Little John's Length North. Occasionally very coarse patches are found in these fine veins and rarely a coarse grained vein (pegmatite) can be seen, e.g. at Hermit's Crag. These coarse grained pegmatites contain Cairngorms or smoky quartzes up to four inches long. All these variations represent stages in the solidification of the granite from a molten magma (lava) several miles below the surface 400 million years ago. After the granite had solidified a series of alteration zones were formed by crushing. These consist of irregular milky quartz crystals set in a dark red matrix and are know as quartz breccias which are best seen just off the path to Mither Tap and below the old mill on the Rushmill Burn.

The glacial history of this area was dominated by a roughly west to east passage of the ice which left glacial striae on the summit of the ridge. As the ice waned, a large slab of stagnant ice was left in the Howe of Alford. As this melted it cut a series of meltwater channels, the most impressive of which is My Lord's Throat.

Economically the area is of little significance. In the past granite was worked in a number of places for building stone, notably to construct Sheerness docks. Today the principal land use is forestry with most of the slopes between 600 and 1000 feet long, being planted with conifers by the Forestry Commission. The summit of the ridge provides an ideal outdoor recreation area within easy reach of Aberdeen.

A BALLAD OF BUCHAN

By John W. Fraser

"Gude speed the plough," the maiden cried—
The Ugie sings as it rins to the sea;
"Speed weel the wark," the man replied,
And the sun glints bright on Bennachie.

The owsen pause on the furrow so red
The Ugie sings as it rins to the sea;
The lark sings loud in the blue o'erhead.
And the sun glints bright on Bennachie.

She has brought him bread right sweet and brown
The Ugie sings as it rins to the sea;
And clear bright ale to wash it down
And the sun glints bright on Bennachie.

He was young and tall and strong—
The Ugie sings as it rins to the sea;
She sweet as e'er was praised in song.
And the sun glints bright on Bennachie.

He looked on her face so bonnie and faire;
The Ugie sings as it rins to the sea;
He looked on her wealth of yellow haire
And the sun glints bright on Bennachie.

He looked in her eyes so kind and blue
The Ugie sings as it rins to the sea;
He clasped her hands so strong and true.
The sun glints bright on Bennachie.

"O, gie me thy plight and troth, sweet May."
The Ugie sings as it rins to the sea;
"And wedded we'll be on St. Fastern's Day."
The sun glints bright on Bennachie.

He has ta'en her his twa strong arms within
The Ugie sings as it rins to the sea;
I wot the maiden made little din
And the sun glints bright on Bennachie.

He has ta'en her his twa strong arms within
The Ugie sings as it rins to the sea;
And kisses laid on her cheek and chin
And the sun glints bright on Bennachie.

"O, I will cherish my ain sweet May,
While Ugie sings as it rins to the sea;
Till the sun gangs down on the world's last day
And nae mair glints bright on Bennachie.

"And tide what may, or gude or bad—
The Ugie sings as it rins to the sea—
I'll aye be true to my ploughman lad,
Till there's nae sun to glint on Bennachie."

MONYMUSK AND ITS PERSONALITIES OF A BYGONE AGE

By the Editor

The inhabitants of Monymusk, the little village of Donside in the shadow of
Bennachie, cannot help but be thirled to the past, because, however modern and
caught-up in the twentieth century they may be, the past encroaches upon them
from all sides. In the background, Bennachie itself—in days of sun, etched blue
against the sky; in time of storm, dark-purple, and wreathed in mist when rain-
clouds threaten—points to the fleetingness of life, and to the centuries of time
and the generations of people that have lived on or around its slopes since it was
formed in the Ice-Age.

The present is thus inextricably bound up with the past. The children play
around the circles of stones that may be relics of past temples or places of
sacrifice or burial—no one can tell. A ploughman of a near-by farm while
ploughing his fields turns up five great slabs of stone that formed the coffin of a
young man of almost two thousand years ago, with the clay beaker that was to
provide him with sustenance on his long journey through the shades. Workmen,
the other day, digging a trench for pipes near the church unearthed the skeleton
of another man, possibly one of the Augustinian monks of long ago.

On Sunday the bell that summons us to church bears the inscription—"Ica
Mowat me fecit vet. Abd. 1748"—"John Mowat of Old Aberdeen made me.
I proclaim the Sabbaths, I toll at funerals," while the clock, high up on the face
of the church tower, has marked the passage of time since William Lunan of
Aberdeen made it in 1792. The stained-glass window in the chancel of the
church is a representation of a Culdee priest, preaching to the "rude forefathers"
of our hamlet, with Bennachie in the far background. This reminds us of the
beginning of the Christian way of life in our village, when the Keledeii—
"servants of God"—followed in the wake of Saint Ninian, came here in the sixth
or seventh century and built their crude cells and church.

But it is at night, when the stained-glass window is obscured, and flickering
candles light up the beauty of the old twelfth century sandstone arch, that the
loveliness and age of this little church is apparent. History comes alive again.
We go back in time to the year 1078 and hear the impassioned tones of Scotland's mighty warrior-king, Malcolm Canmore, kneeling on this very spot,
beseeching God to grant him the victory on the morrow against his enemy, the
Mormaer of Moray, vowing, if his life was spared and victory his, to build a

church here to the glory of God and the Blessed Mary of Monymusk. Victory was his and so our church was built, the arches of which, in many details, resemble those of Dunfermline Abbey, built by Malcolm's Queen, Margaret. Here at appointed hours of the day and night, from the priests' door in the chancel, filed in the twelve Culdees and their Prior, to worship in the chancel, while the nave was reserved for the worship of the laity and their vicar. Both parishioner and monk lie mingled in death in the churchyard. The Culdees in time were superseded by or transformed into the Augustinian Canons Regular, largely due to the influence of Queen Margaret and her three sons, and as centuries went by, at the time of the Reformation, Catholicism also gave way to Presbyterianism.

When we sing hymns or psalms on Sunday and listen to the minister in the pulpit, it requires a conscious effort to realise that underneath the wooden floor on which we tread is a graveyard of dead Prelates, Priors, Vicars, and Ministers. From the first Church Records we learn of the death and burial in the church of the minister, Mr John Burnett, who died in 1728 and was "buried in the middle of ye church floor before the latron," after a ministry of over 49 years. It was during his ministry that the six beautiful silver Communion cups were bought— the Dutch beaker type peculiar to the North-East at that time—still carried in procession by our elders on Communion Sunday. The last burial inside the church, that of the Rev. Alexander Duff who died in 1814, only took place there because of the intervention of the Keithhall minister who, on hearing that his friend was not to be buried inside the church where he had ministered for over thirty-three years, took up the spade and began to dig the grave himself. The burial place of the Grant family from 1712 is in the roofless part of the chancel outside the east-end of the present church.

How we know so much about the history of our Church and Parish is largely due to the efforts of Dr William Mearns MacPherson, parish minister from 1867 until his death in 1911. His book, "Materials for a History of the Church and Priory of Monymusk," the chapters of which were originally written to amuse and instruct his parishioners of a Sunday Evening, must be the result of a life-time of pains-taking research. We owe much, too, to the labours of two other eminent ministers, Dr William Walker, the Episcopalian minister, who lived in the Rectory near the Clyans Burn, and Dr James Stark, who lived in the Braes O' Bennachie, near My Lord's Throat on the road to Keig. Largely owing to the efforts of these two authors the personalities of the 18th century emerge.

Up till now the fame of our small village rested solely upon the importance of our Church and its Priory, its affiliation to the Culdee, later Augustinian Priory of St. Andrews, and also because it was directly under the protection of the Pope during mediaeval times. Now, however, from the 18th to the 20th century its fame rests upon its personalities, the people living there, either as lairds, ministers, schoolmasters or Scotland's Pride—the lad o' pairts.

Of the late 17th and early 18th century personalities, in the forefront is Sir Francis Grant, later Lord Cullen, advocate and judge, of whom it is said that he was "a gentleman possessed of the most profound erudition and inflexible integrity"—also that he "kept a quiet heart in a troubled time." He went to King's College, Aberdeen, at the age of 15 and thereafter to study Law at Leyden University where Professor Voet, lauding him as an example to his other

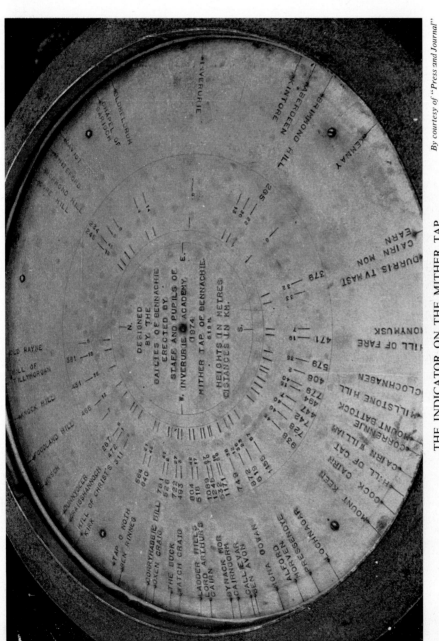

THE INDICATOR ON THE MITHER TAP.

By courtesy of "Press and Journal"

By courtesy of "Press and Journal"

The unveiling of the Indicator 15th July, 1974

THE COUNCIL (*From left to right*): William Taylor, Algy Watson, Leslie Anderson, Helen Fraser, Johnstone Hay, Danny Gordon, John Stephen, Lady Grant, James Gill, James MacKay.

students said of him "he shed lustre upon this classroom." On his return to
Scotland, he went to Edinburgh and passed as an advocate and along with
Sir George Gordon of Haddo, First Earl of Aberdeen, Sir George Nicolson of
Kemnay and many others from the North-East, became Senator of the College
of Justice. Lord Cullen played a prominent part in the Revolution of 1688 when
Scotland offered the crown to William and Mary. He played, also, a major part
in advocating the Union of Parliaments in 1707 for which service Queen Anne
made him a Baronet of Scotland and Nova Scotia; and a year later appointed
him one of the Senators of the College of Justice, with the title of Lord Cullen.
Lord Cullen who lived in Edinburgh, in Lord Cullen's Close in the Lawnmarket
for 14 years, must have spent the closing part of each summer when the Court of
Session rose, and the whole of the autumn, in Monymusk. While his son,
Archibald, improved the property, planting trees, putting up fences and en-
trenching the ground, and rebuilding houses (hitherto "all poor, dirty hutts!"),
Lord Cullen, as was customary with him, sought to improve the lives of the
people. He was of a like-mind with Alexander Jaffray, Quaker Provost of
Aberdeen, and friend of Cromwell, who wrote in his diary of "the great advantage there is in breeding young ones timely in the fear of God and keeping them
closely and diligently at their studies!" It concerned Lord Cullen that great
numbers of children and servants "are tied to labour during daylight in winter
season as in summer" and that they had no opportunity of schooling or of
attending church or of being catechised. He drew up a deed by which he left
two chalders of meal yearly for educational purposes, adding that the fund
should also be used for buying Bibles and good books for the poor. Later on,
out of the funds which had accumulated, Lord Cullen's School was built at
Abersnithack. It lasted for 60 years and was afterwards superseded by Sir
Arthur Grant's School at Blairdaff.

After Lord Cullen's death came Sir Archibald Grant, his eldest son—a famous
son of a famous father, although in a different way—for Sir Archibald achieved
fame by bringing in modern methods of agriculture in a backward age. We are
told—"His practical genius and enterprise soon turned a bare, bleak country
into a region of fertility and beauty." His father's influence on him was shown
by his "Memorandum to the Tenants of Monymusk, 1756" where along with
advice as to the management and improvement of their farms and offers of
"pecuniary assistance, premiums in carts, tools and seeds," he mentions some
of their "prevailing vices" and urges on them "a virtuous conduct, as one great
means of success, by drawing down a blessing on their endeavours." Sir Archibald is reputed to have planted something in the region of 50 million trees
although that was not appreciated by his fourth wife, Lady Jane, who, in reply
to the philosopher Hume's mention of Sir Archibald's "extensive and noble
planting," said she thought planting was his folly and that people ought to take
care lest their concern for Posterity should hurt themselves! They were a
very devoted couple and so popular in Edinburgh society that the violinist
Daniel Gow composed the well-known Monymusk Reel in their honour. Lady
Jane donated the silver christening bowl still in use in the church and also left
money for the poor of the parish.

Many inhabitants in Monymusk in Sir Archibald's time eked out a livelihood
by weaving 'serges' or knitting woollen stockings. This source of money supply

gradually dwindled away after the Union of 1707, when the removal of trade barriers between the two countries brought an influx of fine English woollen goods into Scotland. To counteract this depression in the wool trade, Sir Archibald turned his attention to the cultivation of flax and built a large Lint Mill at Gloies. One of the fields nearby is still known as "Bleachfield." He also set up a lapidary in the village for polishing stones of granite. This was later, in 1801, transformed into an Episcopalian Church and now stands boarded-up and empty. At Enzean he also built a factory for making glass bottles, some of which bearing his initials were dug up in the fields a long time afterwards. According to the Church Records, however, in 1792, the kiln was burned to the ground and four men perished in the flames. There was, also, a lace factory in a house near the village. After accomplishing so much for the land he inherited and the people of Monymusk who lived there, Sir Archibald Grant departed this life in 1778 at the age of 82, leaving his name indelibly printed on the pages of its history.

In 1739, when Sir Archibald was 43 years old, there came to our village to act as assistant schoolmaster, John Skinner, a gay, carefree young man of 17, fresh from his graduation at Marischal College and after a brief spell of teaching at Kemnay. John Skinner, in later days famous as Dean Skinner of Aberdeen, eminent Episcopalian Churchman in the times of persecution after the second Jacobite Rebellion, is chiefly remembered by posterity for his poems and consequent association with Burns. It was at Monymusk, in the ebullience of youth, that his best-remembered poems were written—such poems as "The Ewie wi' the Crookit Horn" and "Tullochgorum" which Burns affirmed to be "the best Scotch song that Scotland ever saw!" Of particular interest to us is the "Monymusk Christmas Ba'aing" which refers to the games of football played by the men and boys of the village over the graves in the kirkyard during the three-days' holiday at Christmas. It was written in heroic vein, in imitation of James I's "Chryste Kirk on the Green" which John had learned by heart when he was twelve years of age, and later translated into Latin. It tells of the feats of strength performed by the village heroes and the grievous mishaps of others. In the poem he describes himself as an "Insett Dominie" (a schoolmaster substitute) and tells us of his prowess in the game.

> "A young Mess John as ane might see
> was neither saint nor sinner,
> A brattlin' band unhappily
> Cam' o'er him wi' a binner,
> And heelster-gowdie coupit he,
> And reeved his gweed horn penner."

One Sunday, John Skinner was taken by a lady-member of the congregation to the heather-thatched Episcopalian Church at Blairdaff, to hear the Rev. Alexander Lunan preach. There Skinner was so enamoured by the service that he gave up being a Presbyterian and joined the Episcopal Church instead. As a result he had to leave his teaching post in the Parish School and abandon any chance of his promotion to parish minister. Later on he must have looked back upon his happy, carefree time at Monymusk, as a period of Halcyon days, for in a few years he entered stormy waters indeed, particularly in the year 1746, when for three months Scotland was under military rule. Parties of soldiers scoured the countryside with a commission to burn, wreck and destroy everything pertaining to the Episcopal Church. John Skinner who had been ordained Episcopal minister at Longside, Aberdeenshire, four years previously, had to suffer the outrage of having a contingent of Cumberland's soldiers, the Campbells, armed with bayonets, burst into his home at night when his wife and children were in bed and pillaged the whole house, leaving them "scarce a change of shift." The next day they put bundles of straw round his church and burnt it down, being exhorted to further efforts by a lady of rank who rode round the blazing building urging the soldiers to throw in the prayer books. As the Episcopal Church of New Deer was blazing away at the same time, she mounted the Hill of Coynach to see both fires, clapping her hands in glee and exclaiming: "The Wark o' Guid gangs bonnily on!" Skinner lampooned her in verses, comparing her to Jezebel, whereupon she retaliated by reporting him for holding services in his home. The result of this was that Skinner was transferred to the jail in Old Aberdeen where he lived for six months. Had he transgressed a second time he would have been transported to the Colonies for life. However he lived through this period of persecution to more peaceful times and after a ministry of 70 years, 62 of which he spent at Longside, he died in Aberdeen in the house of his son, then Bishop of Aberdeen.

One May day in the year 1765, Archibald Robertson, eldest son of William Robertson of Drumnahoy, was born in his mother's old home, Balnagowan, in Monymusk. William Robertson's family had farmed the farm of Drumnahoy in the Parish of Cluny for almost 200 years, yet the child, born in Monymusk, was to depart from the pattern of life of his forebears to become one of the most famous portrait painters in oils and miniature of his day, being known as the Sir Joshua Reynolds of Scotland. His two younger brothers also achieved fame as minature painters, so that this flowering of artistic talent must have come from his mother, Jean Ross of Balnagowan. He was educated at King's College, later on had instruction in Edinburgh in oil and water-colour painting and when 21 went to London where he studied under Sir Joshua Reynolds. He was recalled home because of his father's illness and once there had to support his mother, two delicate sisters and a mentally-defective brother. A few years later, the Earl of Buchan sent him to America to paint the portrait in oils of President Washington. The Earl gave him a letter of introduction and a silver-mounted box made of the oak that sheltered Sir William Wallace after the Battle of Falkirk as a present for Washington. Robertson received such acclaim for his painting that he decided to stay in America and on the arrival of his brother Alexander, founded the Academy of Fine Arts in New York. His last public enterprise was designing badges and medallions along with maps and drawings on the occasion of the formal opening of the Erie Canal. He went blind a few years before his death which occurred in 1835.

Another interesting personality was Alexander Nicoll who was born in one of the village houses in 1793. After receiving his early education at Monymusk under Louis Duff, son of the last minister to be buried under the floor of the Church, he entered Marischal College at the age of 12 years and was awarded the outstanding prize for Greek, the silver pen donated by the Earl of Buchan. After two years there, encouraged by Bishop Skinner, son of the famous Dean, he went to Balliol College, Oxford, on a Snell Exhibition being then, as his memorial states "paene puer," little more than a boy, only fourteen years of age. After graduating B.A. and M.A. of Oxford in 1822 he became Regius Professor of Hebrew and Oriental Languages and Canon of Christ Church. He had the reputation of being the best Oriental scholar in England and his mastery of languages was such that it was said of him, "he could speak his way to the Wall of China." Dr Nicoll was as humble as he was learned, for when he received a letter from the Earl of Liverpool offering him the appointment of Professor of Oriental Languages, on "account of your high reputation and the value attached to your labours," he thought the letter was a hoax and carried it about in a pocket for ten days till a friend convinced him it was genuine. He died at the early age of 36 from bronchitis, though Mrs Cruickshank who lived at Pitfichie imputed his death partly at least to the shock of grief he sustained three years earlier on the sudden death of his first wife, the day after their marriage. Mrs Cruickshank told also the story that Dr Nicoll, on a visit home, went to see her husband, who didn't recognise the friend of his youth in the stranger, when the Professor said: "What, don't you know Dawson Girds?" his nickname as a boy, trundling his gird or hoop through the village. Little "Dawson Girds" lives for all time in the memorial on the wall of Christ Church Cathedral, Oxford:

"Memoriae
Alexandri Nicoll
Domo Monymusk Abredonensi."

In 1854 there came to the Parish School of Monymusk a most dynamic young schoolmaster who was to teach there for eighteen years—Alexander Ogilvie, one of the famous dynasty of dominies whose names were a household word in the North-East in the last quarter of the 19th century. After teaching for a period of years in Monymusk, he introduced into the school what was then a most daring innovation—a female infant teacher! He wrote "We have in full play an element that softens the rigour of Education, refines and elevates the tone and enters with sympathetic appreciation into the feelings, thoughts, troubles and difficulties of the young and tender pupil." After 18 years in Monymusk he was appointed to the Headship of Robert Gordon's Hospital where he enhanced the reputation of this great school by bringing it into line with modern ways and changing it from a Hospital into a College or Day School. During the years 1884-86, the small son of the farmer at Pitfichie, John Ferguson, attended Robert Gordon's College. One day, Dr Ogilvie caught him in the act of trying to throw a boy downstairs and summoned him to his room. In his own words, "I had no hope of escaping with my life but I felt I ought to die game." The first question shot at me was, "What is your name?" I believe I answered correctly. "Where do you come from?" was the next query. I answered "Monymusk." A curious gleam shone for a moment in his eyes and putting his hand on my shoulder, he said: "You'll promise me, on your honour, that you'll never do a dangerous thing like that again. And how are your father and mother?" This boy from Pitfichie became Sir John Ferguson, K.B.E., Manager of Lloyd's Bank, London.

At this time, where sons of Monymusk were concerned, knighthoods were fairly thick on the ground, for Francis Grant Ogilvie of the Schoolhouse, eldest son of Dr Ogilvie, received this honour, while the son of the Land Steward at Beech Lodge became Sir James Porter, K.C.B., M.D., both of whom were taught in the village school by Dr Ogilvie. Sir Francis Ogilvie in writing to Sir James to congratulate him on the honour spoke of it as the "jelly on the piece," while his father, Dr Ogilvie, wrote to his ex-pupil that his wife and he were "back in memory of his early days in the quiet village of dear old Monymusk."

In a letter to Sir James Porter, dated 13 November, 1911, Sir Arthur Grant, the laird, tells him about the changes in the village. "About Monymusk, it is greatly changed since I went there. I have spent £60,000 on buildings, I have rebuilt, built or added to nearly every farm and house on the estate. The whole village is rebuilt in stone and slate. The inn is now four cottages. A new school was built three years ago and the old school is now the Public Hall. I had to pull down the spire of the kirk and put a battlement up as it was dangerous to the children below."

Now once again the houses in the Village Square, that for about a decade were abandoned after the inhabitants were transferred to the County Council houses built on the Glebe, under the modernisation scheme of Lady Grant, are lived in and the lights shine out as in days gone by through the leaded panes of the windows, while the inn, with its ancient pend, that had ceased to function for over 70 years, is now once more in constant use.

And so, using the nostalgic phraseology of Dr Ogilvie and of her absent sons and daughters, the "quiet village of dear old Monymusk" that began as six cottar houses with their gardens for the dependants of the Priory, is now a stirring village of the 20th century, with the character of the old houses preserved, and flanked by the many new houses that ensure its future in the years to come.

*   *   *   *

When Dee and Don shall run in one
And Tweed shall run in Tay
And the bonnie water o' Ury
Shall bear the Bass away.

EXCERPTS FROM

"THE MONYMUSK CHRISTMAS BA'ING"

By Dean John Skinner, author of "Tullochgorum"

Has ne'er in a' this Countra been
Sic shou'dering and sic fa'ing,
As happen'd but few ouks sinsyne,
Here at the Christmas Ba'ing'

* * *

Like bumbees bizzing frae a byke,
Whan hirds their riggins tirr;
The swankies[1] lap thro' mire and syke[2],
Wow as their heads did birr[3].

They yowff'd the ba' frae dyke to dyke
Wi' unco speed and virr[4];
Some baith their shou'ders up did fyke[5]
For blythness some did flirr[6]
Their teeth that day.

The sutor like tod-lowrie[7] lap,
Three fit at ilka stend[8];
He didna miss the ba' a chap,
Ilk ane did him commend.
But a lang trypall[9] there was Snap,
Cam' on him wi' a bend;
Gart him, ere ever he wist, cry clap
Upon his nether end
And there he lay.

* * *

The parish-clark came up the yard,
A man fu' meek o' min;
Right jinch[10] he was, and fell well-fawr'd,
His claithing was fu' fine.
Just whare their feet the dubs had glawr'd[11],
And barkened[12] them like bryne,
Gley'd Gibby Gun wi' a derf[13] dawrd[14],
Beft[15] o'er the grave divine.

When a' were pitying his mishap,
And swarm'd about the clark,
Wi' whittles soon his hat did scraip,
Some dighted[16] down his sark.

Will Winter gae the ba' a chap,
He ween'd he did a wark,
While Sawny, wi' a weel-wyled wap,
Youff'd her in o'er the park
A space and mair.

Wi' that Rob Roy gae a rair[17],
A rierfu' rout[18] rais'd he
'Twas heard, they said, three mile and mair,
Wha likes may credit gie.

* * *

Syne a' consented to be freen's,
And lap like sucking fillies;
Some red[19] their hair, some maened[20] their banes,
Some banned the bensome[21] billies.
The pensy[22] blades dossed down on stanes,
Whipt out their sneishin millies;
And a' were blythe to tak' their einds[23],
And club a pint o' Lillies
Best ale that day.

[1]Active chaps.	[7]The fox.	[12]Coated over.	[18]Loud noise.
[2]Bog.	[8]Stride.	[13]Stout.	[19]Combed.
[3]Sing with excitement.	[9]Tall, slim,	[14]Push.	[20]Bemoaned.
[4]Force.	ill-knit fellow.	[15]Threw.	[21]Quarrelsome.
[5]Shrug.	[10]Neat.	[16]Brushed down.	[22]Foppish, spruce.
[6]Gnash.	[11]Made slippery.	[17]Roar.	[23]Refreshment.

Footnote—The above poem depicting a game of football, played with much vigour and rough enthusiasm over the grave-stones in the Church-Yard around the old 12th century Norman Parish Church of Monymusk, by the local worthies of the day, was written when Dean Skinner was assistant-schoolmaster at Monymusk.

I make no apology for adding a glossary!—The Editor.

THE PARISH OF KEIG

By the Master of Forbes

For several centuries the clan Forbes has occupied lands, strongholds, castles and houses in and around the Don Valley area of Aberdeenshire, and today members of the clan from all over the world return each year to this part of the north-east to visit their "homeland." And here, in the small agricultural parish of Keig, they can still find the seat of their chief.

Castle Forbes itself was built by the 18th Lord Forbes in 1815 as an extension to an older house and is superbly sited on a level plateau on the north banks of the Don commanding wide views to the south and west. Behind, and providing a natural barrier from the icy north-easterly blast, looms Bennachie, the top of which in darker ages afforded the only safe refuge in the district for adversaries of the Forbes clan.

Designed by Archibald Simpson—it was the Aberdonian's first independent commission since his training in the London office of Robert Lugar—Castle Forbes is constructed almost exclusively of roughly-dressed local granite which shows no sign of weathering, the greater part of which came from a wood a few hundred yards from the site. And as a local labourer employed on the project wrote later: "the rest came from Bennachie and being of a better description was used for the mouldings of the windows, etc."

The Castle has until recently—apart from being used briefly as a wartime auxiliary hospital—been the residence of the clan chief's family. At the time of writing, however, it has joined the long list of country homes in Britain whose owners have found them to be impractical and is leased by an American company involved in the search for oil in the North Sea.

It was at about the same time as the Castle itself was being built that Telford's magnificent single-arch stone bridge over the Don at the present front entrance to the Castle policy grounds was being constructed.

The parish of Keig also contains two fine examples of stone circles, the main stone of that at Old Keig having been estimated to weigh over ninety tons. The other circle, set in a glade in a young plantation near Castle Forbes, has two very fine flanking pillars at either end of the recumbent "altar" stone.

Around Bennachie there are no less than six hill forts, including the Barmekin of Keig (929 ft.) somewhat similar to the one at Echt. What these forts were used for remains a mystery to this day but one can readily guess that they were places of refuge for the Pictish inhabitants from possible attacks by the Romans.

Keig has had many notable sons but perhaps one of the most illustrious was the Rev. Robertson Smith, who was born in 1846 in what was in former years the Keig South Church Manse. He was an outstanding Hebrew scholar and occupied the Chair of Hebrew in the Free Church College, Aberdeen; but owing to his so-called unorthodox views he was removed from office. Afterwards, he became Professor of Hebrew at Cambridge and his advanced ideas are now almost wholly accepted in our Divinity Schools. His literary eminence was recognised when he was appointed editor of the Ninth Edition of the Encyclopaedia Britannica.

The whole of the South-West slope of Bennachie lies in the Parish of Keig. The parish, although in so many ways typical of many farming communities of north-east Scotland, has a particular charm brought about by many years of carefully blending agricultural and forestry practice combined with the natural beauty of the hills, the Don valley and the river itself.

ANTIQUITIES IN THE PARISH OF CHAPEL OF GARIOCH

(formerly called the Parish of Logie Durno, until united with Balquhain and Fetternear)

By Mrs M. Erica Smith of Pittodrie

The History of the Garioch can be traced to prehistoric times—at least to the Iron Age and possibly before—as witnessed by a stone coffin found at Crowmallie (formerly Knockollochie); an urn burial cist at Newlands; and another at Drumdurno. In addition there are two stone circles within the Parish boundaries—one at Balquhain—and a fine one situated immediately behind Aquahorthies. Also there are three prehistoric carved stones at Logie Elphinstone and one at Drimmies, as well as the better known one, known as the Maiden Stone at Pittodrie.

Perhaps the most interesting of the mediaeval buildings remaining is the ruined castle of Balquhain, the demesne of the ancient family of Leslie, the first Baron of that name being created in 1314, and the last (being the 39th Baron) died only about 30 years ago. The family were all successively Counts of the Holy Roman Empire. At some time they removed from Balquhain, which was destroyed by the Duke of Cumberland in 1745, to build the mansion house of Fetternear which in its turn was destroyed (in this case by fire) in the early years of the present century. The later members of the Leslie family built the House of Aquahorthies as a seminary for priests—which having proved too small, was moved to Blairs College on the Dee where it still exists.

Queen Mary of Scotland is reputed to have slept the night at the Castle of Balquhain before hearing Mass at the Chapel of Our Lady of the Garioch during her disastrous expedition against the Earl of Huntly.

The present church at Chapel is of little interest, the original building having been destroyed some time after the Reformation. It is believed to have stood a little to the south of the present church where the burial place of the Erskines of Pittodrie now stands, of which the vault may well be the crypt of the old church. One cannot but deplore the vandalism which destroyed so wantonly all the churches of the Garioch with the sole exception of Monymusk.

Another ruin worthy of mention is Tullos, now almost completely decayed, but said to be the birthplace of Field-Marshal Alexander Leslie, one of the Scottish soldiers of fortune employed by King Gustavus Adolphus of Sweden in the thirty years war. He was a natural son of the Leslies of Balquhain, afterwards created Lord Leven.

There exists also the foundation of the ancient hermitage and chapel of Braco, where prayers were said for those who fell at the battle of Harlaw in the year 1411, and where some of the victims took sanctuary.

Older still must be the remains of the chapel dedicated to St. Apollinaris, the mausoleum of the family of the Gordons of Manar. St. Apollinaris was an early Roman Saint whose shrine at Ravenna attracted the notice and reverence of a member of the great family of Balliol, David Earl of Huntingdon, who in the event of his safe return from a crusade promised to endow a monastery in the saint's honour. This he actually did, thus importing into the local place names of far-distant Scotland, the slightly perverted version of "Polnar's Chapel," "Polnar's dam" and others.

There remains to be mentioned the total ruin of Maiden Castle on Bennachie. This was given to the Erskines of the House of Mar for services rendered to King Robert at the Battle of Bannockburn in 1314. Legend has it that at some time the family abandoned this site and used the stone to build the old part of Pittodrie House. The first date we have for this is 1490. The house was later burned down by Montrose in his covenanting days. The Erskines must have rebuilt the house as the next date extant is 1675. The Erskine family thus owned Pittodrie and Balhaggerdy from 1314 until 1900.

One must also mention the interesting discovery this year by Dr St. Joseph of an extensive Roman Camp at Logie Elphinstone possibly connected with the battle of Mons Graupius under Agricola, as described by Tacitus.

Perhaps the most cheerful note on which to end this very brief history of the parish of the Garioch is to mention Pitcaple Castle, erect and unruined—owned and lived in by the Lumsdens who are descended from the ancient family of Leslie of that Ilk.

*   *   *   *

"ABERDEENSHIRE BY MOONLIGHT"

By Innes White

"The same moon shines no less on Bennachie
And at the thought a yearning takes me west
And in the mind's enchanted eye I see
The Mither Tap whose slopes I love the best.
Perchance a star is nestling at her breast:
Perchance the Gadie, dancing to the moon
With fairy ripples, murmurs 'here is rest,'
I may not tarry now, sweet stream, but soon
I'll come and on your banks await a golden noon."

Reproduced by Courtesy of The Deeside Field Club.

DUNNIDEER   *Illustrations by* HENRY J. L. MANTELL, A.R.I.B.A.

INSCH—BEFORE THE "CHARTER"

By Dr Douglas L. Stewart

To the north-west of Bennachie, overlooked from the west by the hill of
Dunnideer, lies the village of Insch, the parish extending north to include the
Foudland hills. In 1178, in the Charters of Lindores, the name was Inchma-
banin; in 1275, in the Episcopal Register of Aberdeen, the name was Insula; in
1291, Ingemabin; in 1366 Inchmacbany; in 1536, Inchis and in 1550 in the
Charter of the Burgh of Barony, the spelling is Inche. This is from Innis, a
meadow or haugh of Mabanin, an unidentified name, possibly of a Saint.
"Henry and Mary, King and Queen of the Scots in (1565) in regard to the good
faithful and acceptable service rendered to us by Andrew Leslie, son and heir
of William, of New Leslie, on behalf of ourselves and our successors for ever,
we make, create amd incorporate all and whole the said lands of Inche with
their pertinents into a whole and free burgh of barony, to be called the Burgh of
Inche in all future time." The charter goes on to outline the method of election
of bailies and officers and their powers to hold courts and administer justice
among the inhabitants, of making and composing acts, statutes and consti-
tutions "for the advantage of the said burgh and our aforesaid lieges."

In the immediate surroundings of Insch there is a most interesting collection
of objects dating from pre-history, so let us go back to find what we can of life
in the district before the granting of the Charter.

From the Stone Age, first of all, a Flint Smiddy was found on the north face
of Foudland; flint arrow-heads were found near Whitehall; short cist burial

sites have been identified on the south slope of the Candle Hill near Coldhome and near Brankstone.

From the Bronze Age, many urn burial sites have been found—on the slopes of Dunnideer, near Williamston, near Greenlaw, at Colpy Farm, at Fallow Hill, Wrangham and recently near Largie. Also from the Bronze Age are the Stone circles, often with a recumbent stone, found only in the north-east of Scotland. Remains of circles are in abundance—at Druidstone, Premnay, Wantonwells, Dunnideer, Stonehead, Candle Hill, Inschfield, Colpy Farm. Now we enter areas of great and interesting controversy. Are these circles and stones connected in any way with Druids? Who were the Druids? Were these recumbent stones altar stones? Were the circles burial grounds—at the time they were built or later? Archaeologists think that the recumbent stone circles are developed from the ring cairns found at Clava, near Culloden and that these chambered cairns were tombs and centres for practising magic rituals in the Neolithic and early Bronze Age of 2000–1500 B.C. There is evidence that the stone circles were used much later as places of assembly for the Episcopal Register of Aberdeen in 1275 tells us—a certain William de St. Michael is to appear "ad unum diem legitimum per juris ordines ordinatum apud stantes

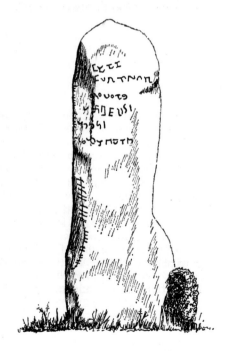 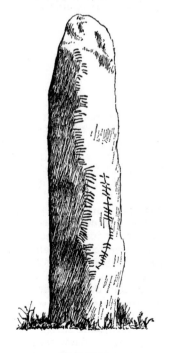

Front View   Side View

Newton Stone showing Ogam Script.

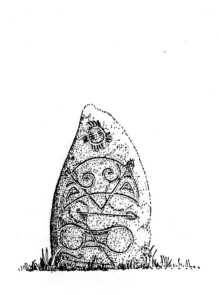

Logie Stone   Picardy Stone

lapides de Rane en le Garuiach" where the Bishop and his retinue were to be present with the "Kings Chief Justiciar benorth the Forth."

As well as the stone circles, there are in the vicinity of Insch three notable examples of sculptured stones—the Picardy Stone at Myreton, the Newton Stone and the Logie Stone. Whereas the stone circles stand sullen, silent, mysterious, the sculptured stones are alive with action and make one feel in the presence of skilled craftsmen of long ago. No sculptured stones are found in any druids' circle. The sculptures are done on natural flattish surfaces of the stones; they are of stylised geometric figures and of symbolic animals. The figures and animals are repeated on different stones although in different groupings. The illustrations show Z-rods, V-rod, double discs, mirror, comb and crescent—all in the same apparently conventional and distinctive manner. These are not religious symbols and are peculiar to the north-east of Scotland, by far the greatest number being in Aberdeenshire, whereas in Forfarshire the sculpturing is more of Celtic crosses as seen in considerable number at Meigle. These in turn are different from the sculptured stones in Ireland, like those at Monasterboice which are in the shape of beautiful Celtic crosses and decorated with friezes of allegorical figures; connecting links are found in the stones in Iona and Argyllshire.

Pictish Stones they are called in the north of Scotland, but archaeologists are by no means agreed that they are Pictish. And what is their age? The Newton Stone with the Ogam writing and other script on it is important here for it is standing beside (and was found beside) a sculptured stone of the same material, gneiss, and that Newton Stone is renowned for the intense interest it has given to philosophers and philologists and it still baffles them. The script is supposed by some to be a translation of the Ogam; by others the script is supposed to have been written first; it is surely unlikely that the two messages are entirely unconnected. But what is the script? Is it a debased Roman or Greek script? One theory is that it is Phoenician and if so this stone is from about 1500 B.C. whereas the sculptured stones are supposed by some to be of 600–800 A.D. Now on the Logie Stone there is ogam writing round a circle at the top of the stone, with the crescent and V-rod, etc. below; the work on the Logie Stone would therefore have to be of the period 1500 B.C. The whole matter is most fascinating. Perhaps a north-east equivalent of the Rosetta Stone will be found to give us definite information about the script just as the Book of Ballymote in Ireland provides a key to the ogam alphabet.

Overlooking Insch from the west is the familiar and picturesque hill of Dunnideer with the conspicuous landmark of its castle, a vitrified fort and an even older set of turf ramparts and ditches; Dunnideer must have been a centre of local life for many a century. The Earls of Mar, Lords of the Garioch held their Courts here in the 15th century; the hill is mentioned in the Harlaw ballad; it was said by Hector Boece to have got its name from being the hill of gold—Dun o' d'or—because there was said to be gold in the hill and that the teeth of the sheep that grazed there turned yellow. Surely an unlikely story; if Mr Mackie's Suffolk tups had gold-plated teeth, he would have noticed and doubtless have told someone!

Dunnideer Castle was, with Balquhain Castle, one of the chief strongholds in the Earldom of the Garioch and is recorded as the "Castrum de Dunidor" as the seat of Sir Joscelyn de Baliol, so the gaunt wall, pierced by a ruined window is all that remains of a 13th century square tower. However, this theory about its age is contested by some who claim that the style of building with the packing of flat chips between the courses, is a feature of buildings of the 16th century. But it is suggested that it was at one time the residence of Gregory the Great, King of Scotland and that he died there in 1393. It must have been uninhabited for many centuries for no record is ever found of inmates of Dunnideer being involved in the troubles and wars in the north of Scotland when occupants of neighbouring castles, now in ruins, were being mentioned in history.

Considerable parts of the wall of the vitrified fort are still in existence. This type of building was practised by the ancient Gaels and characteristic of the north-east of Scotland and of Aberdeenshire in particular, the prime examples being the fort on

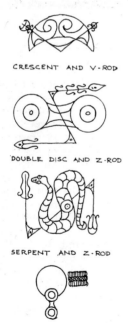

CRESCENT AND V-ROD

DOUBLE DISC AND Z-ROD

SERPENT AND Z-ROD

MIRROR AND COMB

Pictish Symbols

Tap o' Noth. It is unlikely, as some have suggested, that the vitrification happened when a besieging force tried to burn the fort, for the materials found on the hill are not vitrifiable, but a very fusible rock is to be found in the surrounding land. The inference is that those who built the wall used this stone so that it could be vitrified.

So, briefly, some thought-provoking ideas and facts about the Insch of long ago. It is of interest that the constitution and functions of the Council of the Burgh of Barony of Insch have been fairly closely followed in the creation of the new Community Councils. There is still plenty to interest and fascinate in Insch and its surroundings, at the back o' Bennachie.

THE PARISH OF LESLIE

By William Leslie Gavin

Describe a circle on whose perimeter lie the towns of Kennethmont, Insch, Premnay, Keig, Tullynessle and Clatt. Within that circle is the parish of Leslie. The most ancient name of the parish was Lesly. The tradition is that Bartholomew de Leslyn, a noble Hungarian, came to Scotland with Queen Margaret about the year 1067; that he was the son of Walter de Leslyn, who had his name from the Castle of Leslyn in Hungary. Other sources, however, attribute the name—with the spelling 'Lesslyn' to the local topography, the word signifying the fort of the pool; a fort may have stood where the castle was later built, on what would then have been a marshy haugh on the banks of the Gadie. Whatever the origin of the name, it seems clear that it was not derived from that of the family Leslie, rather that the family name was a contraction of Leslyn or Lesslyn. The earliest ancestor of the Leslie family is said to have been one Bartolf, a Fleming, who acquired lands in the Garioch and fixed his residence in what we now call Leslie. However, the date 1067, when he is said to have landed in Scotland, suggests that Bartolf and Bartholomew, whether Flemish or Hungarian, were one and the same. His son Malcolm received a grant of the lands in the 12th century, and thereafter, as the charters show, the family lineage can be traced to the first bearer of the surname Leslie, Sir Norman de Leslie, proprietor in 1282.

By the end of the 16th century the fortunes of the Leslies began to wane. When the last Leslie to hold the lands died, his widow married William Forbes, a son of the Laird of Monymusk, and the lands of Leslie passed into the Forbes family. At that date, about 1620, the original castle or fort was in a state of ruin. The new proprietor pulled it down and the foundations of the present castle were laid in 1661. John Forbes, his son, succeeded to the estate, but during his lifetime it became, by purchase, the property of the Leiths of Leith Hall, in whose possession it has remained. The Leiths had previously obtained the barony of New Leslie. Today the original estate is largely broken up; the Leslie and Duncanstone portions were sold to the tenants during the last half-century.

The Castle of Leslie, now sadly a ruin, has been ranked as one of the most interesting and valuable specimens of ancient domestic architecture in Scotland. Although it was built long after the period when fortification was an essential feature of Scottish castles, it was designed on a traditional L-shaped pattern, incorporating many of the defensive characteristics of a feudal castle. There are shotholes, for example, those at ground level being ornamented horizontal slits, an older design than the plain shotholes which appear in the turrets. The castle presented a combination of the older features of fortification with the latest improvements in domestic architecture. The stair tower, for example, is large, to provide space for a broad—four feet wide—stair, not the traditional awkward spiral but a fine square stair ascending in alternate short flights and landings arranged round a square newel. At the foot of the newel was a small opening like a fireplace, above which the hollow centre of the newel resembled a flue. The purpose of this device, however, was to provide light, the newel being pierced at different levels, so that a lamp placed at the bottom reflected through the openings and lighted the stairs all the way to the top. This perhaps more than any other feature of the castle that we know of, is evocative of an atmosphere and an age—thin light filtering on to the stone steps that provided a comfortable civilized ascent for women in long skirts. One needs to go no further than this to imagine the castle occupied, the sound and motion of people going about their daily lives, each one in his station, servants making haste up the small domestic stair that led from kitchen and wine cellar to the long hall above, a fire burning in the big fireplace which backed on to the west gable.

The hall gave access to a drawing room, and there was a third room on the same floor, possibly a private family room, to the south east. From this floor there must have been a little stair leading to the garden because there is a door in the centre of the east wall; we know from the position of the old moat, a relic of the former castle, that there was a considerable area of ground on that side, which no doubt incorporated a garden. There had also been buildings extending from the south wall to the moat, probably containing necessary offices, but this extension has long ago crumbled away. We are left at the present day with a shell, sadly neglected, many of the internal features of which might have been preserved. One can still see that there were two storeys above the first floor, that the stair tower rose a storey higher, within which a small stair on one wall led to a living room at the top. There may have been a parapet above, or there may have been a pyramidical roof matching those of the turrets. The external features of the castle are a mixture of Scottish and English architecture; in the main it is distinctively Scottish, but the omission of crow-stepping on the gables, and the separate diagonal chimney stacks instead of a single chimney head on each gable, are distinctively English. Only two of the chimneys now remain. Although some of the topmost masonry still miraculously stands, there has been extensive deterioration during the last fifty years. All the fine corbelled turrets have lost their roofs, and the north-east corner of the castle has been allowed to crumble away. For this neglect 20th century man deserves no better than the 20th century houses farther along the road. At a certain point as one travels east the field of vision encompasses 17th and 20th centuries. The experience is grotesque and unnerving. It is not recommended.

Leslie is a parish of hills and rock. Between the northern ridge with its high

The carters with the wood off Bennachie at Oyne Railway Station
at the end of the First World War.

Cuthbert Graham, Flo Garry, Danny Gordon,
at the Verse Speaking Tryst on Bennachie, 4th October, 1975.

By courtesy of "Press and Journal"

By courtesy of "Press and Journal"

The First Summer Rally — July, 1973.

rounded caps, and the high range that runs from Bennachie westward, the Gadie flows in its fertile valley. It has its source in the adjoining parish of Clatt, and flows into the Ury in the parish of Oyne. Only a small stream perhaps, but an important one for the agricultural prosperity of the region. Its romantic associations, immortalised in the famous song, are evocative of remote idyllic summers in a past age, before the present day harbingers of an ice-age, before any ordinary body could suspect that summer would not always be a season of cloudless days and the sun high and constant in a bright sky.

There are at least five versions of 'Where Gadie Rins.' The one believed to be the oldest, by an author unknown, is a melancholy ballad, a lament by a young woman for her two lost loves:

> The tane was killed at Lowran Fair,
> An' the ither was drooned in Dee.

The version ascribed to Dr Arthur Johnston, who was at one time proprietor of the Castle and lands of New Leslie and Rector of King's College in 1637, is a young man's rhyme in which the singer dreams of his betrothed 'At the back of Bennachie.' The best known version of the song is a departure from the ballad, a nostalgic cry for the idyllic days of youth. The second verse is probably the most familiar:

> Ance mair to hear the wild birds' sang;
> To wander birks and braes amang,
> Wi' frien's an' fav'rites left so lang
> At the back o' Bennachie.

Unlike the earlier forms, all the verses in this version end with the same line. It has been ascribed to Dr Johnston, to the Rev. Dr. John Park of St. Andrews, and to the Rev. Mr Barclay, a minister of Cruden.

In another version the word 'foot' takes the place of 'back' in the phrase 'back of Bennachie.' This seems less effective as an evocation of the remote in time and place. On the other hand this version has many attractions:

> When bud and blossom sprout in spring,
> And gar the birdies wag their wing,
> They blithely bob, and soar, and sing,
> By the foot o' Bennachie.

And 'foot' in this context is exactly right. The author, John Imlah of Aberdeen, who died in distant Jamaica in 1844 at the age of forty-five, did not confine his memories to the lush fertility and romance of summer. The reader who thinks of the back of Bennachie as a bleak windswept glen, will find echoes in the verse:

> When winter winds blaw sharp and shrill,
> O'er icy burn and sheeted hill,
> The ingle-neuk is gleesome still
> At the foot o' Bennachie.

Yet another, later version, rather similar to the well-known one, contains eight verses, and reverts to the use of 'back.' Such is the veneration accorded to this old song that it is said that after the siege of Pondicherry, a Scottish regiment marching into the town stopped abruptly and stood to listen as a Scotswoman at an open window sang 'The Gadie Rins.'

In the distant past there had been a 'town' as well as a parish of Leslie. James II granted a charter erecting the town of Leslie into a Burgh of Barony, with the privilege of a weekly market on Thursday and a yearly fair at Michaelmas. Today there are neither markets nor fairs, Duncanstone as well as Leslie has lost its shop, and at New Leslie, which was a thriving hamlet in the 19th century, only three farms remain. Agriculture is still the chief industry. A century ago there were at least four mills on the Gadie, at Auchleven, Leslie, Auchmar and Clatt. Of those remaining none is working at the present day. The Mill of Leslie, which produced the staple fare of the community for generations, ceased production of oatmeal in 1927. The water wheel did continue in use for the production of electricity, but that too is now of the past.

Down through the centuries Leslie has had its share of strife and misfortune. The first Jacobite rising sent its waves reverberating through this as through other parishes. In 1745, we are told, there were no recruits from Leslie, but rebels from other neighbourhoods were a source of many rousing tales by old men who in their youth had spoken to the last followers of the Prince's cause. In the 17th and 18th centuries cattle-lifters and smugglers plied their trades, and an incident is recorded about the year 1820 when a fight took place on the public road near Millfield. The gauger found himself outnumbered, and was driven off by the smugglers. Although help was subsequently forthcoming, the smugglers had by that time managed to secrete their kegs of whisky on the premises of an obliging farmer, and authority was outwitted. Like other districts, Leslie did not escape the resurrectionist scare, and for several weeks the parishioners had to do watch duty at new graves. In 1829 came the notorious 'muckle spate,' recorded so colourfully for posterity by David Grant, and in 1837-38 there was the 'big snaw.'

Records of the ecclesiastical history of Leslie date back to 1698. In an earlier century the parish was served by 'Readers.' There was, too, at one time a Roman Catholic Chapel, hence the name Chapelton. The first church stood further to the south than the present one, in what is now the churchyard. It dated from 1635, and on its demolition in 1855, when the fabric was no longer considered to be safe, the belfry (bearing the date 1635) and the bell were transferred to the new church. Two silver communion cups, beautifully wrought and inscribed, were gifted to the parish by the Rev. Mr William Watson, an Episcopalian, whose ministry dated from 1681-98.

The Kirk Session records provide the earliest picture of life in the community. Some of the accounts of the charges for Sabbath-breaking, and of the discipline administered by the Session fall strangely upon our ears today. It may not seem too incongruous for a woman to be charged with washing or even drying clothes on the Sabbath, but other charges referred to 'publick and scandalous laughing upon the Lord's Day at the Kirk door immediately after service;' 'vaiging and travailing through the parish without any necessity.' Even in 1705, 'abuses at pennie weddings by reason of pipeing and dancing' rendered all the parties concerned liable to censure.

The old Church was a plain building, its best feature probably its fine leaded windows. Unfortunately not all of the originals survive. The first Free Church was built just outside the boundary of the parish at Waulkmill in 1844. In 1876 it was replaced by a handsome building with a fine belfry—almost a modified steeple—a graceful arched door and gothic-style windows. Today, while the old Church is still in use—a single minister now serves Oyne, Premnay and Leslie—the architecturally finer Free Church has been abandoned to legalised vandalism, even its entrance enlarged to admit the implements of mechanised farming. Leslie has not escaped the present-day mania for tarting-up old buildings to the complete destruction of their character. The Free Church manse, built in the traditional north-east country style, is now a sad and mutilated spectacle. The Parish Church manse, which has a graceful bell-mouthed stair to its front door, is largely untouched, but since its sale neglected and delapidated, and a nasty flush board now does service as a front door. Some desecration is irreversible; the rest one hopes may some day be undone in the interests of posterity.

The parish is not without its legends and antiquities. On the farm of Chapelton, on the road leading to Tullynessle over the shoulder of Knock Saul, there is a point on the march boundary known as the 'Four Lords' Seat.' It is said that on one occasion the Lord of Leslie, Lord Glamis, the Lord of Putachie (Castle Forbes), and the Bishop of Aberdeen met there and dined, each sitting on his own land. Other sources suggest that besides the four Lords, the Lairds of Montgarrie and Balgowan also dined, each of the six proprietors sitting on his own land. On this same farm of Chapelton there is said to have been a Druidical circle or temple. Traces of two other circles were found on the farms of Braehead and Johnston. A large slab of red granite sculptured on one side with the form of a dog or wolf and other markings, was found at Newbigging, and is preserved in the grounds of Leith-hall. It is sad that agricultural developments during the past century must have denuded the parish of much that was of archaeological value.

Records of schooling in Leslie show that several buildings have at different times served the educational needs of the community. The first school is thought to be the one which stood within the precincts of the present church-yard, its playground extending to the Gadie. Around 1828 it was transferred to a new building, later to become the merchant's shop at the bridge. The children at that time were responsible for providing their own fuel, and woe betide the child who forgot to bring his peat, or who was caught filching one on the way from a convenient stack! In 1857 a final transfer was made to the building which closed only in 1964. It is now used as a community centre. Both school and schoolhouse, a single structure, are built in an attractive architectural style—in contrast to the faceless blocks of the present day. Happily, alterations to the old buildings have not marred their character. Not so with the old shop, which is now a house. Robbed of its gable chimney-heads, it reminds one of an animal shorn of its ears.

As with so many place names, the traditional and local pronunciation of the name Leslie has suffered in general usage from anglification. The old 'Leslyn,' or more particularly the form 'Lesslyn,' leave little doubt that a soft 's' is intended, and 'Lesley' as a woman's name is generally pronounced in this way. But 'Leslie,' which is more common even as a woman's name, tends to be anglified, at least furth of Scotland but also regrettably by Scots themselves, by the use of a hard 's.' Being born at the Mill of Leslie, the writer and his twin sister were both blessed with the name, and in his own case although 'Leslie' is a middle name, it has been the one most favoured by family and friends. But mispronunciation is a legacy. Perhaps those who belong to Leslie, and those who bear the name, should more zealously strive for preservation of the old pronunciation. The parish may change, but at least let us take a stand for its ancient and venerable name.

The writer would like to express his thanks to Mr William Morrison of the Mill of Leslie for his help in the preparation of this article.

WHERE GADIE RINS

By John Imlah

O gin I were where Gadie rins,
Where Gadie rins, where Gadie rins,
O gin I were where Gadie rins
    By the foot o' Bennachie.

I've roamed by Tweed, I've roamed by Tay,
By Border Nith and Highland Spey,
But dearer far to me than they
    The braes o' Bennachie.

When blade and blossoms sprout in spring,
And bid the birdies wag the wing.
They blythely bob and soar and sing
    By the foot o' Bennachie.

When simmer cleads the varied scene
Wi' licht o' gowd and leaves o' green,
I fain wad be where aft I've been,
    At the foot o' Bennachie.

When autumn's yellow sheaf is shorn,
And barnyards stor'd wi' stooks o' corn,
'Tis blythe to teem the clyack horn
    At the foot o' Bennachie.

When winter winds blaw sharp and shrill
O'er icy burn and sheeted hill,
The ingle-neuk is gleesome still
    At the foot o' Bennachie.

Though few to welcome me remain,
Though a' I loved be dead and gane,
I'll back, though I should live alane,
    To the foot o' Bennachie.

O gin I were where Gadie rins,
Where Gadie rins, where Gadie rins—
O gin I were where Gadie rins,
    By the foot o' Bennachie.

ON THE HIGH TOPS

By Frank G. S. Davidson, Advocate

"Bennachie" to me a native of the North East is like the personification of life itself. My world has revolved round it from my earliest days. Shethin, Tarves, nearly five hundred acres of the finest land in Aberdeenshire, the home of my ancestors was the place from where I first glimpsed the "Mither Tap." From the dining room it was always in view. The vista left open through the ancient ash and sycamore trees.

Years passed ere my greenheart rod first caught the Don trout in the Vale of Alford in 1925. And days and nights in sunshine and April showers and even snow showers always under the watchful spirit of the "Ben," the Don has yielded my share of her speckled beauties to the dry fly and the occasional salmon has failed to return to the sea.

To the "Tap" and the moss lying between it and the "Owsen Crag" there on the Twelfth the grouse lie canty and snug, their privacy is invaded by the black labradors. Their masters pause and relish the breeze fresh from the Atlantic or the North Pole bringing with it the tang of heather honey. Handsome Syd, no mean labrador, distinguished by his seal head and otter tail soon signals a covey is at hand and the guns take their toll. No Cheepers here—all well grown birds in beautiful plumage including the patriarch himself with his red wattle above his eye

The moss retains its winter moisture which during the long summer days gently fills the wells, the burns, the Gadie and the Don. The very source of life.

At the spring the shooters halt for lunch. There also they stay to allay their thirst. Such water is fit to christen the ancient malt from the Braes of Glenlivet still with the bead as it is poured from the flask.

Now Roy Milne, the Pittodrie keeper sets our course for the summit and as I climb the rocky edifice I unload my gun as a precaution. The coveys calling "go back, go back" depart unscathed.

Immediately below the summit a hen grouse has nested and safely brought off her brood. What a view point for a sitting bird!

As the afternoon wears on, the bag fills slowly. Numbers do not count in these surroundings. What counts is the setting—the dream world of the exiled Scot so ably portrayed by "Hamewith" coupled with the companionship of my clansmen, guests Milne, Watson and the faithful four-footed friends. A happy and understanding partnership enjoying the spell of the "Mither Tap."

So to tea with Mrs Milne at the bottom of the hill to be greeted with the aroma of new baked scones and crumpets. Lashings of tea and our pieces are spread with farm butter and covered with yellow raspberry jam made from berries gathered at the back of the cottage.

Our labradors relax on the back seat as my clansman and I drive slowly down the Pittodrie Avenue. I wait for Donald's usual cryptic comment "Another day plucked from the Gods"—and who can deny it?

THE STORY OF "THE COLONY" ON BENNACHIE

By the Rev. N. L. A. Campbell, M.A., of Chapel of Garioch, 23rd July, 1939

As you approach Bennachie from the South-East, your eye is caught by a little patch of brightest green among the greys and browns of the rocks and heather. This is the story of that green patch and in telling it there is told the history of three generations of the Esson family.

The Squatters

The Hill of Bennachie was what was known as a Royal or Free Forest, that is, a commonty. The local inhabitants had rights of grazing, and if they needed stones or peat or wood, well, these were there on the commonty of Bennachie for the taking and taken away they were by all and sundry. But in 1801 there arose a new development, for in that year a certain man took his pick and shovel and climbed the slope of the hill till he came to a spot on the left bank of the Clachie Burn about 700 feet up; there he began to build for himself a simple dwelling and to "rive in a bit grun' " to eke out his living. That man was the first squatter on the commonty of Bennachie. His daughter married John Esson who, in 1826, with his wife and little son (John aged five) joined his father-in-law. This John Esson was a mason; he built a house with walls of stones and clay, and a roof of divots thatched with broom or heather, and began to break in from the wild that patch which is so green today. He was followed by others till there grew up on this slope of Bennachie a group of squatters known throughout the whole country side as "The Colony."

The Colony

In "The Colony" there was no trouble about title deeds. As a man's family increased it was an easy matter to increase the number of the rooms, and even the greater problem of building a new house for a new settler presented little difficulty. The materials were to hand in plenty and the story is told how once the neighbours completed a house for a new settler in a single day and celebrated the event by a supper that same evening in the newly erected home. The Colonists were a community unto themselves; they lived on the borders of Chapel and Oyne but, because of Poor Law Liabilities, neither parish would own them. Chapel said they were in Oyne and proclaimed them as such, while Oyne said they were in Chapel and, equally so, proclaimed them; in the end Oyne had to accept them. And the Colonists, likewise, were a law unto themselves. They had their private supply of whiskey which paid no duty and as to other forms of private property, well, some of them had their own ideas—and these ideas rather vague concerning thine and mine. But the great majority of the Squatters were hard-working respectable people who, to eke out their meagre wages as day labourers, gave their leisure and their strength to win their little fields from the bare and barren hill. Amongst these were: The Essons, masons and famous dykers; Macdonald, a retired contractor; two or three families of Littlejohns, thatchers; Sandy Lindsay, the fish cadger; Gardens in the highest croft; and Christies, Findlaters, Mitchells and Beverleys. In 1859, there were in "The Colony" some twelve or more households and nigh on sixty people, a considerably bigger population than there is in the Kirktown of Chapel today. But in 1939, of all these only one remained—George Esson, third of his line, and now he too is gone.

The Partition of The Commonty

Of the long, sad and bad story of the partition of the commonty of Bennachie by the neighbouring landowners it is sufficient to note that the final decree of the Court of Session was signed on March 5th, 1859 (80 years ago) and that by it the Colonists found that they were no longer squatting on common ground but were settled on the estate of Fetternear. No drastic action was taken immediately; small rents were imposed and the squatters became tenants at will. Probably the rent was 5/- for householders, for that was the rent paid by Sandy Porter who had built himself a house and enclosed a garden at Kewlie, just below the commonty on the Fetternear estate. And they, like him, in return for their half-crown each half-year would receive as much as they could eat of the grand rent-day dinner. But the crofters—they had to pay according to their industry, and on 6th August, 1859, five months after the Court of Session decree, John Esson signed a lease waiving all claim to compensation and agreeing to pay £2 10/- a year for the privilege of using the house his own hands had built and tilling the fields, five and a half acres, which by the sweat of his brow he had fenced and trenched from the hill.

In the later Seventies, with the fall of prices, the crofters began to go, so that in 1878 John Esson paid £2 for the grazing of what had been the Garden and the Macdonald Crofts. In that year, also, occurred the 'famous' evictions. The Littlejohns, Hugh and James, had stopped paying—or been unable to continue paying—the rent of £2, yet refused to move. So they were forcibly removed, by a sheriff's officer and two policemen and several estate workers; their few pieces of furniture, and amongst them the old man himself as he lay on his bed, were lifted out and set by the roadside. On a course of masonry being removed, the houses collapsed and the homesteads of fifty years ceased to be. In the lean times of the 'Eighties' the Colony grew less and less till only John Esson remained.

George Esson

In 1891 John Esson, the second, who had gone to the Hill as a boy of five died at the age of seventy. His youngest son, George, had been in America but had come home for health reasons and, being at home, he took over the croft which for the next eight and forty years was to be his home, his castle. He, too, like father and grandfather, was a mason and famous as a dyker. No distance was too great for him to walk to work, and samples of his work, of which he was rightly proud, are to be found on all the neighbouring estates. But he always returned at night to the croft, his eagle's nest from which he watched the world of lesser men. The Hill was his true background; it would have been difficult to say whether the croft belonged to him or he to the croft; for he was a strange man with strange ideas, essentially a solitary and with independence almost a fetish—his avowed creed "I beg and bow to no man and no man begs and bows to me." More and more he grew a part of the hill, every stone and tuft of which he knew, and more and more he became a survival from an age that was gone, until at last the heart that had been strained by a life of incessant and arduous toil gave way and he slipped quietly into that sleep from which there is no waking. With the laying to rest of his body in Chapel Church- yard on May 31st, 1939, there ended 'The Bennachie Experiment.'

A hundred years of history! Climb the Hill today up past the patch of green that is the Esson croft, keep your eyes open for the holly tree, the laurel. the honeysuckle and the berry bushes—the people and the houses alike are gone, but the honeysuckle and the berry bushes, these remain—and in their midst you will find the stones that were once the homesteads of the 'Colony' of Bennachie. Seeing, you may say, "To what end?" Out of the hill; back to the hill, their labour all in vain! No. Working early and late, summer and winter, enclosing, trenching, draining, waging a hard unending warfare with nature, they turned moor and bog into smiling little fields and in the doing so, even if the fields have gone back to moor, in the doing so, they won for themselves and their descendants that grit and indomitable perseverance that characterise the people of the North-East. The true memorial of the "Colony" that once was there, and is no more, is nothing less than the hundreds of men and women, in our own land and in lands across the seas, who have in their blood something strong and clean, hard maybe but true, something that has come to them from their forebears who once upon a time squatted on the rugged shoulder of Bennachie.

Reproduced by the courtesy of Mrs Campbell, Helensburgh.

*   *   *   *

BENACHIE

Anon.

Oh, ye was aince a monarch hill,
To freedom's footsteps free,
But, noo, unless their honours will,
We daurna tread on thee.
Alas, the heather on thy broo
Will bloom nae mair for me;
The lairds aroon' hae ta'en ye noo,
Ye're nae oor Benachie.

BLAIRDAFF AND ITS KIRK AND SOME SIDELIGHTS OF OLD CHURCH RESPONSIBILITIES AND CUSTOMS

By James Smith

From a talk given twenty years ago

Blairdaff as we know it today is a very different district from what it was about 120 to 130 years ago.

Then it was a much more populated district dotted with numerous crofts and smallholdings, now mostly out of existence, and in all with a population of about 1,000 people. A fairly large part of the parishes of Oyne and Monymusk intersected it, and as they and a large portion of the south of the parish of Chapel of Garioch were far removed from their centres of religious life, a very real want was felt by the humble people who had their daily life to lead.

Religion played a big part in those times, there being very little else to divert their attention, and in the beginning of the 19th century in particular.

Adherents of the Episcopalian and Roman Catholic faiths were better catered for, as an Episcopalian chapel stood at one time near to where the Blairdaff Church now is, and for centuries a Catholic chapel existed at Fetternear, where the now ruined Fetternear House was the bishop's summer palace.

Around 1838-39 a movement was set afoot to procure a "Chapel of Ease" for the district, and a piece of ground in a most picturesque spot was gifted by Robert Grant, Esq., of Tillyfoure as a site to the Minister and elders of Chapel of Garioch. The ground on which the church stands consists of a Scotch acre and was beautifully surrounded with wood, as it now is again.

In 1839 the church was built capable of seating 500 people. The cost of building was £500 and was defrayed by subscriptions from some of the heritors and parishioners of Chapel of Garioch, Oyne and Monymusk, from Ministers of the Presbytery of Garioch and other charitable individuals connected with this part of the country, and also from a liberal grant from the General Assembly's Church Extension Fund, insomuch that it was clear of debt when it was opened for public worship on the 9th June, 1839. At the communion in 1840 there were 318 communicants.

The feuduty for the ground is 1 penny Scotch if called for.

The Church is typical of the ecclesiastic architecture of the early 19th century. It is a well-built building of native stone and has a birdcage steeple on the west end. It has galleries round three sides, with the pulpit on the south side, and the choir below in the middle. It had all the austere severity and comfortlessness of the time; nevertheless it served the community well for over a hundred years, and the walls will stand for ages yet to come.

The first Minister to serve the new congregation was the Rev. David Mitchell who was installed in 1841. Previous to this the Church was served by the parish Ministers and various probationers when available.

At the disruption of 1843, he came out, along with many of the congregation and formed the Free Church of Blairdaff of which I will mention later.

He died in 1876. He was succeeded in 1843 by the Rev. Mr Thomson, who in 1846 gave place to the Rev. Gordon Smart, M.A., who was also teacher of Lord Cullen's School, now better known as Abersnethick. In 1849 Mr Smart became Minister of the parish of the Cabrach and was succeeded in both Blairdaff appointments by the Rev. Jas. Mitchell Laing, M.A.

Mr Laing was a well-loved pastor and schoolmaster. His gentle manner and encouraging advice proved a stimulus to many of his scholars who remembered him with affection.

He died in 1886 at the age of 71 and was buried in Blairdaff Churchyard. He was succeeded by the Rev. Geo. Keith who later emigrated to New South Wales. He was likewise followed in 1889 by Rev. Alexander Wilson but he removed to Ythanwells the following year. His successor was the Rev. Richard Robb who was minister till the union. The churchyard was laid out in 1875, after the old churchyard of St. Ninians at Fetternear ceased to be used as a parish burying ground.

The first interment was commemorated by erecting a tombstone by public subscription in 1875, the Rev. J. M. Laing officiating.

Blairdaff Church continued as a Chapel of Ease till March 1895 when sufficient endowment having been secured it was raised to the status of a quoad sacra.

At the disruption of the Church of Scotland in 1843 the Rev. David Mitchell came out, as the saying of the time was, with a large following of the congregation. The then Slattie Free Church, now the one used, was founded in 1843, on ground originally granted by Sir James Grant, Bart of Monymusk, to a Friendly Society, who disposed of it to the Free Church.

The first Minister, as stated, was the Rev. David Mitchell. He was succeeded in 1876 by the Rev. Alexander Yule, M.A., but his promising career was terminated by his death in 1887 at the early age of 36.

His successor was the Rev. John Stalker, M.A., who ministered well into the present century. His successors in the charge were Revs. Mr Craig, Rev. Mr Murray, Rev. Mr Laing and the Rev. Mr Masson. After the union of 1929 both Churches were used summer and winter alternately but only one is now used. That is about all that there is to say about the quoad sacra parish of Blairdaff, so I will now pass on to the part the Scottish Kirk played in early times among simple folk of the parishes who were its charges.

Before writing this part of the paper I read Edgar's book on Old Church customs in Scotland and find a similarity of customs and procedure existed throughout the length and breadth of the country. The country folk clung to their church with a tenacity which was truly a religious zeal. The buildings were far from comfortable or attractive places and if they were pre-reformation buildings, any embellishments which might have savoured of Romanism, were ruthlessly destroyed.

New buildings were bare, barn-like structures, devoid of any comfort or attractiveness and had no heating of any kind.

The pews were narrow, hard and straight-backed. The only difference was the laird's seat, which generally occupied the space of two seats and was enclosed and cushioned.

The service was long and dreary, timed by hour glass and sand glass, the Minister generally preaching the terrors of the day of judgment rather than the compassion and kindness of a loving Redeemer, but the people liked it. If he had not preached so he would have been considered weak with not enough religious fire in him. The praise was entirely the Psalms of David, anything else was considered the work of man and not fit to be sung in the church. No music was allowed, only the precentor with his tuning fork, and he had only a range of less than a dozen tunes to choose from.

Along with the Minister the elders and the beadle were generally characters to be reckoned with, and a great fund of wit and humour is woven round them in Scottish rural literature of the 18th and 19th centuries.

In this respect the beadle generally figures most, as in olden times he considered himself a personality of some importance in the kirk, and at times was not slow to pass his opinion over Minister, Kirk Session and congregation, if he thought differently. Much native wit, as well as sarcasm was given by them and especially on any young, or pompous Ministers, whom they deemed to be showing off their superior learning. He was also subjected to quite a lot of good-humoured banter, as is the case yet, of which I myself can tell.

To the minister and kirk session fell quite a considerable amount of oversight in the congregation.

There was no Welfare State in those days and the care of the poor fell to their lot. Many churches had bequests left in their charge, the interest to be divided amongst the deserving poor, at stated times. Church collections were deposited in what was termed the poor box. We have still got the original poor box in Kemnay, a crude-made box, locked by two keys, one kept by the minister, the other by the box master, so that the two had to be together before the box could be opened. Often bad money was put into the box. It was kept until a considerable amount was collected then it was sold and the proceeds used for small repairs about the church.

In the country districts the inhabitants who were mostly crofters, and who lived very frugally on the produce of their land were often struck with affliction through bad harvests, or plague among their livestock and ever so often the kirk was called on to relieve their want by supplying them with seed corn in spring or meal from its girnal and to supply money to buy a cow. In session records of Kemnay we have many such instances during the 18th century.

Another call that often was made on the poor box was paying doctors' fees and paying for such medicines as were prescribed for the ailing who were also needy.

The burial of the dead was also a care of the Church.

In olden times the parishioners were most anxious that the dead were decently interred and would live most frugally to save as much as defray all the burial expenses but sometimes this was impossible and again the box had to be resorted to. Likewise to them the use of the mortcloth was granted free of charge. The mortcloth was a large piece of black cloth used to cover the coffin on the journey from the home of the deceased to the churchyard. To those who were more fortunate a charge of 5/- was made.

The kirk session employed the sexton, as the churchyards were under their charge and in old country parishes the minister had the right to let his pony graze in the churchyards.

While on the subject of churchyards, around the 1820's to 1840's the activities of the body snatchers aroused the indignation of the country people and the kirk had to prove its ingenuity to protect the newly-interred remains in the ground which came under its charge. Many schemes were tried. A system of watchers in a watchhouse was tried in many places, but the tediousness of the job in long dark nights and a fondness of the bottle often rendered the guard ineffective. In Kemnay a unique relic still stands, in the form of the vault, where the remains were deposited on iron shelves for six weeks before being laid in the ground. It is built of granite of formidable strength, every stone being joined to the next with an iron clamp. The door is about two inches thick of solid iron and locked with three locks, a key to each lock being kept by a separate person, so that all had to be together to open it.

Another of the duties in times past as at present, though not heard of nowadays to the same extent, was discipline.

Old session records all over Scotland contain long accounts of defaulters and their punishments, such as sitting on the stool of repentance, or standing in the jougs, which was an iron collar on a chain at the church door. All these humiliations were inflicted on the defaulters for so many Sundays and the defaulters had to be dressed in garments suitable for their misdemeanour.

Likewise offences of intemperance and of unruly behaviour had to be dealt with according to their code of rules.

Few of the old customs of the church now remain with us but one is unique in the districts around here, but which is not to be found in many country districts and that is the ringing of the bell at 10 o'clock on Sunday morning.

In olden times calendars and clocks were few and far from common, and the bell was rung at 8 a.m. to warn the country folk that it was Sunday. They then started to gather at the kirk to await what was termed the reader's bell at 10 a.m.

Education was scarce in those days and few people could read or write but they were far from ignorant and had an eagerness to learn of higher things, so someone who could read, read and explained the Bible to them, for an hour before service time. The ringing of this bell is an old custom which has come down to us unbroken through the ages and one we should uphold, as so many of our old customs have been swept away so readily in these ages of modernisation. Communion times have always been observed with great veneration. Preceding the Sunday set apart for the observance of the Lord's Supper was the fast day which was more or less observed as a Sunday, all common work being suspended. As many members as possible went to Church, and young members, who had been under special instruction from the Minister, and after approval of the kirk session, were admitted, at this meeting, when tokens were distributed to those who intended partaking communion on the Sunday. I have with me some tokens used in Kemnay since very early times. Tokens were the property of the Minister. Much controversy was held in early days about what kind of wine was to be used at the service and it was finally decided to use claret and Edgar in his book tells that it was not by the bottle but by the puncheon that it was bought. The elements were served to the congregation not in their pews, as now, but at the table as at the first Lord's Supper. There are accounts in some old session records for boards and stools for making of the table for the communion and hence the reasons for the services extending over the greater part of the Sunday. The festivals of Christmas and Easter were taken little notice of in the Protestant Church for a greater number of years as the people considered them tainted with Romanism.

Harvest Thanksgiving has always been observed, the congregation assembling at the church and giving of their fruits with reverence and without stint. Baptisms have always been observed in the church and it was a law laid down by the Assembly that it had to be in the church not at home unless there was something wrong with the child that it could not be taken there. At the Reformation it was decreed that it had to be observed in front of the congregation, the font being placed there, not on entering the door as was the way before. In pre-reformation times the font or stoup as it was called was at the door, symbolic of the child entering the christian church by baptism.

Weddings were also solemnized in church but with a certain amount of restraint owing sometimes to over indulgence of the parties concerned. These customs have been gleaned from old session records, which are sometimes tedious to read, many of which are written in old Scots, and in words which are now obsolete, but they are worth the time and trouble needed, as they give us a glimpse of the Scottish life and times in days gone by.

They were days of joy and sorrow, days of poverty and hardship, but in days of plenty the people were not slow to give of their means, to their church. There were no other attractions for them and their church was their one interest outside their humble homes.

FETTERNEAR AS I REMEMBER IT AS A BOY

By Alan Mackie

Life on a farm as I remember it in the thirties when I came with my parents to live in Blairdaff, near the foot of Bennachie, was a hard but happy life.

The day started around 6 a.m. and we often worked right through till about 8 o'clock at night. Saturday was a working day too—and even on a Sunday there was little time for leisure when the cattle and horses were indoors in the winter.

The work on the farm was all done by horses. Tractors were not heard of in this district at that time. A seventy-acre farm had usually one pair of horse with a colt being reared for a replacement; farms of 150 acres or thereby had two pairs of horses and were called "a two-pair toon." The horses were worked by the 1st and 2nd horsemen and the cattle were looked after by the cattleman, known locally as the "Baillie."

During the winter months the horses were kept in the stable when they were not working. They had to be fed in the early morning (before the horseman went to get his breakfast) and would have been allowed about 1½ to 2 hours eating time. The same time would be allowed for eating at the mid-day break. They were fed again about 5.30 p.m. and had a last feed about 9 o'clock at night. This had to be done seven days a week so the men in charge of the horses took turn about at the week-ends to feed them, the one in charge being known as the "Catcher."

Various methods were used for threshing; when farms had no mill of their own in the barn, a steam-engine pulling a threshing mill went round the farms to thrash the corn out of the rucks in the corn-yards. Usually two men operated this kind of mill and they lived in a van, pulled behind the mill by the steam engine. The farmer needed about 16 men to do the work on a "Threshing Mill Day." They were mostly the men from the neighbouring farms. They all helped each other in turn and there was no cash payment for the help given. It was always the Loon's job to carry pails of water from a nearby burn or the "Horse Troch" to keep the steam going in the engine. It needed about 5 to 6 cwts. of coal to fire the engine for one day's threshing. This was supplied by the farmer. Another type of threshing mill was a Horse Mill. It was a lever pulled round in a circle by two horses and called "A Mill Coorse." This operated the mill for threshing. In the early twenties it was quite common on the smaller crofts for the corn to be threshed by a hand mill. This was done by the crofter himself, the sheaves being fed to the mill by his wife. Many farms had water mills for threshing, the water from the dam being allowed to flow down a sluice or mill lade to turn the huge iron wheel.

The Harvest was a time when every available person on the farm or croft had to lend a hand in the Hairst field. In the thirties on most of the larger farms, binders were becoming quite common; but on the crofts the corn was still being cut with the scythe and gathered into sheaves mostly by the women folk, some of the men following and putting the sheaves into stooks. Sometimes the grain was cut by a reaper. Again it had to be gathered into sheaves and stooked in the field. Later on, the sheaves were forked on to a box cart with a frame and taken home to the "cornyard" where they were built into "rucks" (stacks). After the leading was finished rushes were cut with a scythe and taken home. The "rucks" were "thacked" and tied down with "raips" to keep them dry till they were threshed.

In the early thirties in this district 100-150 acre farms would have employed two Horsemen and one Cattleman. Farms of around 50 acres employed a loon just left school.

Wages for the 1st Horseman would have been about £22 to £24 for 6 months and for the 2nd Horseman £18 to £20 (for 6 months). The loon got about £12 (for 6 months). Wages were paid only at the terms Whitsun and Martinmas. These men were employed at the "feeing market." This was an event held twice a year. It took place about the middle of May and the middle of November. It was held in the nearest town. This day was a holiday for all farm workers. Farm workers who wanted to change their employment went to the "feeing market" where they met the farmers on the look-out for Horsemen, Cattlemen, etc.

When the farmer engaged a man to come and work for him, he gave him a shilling or two and said "I'll see you at the term" meaning either the 28th May or 28th November. The handing over of the shilling or two was called "Arles"—the token given to seal a bargain. If the man employed was a married man, a horse and cart were sent to the house he was leaving, for the "Flittin" to take them to their new house. Farm workers—"cottars" as they were called, had very little furniture. It was loaded on to the cart and his wife and bairns sat on the top of the load. The "cottars" were given meal, milk and potatoes along with their wages. The farmer had his own corn made into meal at the local meal mill. Newly threshed corn was taken to the Mill. The weight of a large bag of corn was 1½ cwts., known as a ½ quarter. The meal was made up in Bolls, ½ Bolls and Firlots. The husks left after the meal was taken from the corn was known as "Sids" and were used to make sowens. There was also oatdust and it was used to add to boiled neeps or tatties for feeding hens and pigs.

The single men employed at the farm slept in one room. This was usually built at the end of the steading or it might have been above the stable with a stair leading up to it and was called the "chaumer." There would have been one or two beds in it, depending on the men employed at the farm. These beds were usually box beds fixed to the wall. The mattress was made with "ticking material" (usually black and white striped) in the shape of a big bag. This was filled with "caff" (chaff). Fresh caff was put into this every year at the threshing time, after the bag had been emptied and washed. A chair would have been the only furniture and the man kept his clothes and personal belongings in a "kist" (a trunk). This was used as a seat, when the neighbouring men came along to spend an evening. There was a closed-in black coal stove in the corner.

About Christmas time, the pig was killed, scraped and cut up into portions. Some of these were hung up on the kitchen rafters to cure. Some of the pieces were put into a big earthenware jar and covered with salt. A neighbour usually shared the pig, because it would have been too much for one family to use while it was still in good condition. The food in the farm kitchen was wholesome and plain fare. Breakfast for the men folk was usually brose. This was oatmeal put into a wooden brose-cup. Salt was added and then boiling water which was stirred with the handle of a spoon. Milk was poured on to the top of this.

At dinner time (mid-day meal) potato, cabbage or kale soup, stoved tatties, chappit tatties, a stewed-stuffed rabbit would have been eaten with milk or bread pudding to follow. Meat would seldom have been used except on a Sunday when broth followed by boiled beef was usually the Sunday dinner and on a special occasion the broth would have been made with a hen.

At supper time (the evening meal) it was usually porridge and sometimes pease-meal brose. This would be followed with bread (oatcakes) and cheese and a girdle scone. Loaf, as we know it, was not widely used in the country at this time.

Washing day was quite a task, because very few houses had water from a tap in the house. The water had all to be carried in pails from a nearby well or pumped from the supply near the house. The large washing pot was hung on top of the fire. When the water was hot it was put into a wooden tub, with a water lifter (pan). The tub sat on a four-legged stool in the middle of the kitchen floor. The clothes were scrubbed on a ribbed iron board, called a washing board, till they were clean. They were wrung by hand. The water was emptied out of the tub into a pail and carried outside. Clean cold water was put into the tub to rinse the clothes, which were hung on the washing line to dry.

The fireside in the kitchen would most likely have been an open fire with a swey on which the crooks hung. The kettles and pots had low handles and were hung on to the crook above the fire. The swey had a four-link chain on it, so that the crook could be lowered or raised, depending on the heat needed for cooking. There were "binks" at each side of the fire and on this a kettle or pot could be kept boiling. There was also the kitchen range which had to be polished with black lead everyday. All the steel about it, including the fender in front, had to be scoured with emery paper till it shone like silver.

The floors in the kitchen were mostly of stone. They had to be washed every-day and scrubbed once a week with a scrubbing brush and soap to get them clean. The kitchen table and chairs were made with plain white wood. They also had to be scrubbed often using fine sand to keep the wood white.

Fetternear lies to the south of Bennachie. At one time most of the district was owned by the Leslies of Fetternear House. Many of the farm houses were attractive residences. The crofts, lodges and cottages were mostly built of stone with slated roofs. Very few houses had running water and very few had bath-rooms installed. The estate of about 5,780 acres was sold in the Kintore Arms Hotel, Inverurie, on Wednesday and Thursday, October 5th and 6th, 1932.

The largest farm on the estate was 340 acres, the yearly rent being paid at that time was £207. It was offered for sale at the upset price of £2,755.

A farm of 105 acres—the yearly rent £85—was offered for sale at an upset price of £820.

A farm of 50 acres—the yearly rent £46—was offered for sale at an upset price £445.

The croft of Boghead of Tullos on the slopes of Bennachie extending to 7 acres, was let at a yearly rent of £3 10/-. The upset price was £40 (this was the croft known locally as Esson's Croft).

The cottages each known as a "But an' Ben" with two rooms and a closet with a £6 to £8 rent were offered for sale at an upset price of £60 to £70.

Part of the hill of Bennachie—411 acres—was offered for sale. The upset price was £300. The water supply for most of these farms and cottages was from a well.

The school picnic was held in a field at Burnhervie on the banks of the Don. The children had all kinds of games and races. Parents and children alike enjoyed this afternoon's outing. John Allan of Melanbrae brought a can of milk which was taken along to the picnic with a horse and gig. It was distributed to the children along with a bag of biscuits. The highlight of the afternoon was when the sweets were thrown across the field by George Bisset, Bograxie (who was parents' representative for many years). The bairns scrambled to pick them up to see how many they could get. In the evening an open-air dance was held. A dancing board was laid down on the field for the people to dance on. The Band played, mounted on top of a four-wheeled horse lorry, drawn alongside the dancing board. The Burnhervie Games were also held in the same field for many years.

A Roup was always a special event and it was James Cowie who conducted most of the displenish sales. He kept up the spirits of the people with his pawky humour, cracking a joke as he sold the different items. I can remember on one occasion when selling a scythe, with a blade cut to about 1½ft long he said "Fit's this for?" When there was no reply, he said, "If there's a man here that's feart o' his wife, he'd better buy this thing." On another occasion at a furniture roup, he was selling two bird ornaments, "I dinna ken fit kin o' birds these are, but we'll jist ca' them twa Fetternear Hawks. There's a lot o' them here the day onywye!!" The Fetternear Hawks have never been seen nor heard of since, and this type of Auctioneer seems to have disappeared too.

The letters and daily newspapers were delivered to the door six days a week. The postie was Norman McIntosh. He cycled from Inverurie to Burnhervie, Hill o' Fetternear, Blairdaff, Dalfling, Afforsk, Bograxie, back to Burnhervie Post Office to collect mail then home again to Inverurie. During stormy weather when roads were blocked he walked. It was quite an undertaking and he must have been a very fit man. His cycle had a carrier in front on which he carried the parcels and when it was raining he wore a large oilskin tippet, which extended over the handlebars of his bike and over the parcels. With this he wore oilskin leggings. The postie brought verbal messages from a neighbour—(there was no telephone in this district at that time) such as—when the threshing mill was to be —or if a baby was born—or if any local body had died. He would have carried medicine from the chemist for an "old body" and maybe shared a cup of tea and a "news" with them. I'm sure he was a good samaritan to many families.

It is impossible to refer to everything in detail. The pattern of living and working has changed down the ages, but farming is our oldest industry and from the richest to the poorest we still live from the land.

The thirties passed. 1939 saw the start of the Second World War and now the way of life has changed so completely, that I can scarcely believe I was only a boy, when I saw all I have written about and that this way of life is only a memory. However, the burns still run on, the trees still grow the same and the familiar outline of Bennachie is just as it was when the Iron Age men built the fort on the Mither Tap over 2000 years ago.

THE HUMOUR OF THE GARIOCH

By Dr. D. G. Gordon

Away back in those halycon days before 1914, Dufton Scott, Inverurie bookseller and popular entertainer published his "Humorous Scotch Stories and Sketches." Going into several editions, it found a place in the homes and hearts of Aberdeenshire folk. The foreword was written by his friend, Gavin Greig, dominie at Whitehill of New Deer, the superb collector of the minstrelsy of the North-East. Dufton Scott was born in 1880 and died in 1944. His fellow entertainer was Tom Morrison, manager of the Inverurie Commercial Bank and Town Chamberlain, who was knocked down and killed by a lorry in the black-out of the 1939 war. He was a prolific writer of verse and reporter for the *Aberdeen Journal*. He celebrated many a local occasion in his volume "Murmurings from Ury," published in 1921.

They were a great pair. Up to the Second World War, no concert around Bennachie was complete without them. Tom did the comic songs. Dufton was no Caruso, gave the recitations and sketches. In 1907 at a Rothienorman Tories' Concert, Lord Leith of Fyvie, described Tom as the local Harry Lauder. Perhaps Dufton Scott, more than anyone of his time, captured the essence of the humour of the farm folk. Time has not aged it. The other night on 7th February 1975, the Oldmeldrum bank manager did a Dufton Scott recitation at Bourtie Hall. It was a great evening. The Bourtie folk, led by their local councillor, Forbes Green, were celebrating the opening of their little hall after a thousand pound face-lift, raised by themselves in their tiny but lively community. After the haggis, the tatties and the neeps, the banker brought the house down.

Another Garioch man with a dash of humour, was George Bruce Thomson of Oldmeldrum who wrote the words for three of Wullie Kemp's bothy ballads, published by Kerr of Glasgow in 1950. The revival of folk-song in Scotland about that time was a great joy. Robert Wilson's singing of "The Northern Lights of Old Aberdeen" has gone round the world. The bothy ballads of the North-East have proved a great mine of material for the folk-singers. This has given much pleasure on television in bringing to a younger generation old favourites like "Drumdelgie," "Mormond Braes" and the "Barnyards of Delgaty." Much of the modern material is poorly written, not to be compared with the gusto and the sheer exuberance of George Bruce Thomson's "McGinty's Meal and Ale," "McGinnis and his Cross-Eyed Pet," and "MacFarlane o' the Sprots o' Burnieboozie." They are real cornkisters.

Many Garioch folk consider that Wullie Kemp was the king of ballad singers. He belonged to Oldmeldrum. His family kept the hostelry called Kemp's Hotel. He was succeeded by his brother-in-law, George Morris. Kemp's Hotel was changed to Morris's Hotel, and Kerr the publishers produced two volumes of Buchan bothy ballads collected by George Morris.

Cold print does little for song or story. You need the voice of May Morrison to bring alive William Thom's "Wedded Waters in the Woods of Logie." Grace Leslie and John Mearns have, in the past forty years taken the songs of the Garioch and the whole North-East to the homes and halls and to the wider media to our joy and delight. Just as a song needs its singer, so even more so a tale needs a teller. The tale that brings the children from their play, and the old man from the chimney corner, needs a real raconteur. John Strachan of Crichie was of that ilk. So were Sir James Taggart, Provost of Aberdeen and the 'Wee Twa' Marquess of Aberdeen, who entertained with story-telling competitions in the decade after the first world war. The droolers of bewhiskered chestnuts at the marriage feast are tolerated in an atmosphere of general bonhomie and the full stomach.

There is a wealth of stories about the farmer on Market Day. As the age of the gig and its shalt that knew the way home from Market was followed by the age of the motor, problems arose. The motor car had not the intelligence of the horse. Many farmers, hard-working through the week, took a dram or two or maybe three with their cronies after the weekly cattle sale. On one such occasion two of them had overdone the refreshment at the Black Bull, and thought they would take a run into Aberdeen. As they got on about Bucksburn the one says to the other "We maun be gettin' near Aiberdeen. Ye're knockin' doon a lot mair fouk." "Me knockin' doon mair fouk" was the retort, "it's you that's drivin'."

Another farmer from the skirts of Bennachie always made a day of it at the Inverurie Mart. His wife knew better than to sit up for him. As she said "He'll come hame some time." This night he was later and more under the weather than usual. He stopped the car in the farm close, and managed to find his befuddled way into the pig-sty, where he lay down behind the old sow, and put his arm round her thinking it was his wife. "Maggie" he solemnly asserts, "thirty years we've been mairriet, and this is the first nicht ye've come to bed withoot yer nicht-goon."

Lewis Grassic Gibbon describes the Mearns folk as coarse, meaning possibly the same as we mean by "coorse." Certainly our humour is rural even bucolic, of the earth, earthy, straight and to the point. "If ye dinna fancy a coo or a woman at the first glance, dinna look back, ye were richt the first time," dropped from the shrewd lips of old.

Sandy down Fintray way, his breezy and expressive speech would not have 'graced a Victorian drawing-room,' but he called a spade a spade. Leaning on the travis at the Inverurie Mart ring, when asked what he thought about a couple of stots that breenged into the ring off the weighbridge, he said "their noses are owre near their tails." It wasn't "tails" that he said.

Hamewith knew the farming stock, the breed remaining in the same hundred acre two pair farm, generation by generation. He writes:

> "A harkenin lug, a gyanging fit
> Although they've never filled my kist
> Have brought me wisdom whiles and wit
> Worth mair than a' the siller missed."

Old Daniel Skinner, born at Cotetown of Leslie in 1820 was of that mould. His descendants are scattered over the Garioch to this day. He had the native wit. "Siller is like sand" he would say "the more you grip it, the more you lose." When his old father died, there was a family row over the grandfather clock. It was claimed by the wife of the son left in Cotetown and by the daughter who was married to William Milne of Broomhillock, a farm over the back of the Cotetown hill, the two farms having a joint march dyke along the skyline. The row got very bitter, till Skinner decided to let his sister have the clock, and one fine summer day at the eleven o'clock lowsing time, his two men were dispatched up over the hill to Broomiehillock carrying the clock. Wm. Milne met them in the close and ordered them to take it back to Cotetown. One can imagine that after carrying the great clumsy mahogany case over dykes, and through broom and whins, the Cotetown men did not relish a similar return journey. Besides, Milne wasn't their boss. They had done their job. So they set off back up the hill, followed a couple of hundred yards behind by the two Broomhill men carrying the clock. On the hilltop the four men foregathered, and the clock was set up erect against the march dyke. As they had a friendly smoke, the wag among them suggested starting the pendulum. This was done. To the great joy and delight of the whole of Leslie parish, Skinner's clock rang out the hours for the whole of a fine summer week from the top of Cotetown hill, while the two thrawn farmers let it ring, until Skinner gave in finally and took it home.

Yes, William Milne was the thrawner. He was deeply religious, was precentor at the Duncanstone Congregational Kirk, and held family worship night and morning. He had to upbraid his wife for not singing, and she countered by telling him he was always trying new tunes. For six months they sang Crimond in the morning and the Auld Hundred in the evening. "Lassie" he asked "hiv ye them noo, because I was thinkin' i' trying ither twa."

Into this frugal good-living community around Duncanstone, there came an incomer a generation later, a ne'er-do-well, brother of an illustrious Aberdeen divine, kept well out of sight on a little croft with a ticket-of-leave allowance from his brother. The kindly neighbours did their best to keep his besetting temptation out of his reach, but on a social occasion in company, he had to be offered a dram among the rest. One night when the hostess gave him a very pale weak dram he asked whether she had put in the water or the whisky first. On being told that the whisky had been poured in first, he said "weel, I'll jist ca awa till I come tilt."

In this year of 1976, more than three-quarters of the twentieth century gone, the pace of change has accelerated so rapidly that in the past sixty years the Garioch has changed more than in the three hundred years before. Today we are in such a whirl, that we have gone completely light-headed in painting and sculpture and music. One great blessing remains, we have retained our vernacular doric, our Aberdeenshire tongue, and that too in spite of all the media have done to anglicise our speech. We have lost many of the old words connected with life on the farm, but enough remain to salt our conversation. Listen to this gem of a story. Dr Robert Bruce of Cults, a Garioch man born at Myreton of Insch in 1871 was Colonel of the 7th Gordons, the Deeside batallion in the 1914-18 war. He knew all his men and was bitter at the terrible slaughter in the trenches. One of his sergeants had got the D.C.M. Colonel Bruce asked him if his folks had been proud of his medal. His reply was that "they didna ken yet." "Why not?" queried Bruce. "Weel, it's nae my turn to write."

That story, more than any other story typifies to me the country character of the North-East, the quiet humour born of the discipline of toil from daylight to dark to make ends meet, the men of whom Sir Alexander Gray wrote one Saturday afternoon when he was having his usual high tea at Lairhillock Inn by Newtonhill in "This is my Country." Cuthbert Graham has taken the title for his glorious Saturday articles in the Aberdeen *Press and Journal*. Sir Alexander's lines about "the men who toil here with sweat in their faces—with want an attendant not lightly outpaced" were taken as his text by Professor Raeburn of the Chair of Agriculture at Aberdeen in his inaugural lecture a few years back.

"Bydand," the Gordon motto means "biding, abiding, enduring, tholing." We are slow of speech. In an interview for a top job, the Glaswegian with his fluency and blarney, runs rings round the tongue-tied Aberdonian with his inferiority complex, more apparent than real. Our speech, our doric tongue, native to our soil, is, I feel, the perfect vehicle for our quiet humour, which so often takes a tilt at ourselves. There must be around Bennachie, many stories of our local characters. The Bailies, whose chief aim is conservation, hope to make a collection of these and will be proud and grateful to our readers for their help in searching the crannies of their memories.

I must acknowledge with gratitude the advice given to me by George Scott, who succeeded his father Dufton Scott as an Inverurie bookseller. He was involved for many years with the local entertainment circles, such as the Inverurie Operatic Society. He published James Milne's "Twixt Don and Ury and Round About." In his opinion Sandy Benzie of Premnay, but recently deceased, deserves a niche as a Scots entertainer of real merit. On a similar level, the plays of Daisy Bruce and Mrs Middleton of Clatt rate honourable mention.

He writes: "The history of a people is not the list of dates, kings and warring barons, battles and massacres we had to learn at school, over half-a-century ago, but rather it was how these people endured through turmoil and managed to progress by hard, honest toil to the standard of civilisation we now know in the countryside.

"Through all their labours in transforming the Garioch from a barren wasteland into a fertile plain, native fun and wit must have flourished to lighten the everyday task. But in the passing of story from one generation to another much must have been lost, though the folk song and later bothy ballads have fortunately preserved some of it.

"Cuthbert Graham, in his 'Portrait of Aberdeen and Deeside' puts this point in referring to the ballad of the bloody Battle of Harlaw, with its exaggerations and its recurring refrain 'Wi' a dree dree dronachie drumplie dree' as the Lowlander's mocking of the Highlander and the drone of his bagpipes."

EDUCATION

By Alex. L. Young, C.B.E., M.A., B.SC., ED.B.

Perhaps some day a historian will undertake the task of writing a history of the development of education in the Garioch and the Vale of Alford. He would do well to begin his research with a careful study of Dr Ian J. Simpson's book "Education in Aberdeenshire before 1872" published in 1947 by the Scottish Council for Research in Education.

For the period after 1872 much interesting information can be found in the log books of individual schools. For example I quote the following extracts from the log book of Port Elphinstone School, kindly sent me by the dominie, Mr Peter Nicol, who recently retired.

The first entry is dated 8th November, 1870. "Last night a fire broke out in the school about 8 o'clock. The school buildings were laid in ruins, and school registers, log book, library school books and other items were completely destroyed. Today a corn store has been converted into a school building and the work of the school has been conducted in it." Only five months later we have the entry—

1871 24th April "Entered the new school premises."

1871 2nd Oct. "Girls sewing blinds for windows of new building."

1873 "The Annual Presbytery and Public Examination held."

1873 "Euclid will be taught chiefly outside school hours so that it will not interfere with normal school work."

1873 "School fees collected during half an hour before school opening in order to prevent interference with school work caused by payment of fees during school hours."

1875 Oct. 8th. "The school board has resolved to charge each scholar 2 pence per week during the winter month for coals."

1876 "The school consists of two rooms, 1: 36 feet by 24 feet. 2: 24 feet by 9 feet 4 inches. (This for a roll of 120)."

1884 Oct. 3rd. "Outbreak of smallpox."

1886 "A large menagerie passed through the village, so the 11 o'clock interval was prolonged to allow the children to watch it."

1889 Jan. 28th. "Medical certificate closing the school because of diphtheria. Only 23 children present out of 130."
March 1st. "School re-opened."
April 19th. "Diphtheria again. Samuel Mutch caught diphtheria from clothes sent to him from a distance. They had belonged to an uncle who had died from the disease."

1897 "Earth closets removed and water closets installed."

1898 April. "School closed for three weeks—measles."

1900 March 2nd. "School closed because telegram arrived announcing relief of Ladysmith."

1910 Sept. 9th. "Medical inspection commenced in the County."

1912 "The threshing mill was in the village this week-end. Many people took the opportunity to refill their beds with chaff."

1918 "An aeroplane visited today and children were allowed out to see it."

1919 Feb. 5th. "Half holiday to see a tank."

1919 May 16th. "Lack of boots reason for much irregularity of attendance."

Mr Nicol has also sent me a brief history, written by himself, of the village of Port Elphinstone and its school from which I have taken the following information.

The first school at Port Elphinstone was a single-room structure built by the heritor, the Earl of Kintore, in 1832. It was destroyed by fire in 1870, and very promptly replaced by a building consisting of one large room and one very small one. H.M. Inspector's report for 1892 states that on occasions there are 100 children in one room, and adds "My Lords have ordered a deduction of one tenth on account of overcrowding." The deduction was presumably in the Government grant to the school board. In 1896 the small room was extended and a third room added. In 1950 the school was wired for electricity, but was still "heated" by coal stoves. In winter the temperatures seldom rose above 45°F. The toilets were outside, and often froze in winter. Central heating was installed in 1954. In 1956 inside toilets were provided, another classroom was added, a playing field laid out, and school meals service began. There was a further extension in 1968, and the school is now described by the headmaster as "a 5-teacher school, with bright airy comfortable rooms, a nice general purpose room, and adequate storage and play facilities."

Since 1832 the school has had only eight headmasters. One of them (Mr Coutts) was killed in World War I, having been headmaster only for a very short time, so the others averaged more than twenty years apiece—a remarkable record of stability. One of them, James Ritchie, headmaster for 38 years from 1875, was outstanding both as a teacher and as an antiquary. His son, Professor James Ritchie, who was born in the schoolhouse at Port Elphinstone, wrote of him in a foreword to the publication of the father's papers—"Even in the high standard of teaching in Aberdeenshire, I think he must have been ahead of his times, for we were taught geography with the aid of an oil lantern, and the slides of foreign towns and peoples, made and tinted in colour by himself, stamped pleasant and deep impressions on more than one generation of pupils. For the higher classes, where special subjects were taught, he compiled and duplicated on a jellygraph press, little booklets on geography, agriculture, etc. He gave them to pupils."

Professor James Ritchie was Keeper of the Natural History Department in the Royal Scottish Museum. Then for six years he was Regius Professor of Natural History at Aberdeen University, and then for sixteen years he was Professor of Natural History at Edinburgh University. He was President of the Royal Society of Edinburgh. His son Anthony became Professor of Medicine at St. Andrews University; he is now Secretary and Treasurer of the Carnegie

Trust, and was a member of the Houghton Committee, which in December, 1974, published a notable Report on the Salaries of Teachers in England, Wales, and Scotland.

Other former pupils of Port Elphinstone who rose to positions of eminence included Alexander Gordon, Professor of Literature at St. Andrews University, Anthony Mitchell, Bishop of Aberdeen and Orkney, and Sir James Taggart, Lord Provost of Aberdeen.

The log-book of the neighbouring school at Keithhall throws some interesting side-lights on the day-to-day work of a school, typical of many in the area, in the years from the Education Act of 1872 to the turn of the century.

The first entry, dated October 13th, 1873, records that "School re-opened after the Harvest Holidays." Later entries show that July and August were not holiday months. The autumn holiday began about the end of August and lasted usually for six weeks. In 1877 the holiday began on 1st September and school re-opened on 22nd October, i.e. after seven weeks, and the log-book entry reads "So few came forward on the previous week owing to the late harvest that the opening was postponed." Christmas Day was not a holiday but there was a "Christmas" holiday lasting from a week to a fortnight, beginning on 1st January. There were several shorter breaks. For example:

"Friday, 6th March, 1874. Holiday. Keithhall Spring Fast Day."

"Monday, 9th March, 1874. Holiday. Thanksgiving Day."

And there are similar entries for 24th, 27th and 28th July, 1874.

"4th November, 1874. Thanksgiving day for the late abundant harvest. No school."

"13th April, 1900. On Tuesday school met from 9 a.m. to 1 p.m. to enable children to attend a cinematograph exhibition in the schoolroom at 4.30 p.m."

"8th June, 1900. Half holiday on Wednesday on account of rejoicing for capture of Pretoria."

"17th November, 1905. Holiday in honour of marriage of a School Board Member."

References to infectious disease are common. For example: "Week ending 13th January, 1882. Helen Allan and William Allan, two pupils, died of diphtheria."

9th January, 1885. "The absence of over 50 during the week was chiefly owing to the prevalence of measles."

16th December, 1890 to 19th January, 1891. "School closed on account of the prevalence of scarlatina."

4th December, 1903. "School closed for four weeks by recommendation of County Medical Officer," (The reason was probably whooping cough).

25th June, 1909. "Closed on Thursday and Friday to allow a thorough cleansing of the school, Diphtheria having been discovered in a family, one of whom had been ill and back at school before this was known.

2nd July, 1909. "Regular work as usual but attendance very much affected by the events of last week."

There are many references to school inspections. For example: 21st April, 1874. "Dr Christie, Inspector of Schools for the Milne Bequest Trustees, visited and examined the school"—but there is no record of what he thought of it.

THE BOOK OF BENNACHIE

Every year Her Majesty's Inspector examined the school, and a detailed report was sent to the School Board, and had to be copied *verbatim* into the log-book by the dominie. This must sometimes have been a humbling experience for him, for adverse criticism of his work was not uncommon. Sometimes, however, there was praise. For example: 1878. "The weakness in intelligence of the second and third Standards has been very successfully remedied." It would be interesting to know how that was done!

The use of modern aids was encouraged:

1882. "The frequent and systematic use of the ball frame in the arithmetical exercises of the Infants and the first Standard is strongly recommended in preference to the present very mechanical use of the fingers and strokes on the slate."

Payment depended on results:

1889. "Grammar has been very skilfully and successfully taught and had the Recitation been more expressive, the higher grant for English would have been recommended."

The School Board were reminded of their duties too:

1894. "The children in the senior room suffered great discomfort on the day of inspection owing to the intense cold which the single fire failed entirely to dispel. Something should be done to secure proper heating even on the coldest day."

The 1894 Report says that singing was remarkably good. But in 1895 "a further development of Musical Drill is desirable and for this a piano is necessary." And in 1896, "The lack of a piano however is preventing the due development of the musical side of the instruction and also renders the proper teaching of drill impossible. The highest grant under Article 19 a.3. cannot therefore be recommended, even though the conduct of the children is in every respect satisfactory."

1897. "The desks in the junior room should be replaced. They are much too high and the seats are too narrow with no back rest."

1898. "My Lords have had difficulty in allowing an unreduced grant in view of the fact that H.M. Inspector's remarks in last year's report on the furniture of the infant room have not been attended to. They trust they will receive immediate attention."

1900. "Of the total number of 103 in the school, the Junior Division made up 67, and that in a room built to accommodate 53. Such organisation cannot be considered satisfactory."

1901. "It is unfortunate that in an average attendance of 77 there should have been 39 admissions." These figures illustrate two of the problems that used to beset rural dominies—irregular attendance and the constant movement of pupils from school to school. Living and working conditions for agricultural workers were deplorable, so that they were constantly changing jobs in the forlorn hope of finding better conditions elsewhere.

The first indications in the log-book of the number of pupils in the school occurs in a brief entry dated 22nd July, 1897, "Annual Inspection, 48 boys 58 girls—106. A. Walker, H.M.I.S. and Mr Topping, Sub-Insp." Presumably these were the numbers present on that day. The total roll may have been more. The staff consisted of the head teacher and one assistant. That had been the complement of qualified staff since 1873, with assistance in some years from a pupil teacher. The pupils ranged from infant beginners to senior pupils studying Algebra, Euclid, and Latin.

An entry in the log dated 11th June, 1880, gives the names of six pupils who had begun the study of Latin, one of them being Alexander Pirie. The same A. Pirie appears as a pupil teacher in the staff lists appended to H.M. Inspector's Reports for the year 1883 to 1886. "A. Pirie passed fairly," "A. Pirie passed well," and on 29th October, 1886, "A. Pirie left to attend College."

The rest of the acts of Alexander Pirie are not written in the log-book, but he duly graduated and went on to spend a considerable part of his long teaching career as headmaster of Tarves School, where one of his pupils was Maitland Mackie, later to become successively Chairman of the County Education Committee, Convener of the County, and Lord Lieutenant of Aberdeenshire. Mr Pirie died in 1972, having very nearly reached the age of 105.

Mr Pirie had retired long before I came to Aberdeenshire, but he occasionally wrote letters to me. In one of these, written in the early 1960's, he wrote "I need hardly say how ashamed I am of the actions of some of the present-day members of my profession"—a reference to a group of teachers in Glasgow who had taken the unprecedented action of going on strike! In another, written in 1964, when he was 97 years old, he told me that he had just noticed an interesting arithmetical coincidence. "I began teaching in 1882, which is **82** years ago, and I retired in **1932**, which is **32** years ago." The clarity of mind that prompted an observation like that was still in evidence when I visited him shortly after his hundredth birthday. I found him in full possession of all his faculties except for a slight hardness of hearing. His memory was excellent, and he was keenly interested in, and well informed about, current educational affairs. At the age of 102 he formally opened the Oldmeldrum Sports, and about the same time he went for his first flight in an aeroplane. A truly remarkable man!

Educationally, the big success story in the Garioch has been the expansion of Inverurie Academy. In 1843 the Inverurie Parish School consisted of two rooms, each holding 90 pupils, on the site of the present Market Place School. After the disruption in that year the Free Church built a new school in West High Street. After several extensions and reorganisations the two were combined under one headmaster in 1905. Then a new Higher Grade School was built and formally opened under the name of Inverurie Academy in 1909, with Mr James Philip as its first Rector.

In 1921 Mr Philip was succeeded by Dr Gordon C. Lawson, who, so far as I can recall, was the only member of Aberdeenshire's teaching staff to hold the degree of Doctor of Science. He was small in stature, but had a great booming voice, and he spoke as one having authority—as indeed he had, for he ruled his school with a rod of iron. Under his very successful rectorship the Academy became a full Senior Secondary School, and he established a tradition of presentation of candidates for the Leaving Certificate and University Bursary examinations that has been maintained unbroken from 1922 to the present day.

Dr Lawson retired in January 1948. The last years of his rectorship (and my first year in Aberdeenshire) were spent in the aftermath of the Second World War. The school-leaving age was raised from 14 to 15 in 1947, and more school accommodation was needed everywhere. But a vast backlog of repair work had been accumulating since 1939, and there were shortages of labour and of all kinds of building materials, so no new school building was permitted except for the prefabricated huts erected by the Ministry of Works under the HORSA scheme (Hut Operations for Raising the School Age). The approved programme included six huts for Inverurie, and I well recall Dr Lawson calling on me to argue that he needed not six rooms but eight. He made an excellent case, which I promised to support, and he left my room well satisfied saying that that would meet the needs of Inverurie Academy for a long time to come.

He was wrong. Neither he nor I foresaw the extent of the developments that were to take place in the reign of his successor, Dr Norman Dixon. The roll of the school grew steadily and new subjects and courses were introduced. An extension costing £80,000 was completed in 1956, and in 1967 I had the honour of formally opening a further extension costing over £300,000 which included the replacement of the Horsa Huts and much else besides. Even that was not the end. A swimming pool was added in 1970, a Community Centre in 1973, and a new physics department in 1974. In session 1974-75 the Academy had over 1500 pupils on the roll.

Dr Dixon came to Inverurie from the Royal High School of Edinburgh, where he was Principal Teacher of English. When his application was under consideration, the Rector of the Royal High School, in reply to my enquiry, wrote in glowing terms of Dr Dixon and ended his letter thus: "He would make a job like the one at Inverurie his life work. My only fear is that he would overwork himself in it, for he never spares himself." That is of course precisely what happened. Dr Dixon quickly established an enviable reputation for the detailed knowledge he had of the individual pupils in his school, and his personal interest in their welfare. In addition to guiding the Academy through an unparalleled period of reconstruction and expansion, he found time to give service in other spheres. His work locally and nationally, for the Educational Institute of Scotland was recognised by the award to him of the F.E.I.S. degree in 1965. He became a Justice of the Peace in 1959. He was appointed to the Governing Body of Aberdeen College of Education in 1964 and was Chairman of that body from 1967 to 1971, and for some thirteen years he has been a member of the County Education Committee as a representative of their teaching staff. Inverurie Academy has indeed been fortunate that two such men as Dr Lawson and Dr Dixon have directed its activities for more than fifty years.

Another notable dominie in the area was John Minto Robertson, Headmaster at Kemnay from 1923 to 1948, when Kemnay was a Senior Secondary School. Before his appointment to Kemnay he was Classical Master at Turriff, and after his war services he was responsible for "The War Book of Turriff and Twelve Miles Round"—a record of all who served in the 1914-18 War from the Turriff District. At Kemnay he combined the headmastership with the posts of principal teacher of Classics and of English. One of his former pupils wrote of him "As a teacher he was extremely erratic. Some days it was fun and games. . . . Other days he was gloomy, unpredictable, and unhelpful . . . . while he did not make first-class Latin scholars of us, he did inspire us with an enthusiasm for English as well as Latin Literature. . . . He was a gifted and eloquent speaker. His former pupils, and staff will never forget the addresses he gave them at morning assembly and on other occasions when he had the whole school in front of him."

"Minto" was elected by his colleagues to be the first President of the County Head Teachers' Association when it was formed in 1946, but he will be remembered chiefly for his open air productions of Shakespeare's plays. These were staged in the grounds of Kemnay House each summer of his 25 years in Kemnay. The weather generally favoured him, and if my memory serves me right, I think he told me that he had never had to abandon a performance. I saw the last of these productions and was greatly impressed by it. The play was "The Tempest" and it was quite the best amateur Shakespearian production that I have ever seen.

I seldom think of Bennachie without recalling George Hendry, dominie of the little school at Oyne for nearly 37 years—from February 1927 till the end of 1963. He was the sort of colourful character around whom the legends grow, and it is sometimes difficult to separate fact from fiction. For example, it may or may not have been true that during one of his spells in hospital, when he had been strictly forbidden to take any form of alcohol, he had a supply of whisky handy in a bottle labelled "After-shave lotion."

In 1940 George got into hot water for talk likely to spread alarm and despondency—an offence under war-time regulations. Unfortunately I cannot now remember what it was that he said, though he did tell me. But I do remember the chuckle with which he added that a year or so later Winston Churchill was saying the same thing. He may have criticised the government, but he was not unpatriotic, for in 1940, and again in 1941, he applied to the education authority for permission to volunteer for service in the R.A.F. Permission was required, because at his age (38 or 39) teaching was a "reserved occupation," and on both occasions permission was refused. Had he enlisted without permission, he would have had to resign his teaching appointment. This would have meant that he would not have had the benefit accorded to others of having military pay made up by the authority to the level of civilian pay. It would also have involved relinquishing the tenancy of the schoolhouse, so that his wife and family would have required to find another home, and he would have had no assurance of a post to come back to at the end of the war. Not surprisingly, he let the matter drop. The official view was that the County's teaching force had already been depleted by the call-up to the forces of teachers under the age of 30, and that more teachers were needed because the County was a reception area for children evacuated from the cities as part of the scheme of air-raid precautions.

During most of the time I knew him George was a sick man. Early in 1949 he was told that he required two major surgical operations. Characteristically, his reaction to this information was to throw a party for his friends, on the principle he explained to me, "eat, drink, and be merry, for tomorrow we die." I visited him in hospital after one of the operations, and was much impressed by the fortitude and cheerfulness with which he faced a grim situation. He was off duty for more than a year, and later there was a third operation with other troubles to follow, including diabetes and pneumonia, and troubles of another kind in the death of one of his sons in 1952.

In 1963 he decided to "call it a day" giving his reason simply as "old age," but in fact he was some years under the compulsory retiring age. He retired to St. Andrews to spend the short time that remained to him within sight of the Old Course, though he was no longer able to play golf on it, as he had done in his youth.

I have given most of this chapter to my recollections of a few of the dominies in the area around Bennachie, but I would not like to conclude it without a tribute to the men and women who have given unpaid service—in some cases over many years—on the County Education Committee. The heavier load falls of course on the Chairman, and I count myself lucky indeed in the succession of dedicated chairmen whom it was my privilege to serve for more than 22 years. Outstanding among them was Maitland Mackie, Chairman for no less than fifteen years, and an ideal Chairman he was—a man of absolute integrity, tolerant, with a keen sense of humour and a prodigious appetite for work. Education is only one of his multifarious interests, but in my opinion he has made a more important contribution to education in Aberdeenshire, than any other man of his generation.

THE BONNET LAIRD

By Archie Smith

Ye aa' ken me, JOCK MEERISON, the laird o' Clortymyres
Full saxty acker o' a tack on coontin' hoose an' byres
Abeen's there hings the Larrickbraes oot ower the eemost knowe
On t'ae side Mains o' Yavelstane, on t'ither Sprottyhowe
Hine doon aneth the Teuchit Burn rins jinkin' throu the haugh
Aye skelpin on at sic a rate amang the funs an' saugh
Whilk mairches gaird the fairest Toon fae Fintra'tae Strathdon
Gyang aa' the far'er gin ye like there's nae a place like yon.

It's forty year come Whitsunday sin we took up the yoke
Me wi' ma kist an' collie dog an' HER wi' aa' her troke
The twa three beasts her faither gied's, a horse fae Andra Wid
The mear we stole at Hilly's roup fan naebody wad bid
The scrapins o' the oxter pooch wared cannily on gear
Wis aa' the doonsit that we got fan Meg an' me cam here
Hoo we survived it's hard tae tell—aa' this wis lang lang syne
But noo ye ken that Clortymyres belangs tae me an' mine.

I mind the day the "letter" cam that tore me fae ma wark
She's rankit oot the razor an' ma Sunday breeks an' sark
The pair o's riggit unco smairt—I couldna gyang ma lane
Gin dennertime we're i' the train het-fit for Aiberdeen
"Yer tack's run oot" the Factor said, "Yer doots I'll seen dispel
"It's buy the place or doon the road, for that jist please yersel
"An' furthermore gin ye can pit sae muckle doon anent
"I micht contrive tae eke ye oot at sic an sic per cent."

At lang length Meg thoomt ower the notts we'd keepit hod sae ticht
An' cried me up instanter tae mak siccar aa' wis richt
The Factor billie lookit queer fan I begood tae tirr
I couldna louse the safety preens an' buttons wantin' HER
Come time the "beuk" wis rivven oot, the binder tow an' aa'
An' han't across the muckle dask intae the waitin' claw
He reeshle't throu't sae fleet an' said "Ye've aa' that I desire
"Jist sign upon the dottit line *Jock Meerison Esquire*."

Tho' noo a Laird the wife an' me had still tae tyauve an' scrimp
Things turnt a hantle easier fan Johnnie got's exemp
He wis that cunnin' wi' a snare an' skeely wi' the wan'
The butcher's cairt for months on en' wad nivver come nearhan
Tho' still a littlin he wis stoot an' did the wark o' three
That mair nor justified his keep an' savin' o' a fee
The laddie fair took efter me for smeddum, brains an' force
A term or twa at orra loon an' he took on the horse.

Ther's aye a something, Hamewith said. Fu' weel we ken it's true
For it wis RAB oor younger loon that gied us cause tae rue
He wis that eeseless wi' his han's—we couldna gar him fee
Sae the Dominie got his wye o't an' we loot him tak's degree
He's githert letters till his name like ony alphabet
In fack ye mith mistak him for some speeshul kin' o' Vet
Noo he's a lecturer at "KING'S," a job that fits him fine
As lang's he hisna neeps tae pu' or mash tae feed tae swine.

Ah weel we're barely roadit wi' the bondie aff the place
An' lookin' baith the brookie an' the mullart in the face
Fan oot aboot the rippit starts aa' ower yon Hitler cyard
Aneuch tae rooze the Gordons' birss as nae doot ye'll hae haard
Sae aince again the Terriers gied their pleuchs an' graips a haive
An' mairched awa ahin the pipes—oor Johnnie wi' the laive
The auld fowk an' the bairns were left tae warsle on their lane
An' thole the dirl o' warldly strife wi' nae word o' compleen.

Fan I look back on mony a nicht wi' tire I couldna sleep
Jist hearknin' tae the yokie heels chap-chappin' on the greep
Sair fashed wi' naisty futrats fae this Ministry or that
Aa' creeshy hair an' fountain pens forivver fin'in' faut
Aye even ma verra neepers cockit on the A.E.C.
An' muckle need tae bide at hame wad tell me fat tae dee
Noo that the roar o' battle's stilled an' vanquished lies the foe
It's like waukin' on a Simmer mornin' efter Alford Show.

Oor Johnnie took the place in han' the meenit he cam hame
An' foo he's han'lt things sin' syne fair pits us aa' tae shame
The Fergie fuffin' ower the brae, lang cairts wi' rubber wheels
A tummlin' tam wi' three speed gear an' routh o' glintin' teels

Wad caa the feet fae Mac o' Forgue forbye yon Cooncil fowk
Wha clob the pass wi' birrin' mulls fan they begin tae howk
We're that far forrit wi' the wark sin' aa' this cam aboot
We ken the day an' date but it's the sizzen that's in doot.

It's fifteen year come Michael Fair sin' Clorties gaed T.T.
Ye'll keep in min' that's jist the nowt—it's nae a tag for me
We've swine in beauty parlours, diet strickly a la chart
Maks sure their score gyangs ower the hog at Lawsons or the Mart
An' as for hens an' siclike trash ye havena far tae rax
Tae chance on raws o' poultry sheds tae help haud doon the tax
The beasts an' birds are aff ma han'—I'm oot o' date they say
But Gweed be thankit Bess the bick will nivver say me nay.

Ye'll see we've managed nae that ill tae keep oor heids aboon
We've redd the hoose up an' installt a fancy "sit-ye-doon"
An' fan we pat the lettrick in, losh fat an eese it wiz
We'd bleezin' licht the winter lang tae cheer the hens an' hiz
We've teemt the weskit pooch tae buy a sonsy Jaguar
That's hurlt a gweed curn new fa'en calves an' faith it's nane the waur
The Session hears us wi' respect, we're on the Cooncil tae
An' gin anither hairst be bye we'll sign oorsels Jye Pee

It hisna broken oot yet sae nae wird o' this ootside
But Johnnie's eident makkin' plans for fessin' hame a bride
The quine he's gettin' teaches sae nae doot she'll cairry on
Till something unforeseen occurs—lats houp it be a son
Fan that day daws ye'll unnerstan that Meg an' me maun flit
An' time tillt for ye'll aa' agree we've mair nor deen oor bit
An' syne ye may look forrit for the fylie that I'm spared
Tae hear me blaw aboot the days I wis a BONNET LAIRD.

THE COUNTRY DENTIST

By Thomas R. Angus, L.D.S., R.F.P.S.

Dentistry, like so many other things, has changed considerably since the old days of long ago. Although "Hesi-Rè" the first known dentist practised his art in Egypt around 3000 B.C.—it was not until the 19th century that it came to the Garioch area. It was around 1900 that my late father, William Angus, came to the Royal Burgh of Inverurie and set up his plate. Up to that time, the extraction of teeth or "the pullin o' teeth" was carried out by the local blacksmith or the chemist or the doctor. A strange assortment of instruments were used and as a result (no anaesthetic was provided) there was pain, much laceration of gum tissue and at times a copious flow of blood! It was a question of "sittin doon" and "haudin on!" A new era commenced with the arrival of my late father to Inverurie. Patients requiring extractions could now get a local anaesthetic or a general anaesthetic in the form of gas from a machine called The Guy Ross—and of course, if the total extraction of teeth was necessary, this was carried out at the patient's home. The doctor was in attendance and chloroform or ether was administered. As a result, fear and pain were being pushed somewhat more into the background. Teeth could now be saved by fillings and patients could now be provided with dentures or "Falsers" which was the common term in those days.

Patients were not too keen in those earlier times to have fillings. My late father had quite a struggle educating the public to the advantage of saving their teeth. He was up against one big snag as the years went by and that was the appearance of the non-qualified dentist. They were known as "Quacks." They had never gone to a Dental School or University. They had learnt the art of dentistry on their own! They were really only interested in extraction of teeth and the fitting of dentures. The result was if my late father refused to extract reasonably sound teeth, then those patients used to say: "Well, well, we will just 'ging tae a quacker'!" Fortunately, in 1921 the Dentists' Act was passed. This forbad anyone practising dentistry unless they had a degree. However, it did allow existing non-qualified dentists to continue.

My late father's surgery was gas-lit. His dental chair had a beautiful covering of rich plush material. It was a comfortable chair—as long as you were not being subjected to dental work!! There were nice pictures on the wall—an open fireplace and a bit of carpeting. The drilling of teeth was carried out by the use of a foot engine which my late father pedalled away—just "like pedalling awa' like a bike!"

The waiting room was nicely carpeted—and there were nice pictures on the walls also. There were nice plush armchairs and also a sofa. Many a farmer coming along to see "Willi" Angus on Mart Day (plus a visit to the Butcher's Arms) enjoyed a nap before being summoned to "The Chair of Terror!!" On the death of my father, I took over the practice in January 1939. Electricity had not long come to Inverurie. So I completely modernised the practice. There was now electric light instead of gas-light—an electric drill instead of the old "Patient and quiet foot engine!" The dental chair was now leather fitted—the pictures (reluctantly) came down. All this had to do with the new teaching about hygiene. They were dust gatherers.

I had just been settling down in the family practice when World War II broke out. At that time, apart from the Inverurie practice, I also had a branch practice at Insch and a branch practice at Auchenblae in Kincardineshire. I also did hospital work. Because of this "The powers that be" thought I would be "more valuable" at home! As a result, I was not asked to serve my country. As the War continued, different regiments came to the Garioch Area for training. I was asked to attend to their requirements. Very often "my faithful Lieutenants"—namely Ernie Davidson and Jim Fraser (my two dental technicians) and I were working until 10 o'clock at night! As a result, I gained tremendous experience over those war years because of the many different types of dental work I had to perform and when a Polish Regiment arrived for training, I certainly had to pull out all the stops re gold and bridge work.

The War came to an end in 1945 and there came that "settling back to normal period." Then in 1948, the National Health Service came into being. It had its good points and its bad points. However, it did mean that all types of dental work—including gold and bridge work—was now available to anyone and the patients who took most advantage of the Service were the teenagers. You see, they had started going out socially at an earlier age than my generation and therefore were interested in their appearance. Instead of wanting extractions, they wanted conservative work. As a result, slowly but surely extractions and denture work were taking a back seat. As a result there is not nearly so much of this branch of dentistry carried out to-day.

As the years advanced so did the dental profession. Dental schools became modernised and new techniques came into being. The Jacket Crown—so popular with Hollywood film stars came within reach of the ordinary patient. New equipment was designed and new drugs, such as Brietal and Valium, were introduced to eliminate pain. On my retiral in 1973, I was finding that the dental surgery was becoming a very safe place. The fear that patients used to have had almost been eliminated. Some patients used to say that it was quite a pleasure to keep a dental appointment. As time goes on, there will be further changes—and they will all be for the better. Let us hope that soon going to the dentist will be like going to the Local for a pint of beer.

I had so many interesting experiences in my 35 years of dental practice, it would take a book to relate them all. However, it may be worth while to turn back the clock and relate a few and the interesting thing is that the patients referred to lived in the shadow of the well-known Hill of Bennachie—the Hill that has become even more famous since the formation of The Bailies of Bennachie under the guidance of Senior Bailie, Dr D. G. Gordon. Now Dr Gordon happens to live at a place called Coldwells. It is a beautiful spot. It is not far from Bennachie and overlooks a part of the River Don. How well I know Coldwells! It used to belong to a late uncle of mine called Tom Robertson and my late brothers and I spent many of our childhood years there. My late Uncle Tom was a butcher to trade and he wanted me to follow in his footsteps. However, my late father (I have already mentioned that he was a Dental Surgeon) wanted me to follow in his footsteps. When I chose Dentistry and started practice, quite a few of my patients used to say: "So you are a butcher after all!" My late father used to charge a fee of two shillings for the extraction of a tooth. I thought that perhaps with the march of time and the more modern methods used in Dentistry, I might be entitled to a fee of three shillings. Quite a few remarks were passed like: "Fa dis he think he is—back fae Glasgow (I studied there) wi' big ideas" and also "he'll niver be like his faither!" One patient actually told me that in the old days he used "to get oot his teeth fae Auld Druggist Munro and it was a question of 'being pulled round the fleer three times for a tanner'!"

There was the case of the patient who had to get dentures (on medical advice) at the age of 75. He was a farmer and he thocht there was nae need for "falsers" at this age. He said that it was a ploy between the doctor and the dentist to mak some siller! However, the dear old chap received his "choppers" and it was not long before he returned to the surgery. He said "in nae uncertain terms" that they were nae good at a'. I assured him that patience and perseverence would do the trick. He returned not long after and said that "he still couldna eat onything." However, he did assure me that they were "grand drinkers!!"

In my early days of dental practice, multiple extraction work was carried out at the home of the patient. The kitchen table was placed at the window which produced the best light. Pillows and blankets kept the patient comfortable! The anaesthetic used was ether or chloroform and it was administered by the patient's doctor. I once had a case in local Port Elphinstone where a young lad had to have several milk teeth extracted. I may say that dental operations in those days were carried out on the Sabbath morning! The doctor had called the day before and had given the pre-anaesthesia instructions—early to bed—no food or drink in the morning. The doctor and yours truly duly arrived on that Sabbath morning and immediately the doctor said to the patient's mother: "I trust that you have carried out my instructions," whereupon the mother replied: "Na, na doctor, he hasna hid a meal and nae drink—but just afore ye cam in I gid him a bap and twa jammy pieces." The operation had to be postponed until the following Sabbath—and would you believe it, both the doctor and the dentist missed "their Communion dram!"

I had a little lass from the Midmar area who came to my surgery one day to have one or two teeth removed under anaesthesia. When she was coming out of the anaesthetic I was saying a few encouraging words to her and she was looking into my face plus moustache. When she got home she had said to her mother: "What was that on the dentist's face?" Her mother replied: "Oh, that was jist a bittie o' broom." Her little daughter replied, "Well, well, it will look bonnie when it blooms in the Spring!!"

There was the case of my patient at Insch. I was extracting a tooth one Monday and on this occasion had to be in fairly close contact with the patient's head. All of a sudden I nearly lost my balance. I was at a loss to understand until I saw a beautiful artificial wig swirling around in the running water of my dental spittoon!

It is well known that after certain tooth extractions haemorrhage (bleeding) can continue for some time and on occasions has to be arrested. I remember I once had a patient from the Craigearn District (near Kemnay). This young man had extractions carried out and they were of a difficult nature. I told his mother to contact me should there be any undue bleeding. It was a stormy winter and lots of that white stuff lying about. Late that night I received the call: "This is so-and-so frae Craigearn—come quick the loon's bleeding tae death—it could be ony minute." I packed my dental case and ploughed through the snow to my destination. When I arrived I found my patient sitting in front of a grand fire roaring up the lum. He was leaning over a large bucket. I said to myself: "It must have been a massive bleeding." However, on examination I discovered roughly two drops of blood in that bucket!! The mother said: "Is he awfa bad dentist?" I quietly said that I would nip back to Inverurie for a microscope and look for blood!!

On occasions, patients used to phone the house (separate from my surgery) re dental appointments. This was capably dealt with by my wife Anne. There was the occasion when a certain patient phoned and "winted an appintment to get some teeth drawn." He spoke for about twenty minutes and finished by saying: "I hiv to hae a touch o' the gas." My dear wife just said: "I do not think that this may be a wise idea because if you get any more gas you could explode!"

And so dear Bennachie—so resplendent in the summer and so majestic if you have a coating of snow in the winter, you will continue to look down on the Garioch. You will continue to look down on many more dental patients who are now attending other dental surgeons. I hope that those dental surgeons get as much pleasure and fun with their patients as I did with mine.

"BENNACHIE"

By Michael G. Kidd, M.A.

O Bennachie, O Bennachie,
I maun awa' across the sea,
Gang far fae thee—

Across the sea, awa' fae thee.
Of a' oor hills thou bearst the gree
It seems tae me.

It seems tae me, faure'er I be,
I'll think upon thy heath'ry lea
Faur I clamb free—

Faur I clamb free as honey bee
Up tae thy taps o' tor an' scree.
The view tae see.

That view I'll see in fancy's e'e
File I tyaave on through years that flee
An' dree my dree.

Though I dree my dree, aiblins dee,
In far aff lands across the sea,
I'll sigh for thee.

I'll sigh for thee, and, if't may be,
I'll tak a pree o' barley bree,
An' drink tae thee.

I'll drink tae thee and mind wi' glee
A lass, a love, a stunted tree
Beneath thy scree.

Beneath thy scree, O I'll be ree
Gin God in answer tae my plea
'Turns me tae thee,
O Bennachie.

THE COUNTRY DOCTOR

By Dr D. G. Gordon

The country doctor, the lone figure in the gig, is the finest figure in medicine, said Sir Frederick Treves at the turn of the century. Now who was Sir Frederick? When the old Queen died, shortly after I was born, making me a last minute Victorian, King Edward VII developed appendicitis, a disease but recently diagnosed, and Sir Frederick removed his appendix. It must have been a tricky task. No surgeon likes a fat patient and the years of good living of King Edward must have deposited several inches of fat on the royal abdomen. Apart from some delay in the coronation, all went well—especially for Sir Frederick. His services were in great demand and many a duchess or countess or lesser light demanded this fashionable operation. Sir Frederick became famous. In 1903 the University of Aberdeen made the Serjeant-Surgeon Ordinary to H.M. the King an LL.D. and in 1905, at the time of the University's 400th birthday, he was the University's Rector. On that occasion there was much junketing and wassail and the high jinks of the students were very boisterous indeed. From his Olympian heights Sir Frederick was prevailed upon to address his medical colleagues in Aberdeen at some length but all that has come down to us was his memorable remark about the lone figure in the gig.

It is about these country doctors that I write—a grand breed, men of the soil, weatherbeaten, knickerbockered and be-legginged, rough but kindly, I knew many of them well and it was my fortune to savour a week of their mode of life at Insch in 1925 in a bad snowstorm, riding the Skirts of Foudland and Bennachie on a great bay horse belonging to the vet. The first night, I had my supper off the mantelpiece, standing. At the end of the week I could have sat down on a heap of horse nails. I feel that we doctors of today, of the same breed and bone of their bone, our bags bulging with the best of tools and antibiotics, our sleek rubber-tyred steeds speeding along the tarmac, should remember our medical forebears with pride. They had little but opium, mercury and castor oil but they advanced the cause of medicine in their generation. We owe them a debt.

Yes, they had few drugs but they had one great asset which was faith—the faith of the patient in the doctor, a commodity which sadly has diminished as the better trained doctor of today has become more impersonal in a team screened by receptionists and nurses. This faith had its bad side. Some doctors became little Hitlers in their small, isolated kingdoms. This but rarely for the virtue of faith was therapeutic in its comfort. Comfort, the scholars tell me, means giving strength. As an old wife told me "Ae look at my auld doctor and I was half better."

Fees were small, apart from a guinea a visit from the few lairds in their castles, half a guinea from the big farmers. The common folk paid from half-a-crown to one shilling. Many doctors never rendered an account. Some got a token payment of a fat hen, eggs and butter, and sometimes a load of hay for the doctor's horses. Dr Mitchell of Old Rayne got his fees paid annually at Lowrin Fair, when hospitality was dispensed.

Looking back to the eighteenth century, records of medical practice are rare. There was only one medical man on the main route for fifty miles north of Aberdeen—Dr Beattie of the Garioch. The countryside, rough with boulders, boggy with great peat mosses, uncultivated, with tracks for roads, was passable only on horseback. The doctor set off on his rounds on the Monday morning and was away most of the week. He carried a supply of drugs and surgical instruments and, at night, wore a lantern with horn windows fastened by a strap above his knees. Bleeding was in great demand and used for every malady. Helpful as this may have been to an over-fed, purple-visaged laird with liver large and hobnailed with claret, when threatened with a seizure, it only hastened the death of a girl of twenty dying of consumption. Herbs were the great standby, wormwood and sage and rue. Thyme and marjoram were used to flavour concoctions of crushed slaters and snails. Where doctors were scarce in the country places, "skeely wives," not averse to claiming supernatural help after they had stopped burning the witches, dispensed their potions to the credulous. The Prophet of Bethelnie was a healer of note, described by Dr William Alexander as a deformed being, ignorant and cunning. He was doctor, vet, and a warder-off of witches. In the '45 Rebellion most of the chiefs had their physician out with them. Lochiel's brother, Dr Cameron, was executed at Inverness. From the Garioch, Francis Ross, surgeon in Meldrum, survived Culloden but had a long weary time thereafter, skulking the countryside and, like Lord Pitsligo, hiding in the small cave on the top of Craigshannoch.

By the year 1854, there were well-established doctors in Inverurie, Wartle, Old Rayne, Insch, Alford and Kemnay, caring for the good folk of Central Aberdeenshire round Bennachie. The doyen of medical men, Dr Thomson of Inverurie, was the prime mover in the formation of the Garioch Medical Society which had its first meeting at the Pitcaple Inn on 11th April 1854, with Dr Thomson as Chairman and Dr Mackie of Insch as Secretary, a post he filled for thirty-three years. The next meeting was at Pitmachie Inn where the Benachie Club of 1807 once met. At the meetings, clinical cases were discussed and experience pooled, and a social hour after dinner enjoyed with song and story. The coming of the railway made the Kintore Arms at Inverurie the most convenient howff and there the "Garie" met for seventy years. What a boon for isolated doctors!

"It's no the meat, it's no the wine
It's jist the tang o' auld lang syne
That draws us to the Garie."

As it grew in strength, members were drawn from all over Aberdeenshire and as far as Banff. The University medical professors were proud to become members.

The Wartle practice produced a real character of a country doctor in Dr Samuel Davidson who practised there for sixty years from 1835 to 1895, the last fifteen with the help of his son Dr James Gordon Davidson. Helen Beaton, in her classic "Back o' Bennachie" (1923 edition) has many tales of him. Dr Findlay Pettigrew, M.B.E., last of the Wartle doctors, has his record and account books for the whole of that time. His son, William Leslie Davidson, was our Professor of Logic in 1919. His nickname was "Bourtie" as he had earlier been minister of that parish. Dr Sammy, as he was popularly known, was a tall figure of a man, his portrait in Mrs Beaton's book showing him in choker collar and side-whiskers. Stories about doctors are very often apocryphal. You can hear the same story told about several doctors, especially the more ebullient characters like Dr Fowler of Ellon or Dr McHardy of Banchory. The most famous Davidson story concerned his paying a visit to Mrs Gordon of Newton, wife of the County Convener of that time. The butler was a hypo-chondriac, always complaining about his throat with little cause. As he was helping the doctor off with his coat in the hall, he began with his usual complaint. The doctor ignored him and proceeded upstairs to see his patient. As he left, the butler fussed about, helping him on with his coat. "What about my throat then, Doctor?" The annoyed doctor retorted "Cut it, man."

One night of Lowrin Fair, one of the tinker caravans was wending its way home down the Colpy-Oldmeldrum road, the tink merry-foo sitting up in front sharing his blackened cutty pipe puff about with his wife, whom Dr Davidson had often attended without fee in her confinements. They met the doctor in his smart gig and spanking roadster and showing no recognition. "Divna ye ken my wife the day, Doctor?" "No" was the reply, "but if ye turned her upside down, I might recognise her."

The medical practice of Old Rayne, later incorporated with Insch, was carried on by the Mitchell family for three generations. Dr Alex Mitchell, M.D., started in 1838. He was a farmer as well as doctor, having the farm of Sauchenloan, a common custom for doctors of that time, as it was cheaper to grow hay for their horses than buying it. His oldest son became doctor at Rhynie but a younger son, Patrick, on graduating in 1869, joined his father and later succeeded him, practising until his death in 1914. There is a stained glass window to his memory in the kirk of Rayne. Once he was riding to a cottage at Dunideer in a snowstorm when the roads were blocked. The barbed wires of a fence had been loosened from their short posts and pushed high on long poles to let the carts go through. In the "blin drift" he rode right into the wire, blinding one eye for the rest of his days. He had three sons train as doctors, two becoming surgeons, of whom the eldest was Mr Sandy Mitchell, the well-known Aberdeen orthopaedic surgeon who retired about 1950 to his father's old house, now the Old Rayne Hotel. Dr Patrick's second son, Dr George, came home to help his father in 1909 but decided that Insch was a better centre for the practice and built himself a house there. Like his brothers, he was a good surgeon, becoming the best general practitioner surgeon in the North-East, doing yeoman work in the Insch and District War Memorial Hospital. He died in harness in 1952. So ended the Mitchell dynasty in Aberdeenshire but a great-grandson of the Dr Alex Mitchell of 1838, Dr Henderson of Grantown, carries on the family doctor tradition there.

When I arrived at Insch to be Dr George Mitchell's assistant on the evening of 15th April 1924, after supper there was a call to a farm to see a lad of fifteen with abdominal pain and vomiting. "Funny thing," said Dr Mitchell, "when I started practice here in 1909 I had a call one night to this same farm. The patient was the farmer's daughter who had pain and swelling of the abdomen." The young doctor found she was pregnant and starting labour. He came down-stairs in some trepidation wondering how he would break the bad news to her father, sitting at the kitchen fireside smoking his pipe. "O that's a' is't doctor" he remarked when told. "I thocht it might be one o' thae knots that would hae to be cut awa." The fifteen-year-old we had now been called to see was the "knot." He had an acute appendix. We took him in the back of the car to Insch hospital where we soon had it "cut awa."

The first winter I was at Insch, I had a night call to a little farm, not much bigger than a croft, up on the shoulders of Bennachie. Life was pretty hard for the farm folk and they could not afford fences along the roadside with the result that there were three gates across the road to open and shut. My steed was the old 4-horse Triumph motor bike. This meant dismounting three times, opening the gate, pushing the bike through and shutting the gate again—not calculated to put you in the best of moods. On arriving at the little, low but-and-ben, I made my way into the warm kitchen where the farmer's wife was sitting up in the box bed with a warm smile for her doctor which froze when she saw me. "Gwa hame, laddie. Whaur's Mitchell?" she said. "It was a Mitchell that saw me into the world and it'll be a Mitchell that sees me oot."

Sandy Mitchell loved to tell of the stormiest night he encountered when a young doctor assisting his father at Old Rayne. There was a call to Bainshole, eight miles away in the Glens of Foudland, to the little grocer's shop which had a porter and ale licence. His horse wading to the belly in the drifted snow, a "blin' drift" blizzard in his face, progress was understandably slow but he finally arrived to see the sick bairn in the attic. His job done, and anxious to face the fremt again, he was making for the door when the goodwife told him to sit down a minute and get something to warm him up. From a three-legged black brooky pot on the peat fire she poured him a great jug of hot porter, sugar and ginger. The night was wild as ever, but as Sandy said, the central heating made the journey back feel about half as long.

Son succeeding father in medical practice round Bennachie has been common, as witness the Simpsons of Alford, the Nicols and Gills of Inverurie and in Kemnay, a daughter, Dr Flossie Malcolm, succeeding her father. Dr William Henry of Kemnay, born in Echt in 1853 and practising well into the nineteen twenties, was a great character, blunt of speech, brusque and rather frightening to his patients, but for all that warm hearted. In 1913, when the first panel cheques started to be paid to make up for the bad debts of the hard-up doctors, many of them were able to buy a Model T Ford. Dr Henry bought a motor bike. When the new bike arrived he got it started, mounted and rode round the village for a trial run, much to the joy of the Kemnay wives who came to their doors to see him pass. But back he came in a few minutes and round and round he went for two hours. Finally, when he stopped, an old wife thanked him for giving them such a treat. "Bless you, woman," he retorted "I forgot how to stop the thing and had to keep going till the petrol was finished."

About that time the old Panel Committee of county doctors was formed and the question of pulling teeth for panel patients was posed as to whether it should be part of the service or whether an extra charge of a shilling a tooth should be made. Opinion was divided. Henry sat quiet, a man of few words. "Come on Henry" says Dr David Rorie, the Chairman, who wrote "The Lum Hat Wantin' The Croon," "tell us what you do." "Well," says Henry, "I'm not much bothered with the problem. I take out the biggest forceps I've got, put a

shake on my hand and say I'm not very good at this but I'm helluva strong . . . .
They seldom come back."

Kemnay is a bonny village built of its own grey granite from its own quarry,
but the "fair toun o' Fyvie" is about its equal. There in a thackit cottage by the
Ythan there was a Dr Greig in practice for nearly a hundred years, father and
son. I knew the younger, Dr Charles, quite well as an old doctor, still active
after fifty five years in harness in 1924—the year I graduated. He was a big,
fine looking man with what is known as a presence and made the most of it.
His stories of other days were a delight, but there was one against himself he did
not tell. A young bank clerk developed pneumonia, a dreaded disease at that
time, lasting a week or more and coming to a crisis, when suddenly, if all was
well, the breathing eased, there was profuse sweating, the temperature fell and
the patient felt better. This was not always the happy outcome. One night when
the lad was at his worst and the parents down from Leochel were anxiously
waiting for the doctor's verdict, Dr Greig descended from the sick room and said
in his dramatic way "No hope. No hope." Upstairs, the lad fighting for his
life was conscious enough to hear the words. Fortunately, on that occasion, the
good doctor was the bearer of false tidings. More than sixty years later the
patient was still recounting his experience and embellishing the story with his
own wry comment "Man, it wis richt dishertnin'."

Dr Alexander Nicol, a Fyvie man, graduated in medicine in 1880 and spent
his life in practice at Inverurie where, succeeded by his son Dr Wyness Nicol,
the father and son continuity was to span a period of no less than seventy years.
His daughter, Dr Aileen Nicol, was for long a Medical Officer of Health in
Norwich. One stormy night, Dr Alec. was called to an emergency in the village
of Hatton of Fintray where a woman was reported to be rolling on the bed in
agony. "Come quick, doctor. She'll need an operation" he was told. Pro-
ceeding by car as far as Kintore, he found the fat haughs towards Fintray
blocked with big snowdrifts and had to continue on foot. It was a slow job
with his bag getting heavier all the time. At last, about three o'clock in the
morning, he arrived at the house to find everything in darkness. He walked up
the path and rattled on the door without result. After knocking louder and
louder, eventually an upstairs window was pushed up and a voice enquired "Is
that you, doctor? We're nae needin' ye noo. The wife broke wind and she's
been sleepin. soun' for the last oor. Good nicht, doctor" then down came the
window. Dr Nicol was half-way down the pathway when the window shot up
again and the voice shouted "Ye winna be sendin's a bill for this?"

His colleague in Inverurie, Dr Alexander Forbes, born in 1869 in Leochel, was
of farming stock, of good physique but bald, and was a farmer in quite a big
way as well as a doctor. While still practising in his seventies, he was killed in
the blackout when his car ran into a stationary unlit traction engine by the
roadside. One night he was called to a farmer who had dislocated his shoulder—
what is described in the vernacular as "oot o' the shooder." In those days, to
reduce the dislocation, the patient was laid on the floor flat on his back and the
chest was held firm by a helper. The doctor then removed the appropriate boot,
put his foot in the armpit and pulled hard on the arm, and the shoulder would
go back into place with a clink if the manoeuvre was successful. On this
occasion the farmer was a strong specimen and, though the doctor pulled his

hardest while the farmer roared like a bull in his agony, the doctor had to admit defeat. Wiping the sweat from his brow he said "Man, ye're a poor tholer. I had a young wife had twins last night and she never gave one cry." "Aye doctor" retorted Mains "but if ye'd tried to put them back in again, ye wid hae heard plenty."

"Give us the tools" said Churchill. These medical men who started practice as Queen Victoria was getting old often lived to be old themselves and many survived until after the first world war when my career had just begun. Their tools were few. Their drugs were opium and faith. With this faith went, hand in hand, the affection and implicit trust of their respective human charges scattered far and wide within the magic spell of Bennachie. For those humble creatures, the world of medicine was concentrated, to the exclusion of all else, on the person of the man who "saw them in and saw them oot," each in his day and generation.

Meantime our kindly little mountain, four hundred million years old, looks down serenely upon the ever changing scene, a silent witness to the history of our countryside and days gone by when the doctor's horse went clip-clop through the lonely night.

THE TRIBE O' GALEN

Song composed by Dr David Rorie

Air: *Maggie Lauder* or *The Smith's a Gallant Fireman*

As I was traivlin' by the Bass
An' in through Inverurie,
I heard the soond o' clinkin' glass
An' tongues agaun like fury.
Says I to Jock, "What is't, my cock,
Are Germans in possession?"
"Na, na," says he, "it's a gaithrin o'
The medical profession."

"My sang," says I, d'ye tell me that?
What kin' o' billies are they?"
"There's some," says Jock, "are fair and fat,
An' some are thin an' swarthy;
There's some o' them are surgeons, an'
There's some o' them physeecians,
Wi' general practeetioners,
An' twa-three obstetreecians."

"An' what will a' the toonsfolk dae
The nicht if they're nae weel, man?"
Says Jock, "They'll hae to keep their beds,
An' tak' a Beecham's peel, man,"

"An' what aboot the wifies, noo,
If they be ta'en in labour?"
Says Jock, "They'll hae to ca' awa'
Wi' some auld skeely neighbour."

"Lat's step inside," says I, "an' mark
The tae kin' frae the tither—
Hoo would ye tell a surgeon, noo
Frae his physeecian brither?
Where a' seem keen upon the drink,
An' shovin' doon the crowdie:
Noo, tell me hoo a common man
Could single out a howdie?"

"Weel, lat's begin," says Jock, "an' note
The heid-mark o' a surgeon—
It's wi' the knife he saves your life,
An' nae wi' peels an' purgin'.
If ony o' them mak's a joke,
An' thinks ye dinna prize it,
He gies McBurney's p'int a poke,
To duly emphasise it.

Physeecians, noo, ye want to ken—
Ye needna be in doot, man—
Gin ye hae ony gumption, lad,
Ye'll easy mak' them oot, man;
Just skin your e'e till twa or three
Are fairly fou o' wine, man,
They'll fit their glasses tae their lugs,
An' cry, "Say ninety-nine, man."

"An' noo," says Jock, "I'll tell ye hoo
Ye ken the obstetreecians;
At ilka table aye they tak'
Left lateral poseetions;
Their hands a' shine wi' vaseline,
An' since the day o' Moses,
They aye pit up twa fingers, when
They're gaun to scart their noses."

Noo, I was awfu' sair impressed
Wi' a' that Jock had tel't, man;
My he'rt was duntin' in my breast,
Sic great respeck I felt, man,
An' when I saw them toddlin' oot
What time the thing was skailin',
Says I, "For honest, dacent folk
Gie me the Tribe o' Galen."

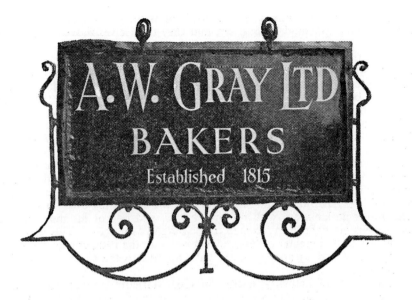

THE STORY OF AN ABERDEENSHIRE BAKERY

By Alexander L. Gray

In his book "Heritage, a Study of the Disruption" the late Professor G. D. Henderson, D.D., D.LITT., of the Chair of Church History in the University of Aberdeen, writes in connection with the social background: "In the second half of the eighteenth century Scotland wakened up and began to flourish. Gradually farmers were persuaded to abandon the ancient run-rig system, to fence and drain the land, and to introduce a suitable rotation of crops, to experiment with artificial grasses and rootcrops, to make proper provision for the winter feeding of cattle, to invest in less primitive implements, to take a more scientific knowledge in breeding, to recognise the value of plantations and hedges and to require terms of tenure which would justify improvements. Conditions of living improved, stone became general in house-building; furnishings, dress, amusements, music, periodicals, all gave evidence of marked advance in taste and in the means of satisfying it." But it may have been some time before all these improvements penetrated to Aberdeenshire and to the Garioch district in particular, which came to be known as the "meal girnal of Aberdeenshire."

It is prior to these improved conditions of living that the first traces of the Gray family with which this story is concerned are to be found. They are mentioned in the "List of Pollable Persons within the Shire of Aberdeen" of 1696 and records exist from 1721, at which date they lived at Cranford, a 40-acre farm now absorbed into Mill of Lumphart. Later, about 1730, Alexander Gray and his wife, Elspet Clerk, leased the farm of Hillhead of

Lethenty, which they ultimately made over to William, the eldest son of their family of three sons and a daughter, and they themselves moved to Inverurie in 1753.

Among title deeds which go back to 1681 is a disposition from George Cruickshank in Balhalgardie to Alexander Gray dated 1753, whereby he "sold to Alexander Gray and Elspet Clerk, his spouse, all and haill, the five roods of land lying betwixt the lands of the Earl of Kintore on the South, the Davoch lands on the West, the lands of William Reedford on the North and the King's Highway or Common Street of the said Burgh of Inverury on the East part." Alexander Gray died on 5th July, 1755, and his wife Elspet on 17th March, 1782, both in their eighties.

In his unsurpassable "Inverurie and the Earldom of the Garioch" (1878) The Reverend John Davidson, D.D., writes of life in a rural burgh in 1600: "Every artizan, or trader, lived as much by the plough and spade as by his urban calling. His house and shop stood at the end of his own burgh roods. These roods he laboured with his own hands, and one of his most valuable interests was his rights as a freeman to the burgh pasturages." This way of life was carried on to a greater or lesser extent well into the 19th, and even the 20th, century and would without a doubt have applied to the Gray family of the 18th century.

William Gray of Lethenty married in 1763 Margaret Cooper from Chapel-hall of Esslemont, Ellon, by whom he had a family of seven daughters and five sons. William died sometime after 1793 and Margaret in 1822. Two of their sons were taken by the Press Gang in Leith. A letter to this effect still exists, but the date is indecipherable as the letter appears to have been carried about for a long time in someone's pocket.

The youngest of this family, Alexander, born in 1789, came into possession of his grandfather's "five roods" in Inverurie. His mother, in a letter written from Aberdeen to a brother in Inverurie on 17th June, 1806, says: "My youngest son, Alexander, is learning the baking trade with James Wyness and is doing well. That I might be nearer the rest of my family in Aberdeen, I have now moved there with my two unmarried daughters, but I still keep my house in Inverurie to go there if I dislike this town." In 1814, at the age of twenty-five, Alexander married Mary Stirling, who belonged to Torry in Aberdeen and whose family were salmon fishers. According to his account books he set up his business as a baker in Inverurie in the following year, 1815, the year of the battle of Waterloo, trading as 'Alexander Gray.' His business records are preserved and reading them he appears to have prospered rapidly, showing a substantial increase in trade each year from 1815 to the 1860's.

This was a time of increasing prosperity for the Royal Burgh, with the opening of the Aberdeenshire Canal in 1805 and later, when that was bought up and replaced by the Great North of Scotland Railway in 1854. There is a tradition that quantities of bread were supplied to the Railway Company for the men making the embankment which stretches over the low lying ground from Keith-hall Road to the paper mills of Thomas Tait & Sons. Where all the material came from—possibly from cuttings in other parts of the line—for such an undertaking and what can have been the labour involved to bring it there by horses and carts are matters for conjecture.

The goods manufactured in the bakehouse at this time consisted mainly of bread and a few other items, although a certain type of biscuit was in demand at christenings and funerals. Hand-made cutters exist for cutting out these biscuits; the large size was called a 'penny bawbee' and the smaller version, costing a halfpenny, a 'bawbee penny.' They are mentioned twice in Mrs Helen Beaton's book "At the Back o' Bennachie" (published in 1915) about life in the Garioch in the 19th century. The baking itself was extremely hard work as all doughs were made by hand. Coal and wood were used as fuel, coke being unknown until after the Gas Company was established in 1839.

Dr Davidson wrote in 1885 his "Recollections of Forty Years," which was really a census of the burgh at the time that he came to it (1844) and which was slipped into the church pews in leaflet form. In it he says "Part of the large burghal property of Stonehouse was possessed by the father of the present proprietor. Alexander Gray, long known as 'baker Gray,' latterly as Bailie Gray, was then a little past the prime of life, a much respected and well-to-do citizen and is still represented in the locality by his children and children's children. Mr Gray's first experience was as much the growing of meal as the making of bread. A local tradition of the trade is that he used to halt in his work on his rigs at intervals, and go down to the shop to see if anyone had come in seeking a loaf. His business life witnessed the development of the change from the ancestral 'cakes' (oatcakes) to 'fite breed.' Mr Gray inherited his Stonehouse upper roods from his father (William), a native of Lethenty and farmer in Fawells, but added some adjacent portions."

Alexander Gray was an outstanding personality in the town. It is said of him that, prior to Council Meetings, he would don a clean white apron, put his coat on above that, and wearing a top-hat go along to the meeting. And he is reputed to have walked into Aberdeen to pay his accounts when the Canal Boat or the "Defiance" Coach were not available. On the premises was a small room known to everyone as Sandy's Parlour, which did duty supposedly as an office, and equally important, no doubt, as a centre for the collection, distribution and discussion of news. He and his wife had their portraits painted, about the year 1830, by William Niddrie, an Aberdeen artist. These portraits are still prized possessions of the family.

At one time the Mercat Cross, recognised centre of the Burgh, stood outside the Kintore Arms Hotel. For convenience the drum used for public proclamations from the Cross, and the mortsafe tackle for the old churchyard were kept in the shop in High Street. In more recent times the mortsafe tackle was given to the local museum by Alexander W. Gray.

Other relics preserved from these earlier days are march stones from the "rigs," removed from their original sitings when ground was ploughed up during the 1939-45 war. And the Bakery Trade flag, over 100 years old, of the Seven Incorporated Trades of Aberdeen, which institution dates from 1457. The flag bears the Bakers' Coat of Arms and motto *Panis nil saturat Deus ni benedicat* (Bread will not satisfy unless God blesses). A beautifully drawn and coloured lithograph by Colin Allen, Aberdeen, of the coats of arms of the Seven Incorporated Trades may have come from an Aberdeen member of the trade related by marriage. A brass weight bearing the date 1709 is also a genuine antique, as are two iron weights dated 1826, which were in use in the early years of the present century. Many years ago the late Lord Kintore gave to the firm a receipt dated 1843 for bread supplied during the time of the great hunts at Keithhall—"the sum of fifty six pounds and sixpence for Bread delivered as per Pass Book." The founder's seal, his gold guard-chain and several other items are still in the possession of the family.

Bailie Gray and his wife and family of seven lived in High Street in one of a row of cottages, numbered 131. One of his sisters resided with her son and daughter close by in one of the still remaining (1885) sidelong rows of thatched cottages standing on their narrow strips of land with the gable to the street. At 129 High Street lived a Barbara Smith, who had only one hand and yet made whalebone stays for the gentry (ladies it is supposed) and whose photograph still exists; it was taken by the father of the later Robert Brown whose sepia work is good to this day.

It is uncertain whether the house and shop at 125-127 High Street were built by this Alexander or by the second Alexander, but an account book of 1814 shows an amount paid for "building a shop and wright work—£48!" Around the window of the old shop at 127 can still be seen the check cut in the granite to take the oak shutters which were put over the window at night.

This, the first baker Gray in Inverurie, died on 31st August, 1874, aged 85, and his wife Mary Stirling on 12th April, 1878, aged 83.

The next generation, their son Alexander, born in 1819, took over the business in 1851, and began rounds with horse-drawn vans. A vanman who worked for the firm about this time was a bit of a worthy known as Aul' Ronal', who was welcomed in cottage and castle alike apparently.

This Alexander in 1861 married Margaret Reid who came from Roquharold, Kemnay. They had seven of a family, four daughters and three sons, one of whom became a doctor and another an architect. Alexander was, to quote a letter to his widow from the United Free Church Deacons' Court at the time of his death, "of a quiet and retiring disposition and lived a singularly peaceful life and was highly esteemed by all who knew him." He built the two houses 117/119 High Street and also owned 121/123 (demolished 1936), 125/127 house and bakery shop and 129 and 131 High Street. In 1897 he built 133 High Street, removing to do so one or more dovecots, and retired there, which is why at that time the south end of High Street was called "Baker Gray's." Each house had its 1¼ Scots acres or thereby of land stretching up to the Manse Road and these he cultivated. At one stage the land was ploughed by oxen, which always pull to the left, hence the curving line of the roods not now visible. Potatoes were planted (seemingly an early version of Edzell Blues) and the drills were sold when in crop to any buyer; those drills left unsold were dug up and the potatoes stored in a large pit. In due course each house retained only a small section of ground, leaving a 10-acre field, now utilised for house-building.

Like many quiet men Alexander was a keen fisher, even making his own rods, an art in which he was a past-master. He was appointed an Honorary Burgess of the Royal Burgh of Inverurie in 1863 and died in 1903. His widow, Margaret Reid, lived to the considerable age of 91, dying in 1929. She is well remembered by the family to this day, as are her anecdotes. One of these tells of one warm summer day when she was "keeping shop," and two very young gentlemen stopped outside. They were the late Lord Kintore, then Lord Falconer, and his elder brother, the late Lord Inverurie. Through the open shop door she heard Lord Inverurie say to his brother "I wonder what I shall have today?" Lord Falconer replied "Try one of these; I had one yesterday and nearly died!" The only thing in the window was a large dish of Eccles cakes, less kindly known as "fly cemeteries." Margaret was very artistic, fond of drawing and all kinds of fine handwork. When she was 91, quite helpless and "dottled," it happened that Mr Fraser of the Aberdeen Library published in the newspaper an article on an old Aberdeen artist, Peter Cleland by name. A daughter asked her "Who used to be your drawing master?" to which the old lady at once answered "Mr Cleland and if I was with him now I would be able to paint."

The successor to Alexander was his eldest son, Alexander William, who was born in 1868. He married in 1901 Mary Ann Valentine of Inverurie and they had two sons and two daughters.

Alexander William replaced the old house at 131 High Street with the present one in 1907 and also acquired land known as "the Doctor's Rig," so-called because, there being no space for a garden at what had been for many years a doctor's house (now 106 High Street), a garden and coach-house had been made on the opposite side of the street where "Red Hythe" now stands. This garden was cultivated as a vegetable garden, but the present family remember in their youth how the walls were covered with soft fruits, especially gooseberries and currants, all of course ripe for eating—surreptitiously! The coach-house, with its cobbled forecourt, was used to store sledge-vans used during snowy spells in the winter.

In his younger days Alexander William was an enthusiastic Volunteer and held the rank of Colour-Sergeant. He was one of the best shots in the local Company and several times represented it at Bisley. He was also a member of the teams which won the Bugle Trophy at Aberdeen in 1900 and the Caledonian Shield at Inverness in 1902. He was interested in all outdoor sports and was a proficient bowler and angler. As one of the Golf Club guarantors he helped to make possible the Golf Course at Inverurie. He was a member of long-standing of the Inverurie Business Men's Club and a deacon of the West Church. His favourite hobby in which he was considered something of an expert and to which he devoted much time was poultry-breeding.

At the outbreak of the 1914-18 war he was mobilised with the 6th Gordons as a National Reservist, and was for some time stationed at Bedford. In his absence members of the family rallied round to help, including an aunt who "volunteered" to drive one of the horse-drawn vans.

In spite of his many interests he successfully developed the business. During his lifetime power-driven machinery was introduced and a new bakehouse built in 1919, while motor vans superseded the horse-drawn ones; and a branch shop was opened in Market Place. Some items manufactured in the 1920's and earlier were the famous white baps, diamond-shaped with a hole in the centre and baked directly on the stone floor of the 100-year-old oven. They were peculiar to this part of Aberdeenshire. Two large pan loaves, four pounds each in weight, were made twice yearly solely for Church Communion. And from the sublime to the ridiculous, on feeing-market days very small currant loaves were made to sell at one penny each, and called "Monkey loaves."

Alexander William died in 1930 and his widow, Mary Ann, in 1939. After his death the business was carried on by his two sons, Alexander Leslie and Edward. For the first time in its history the firm had two partners, and the management was equally divided between the two brothers, who added in due course branches at Monymusk and at Oldmeldrum.

Alexander Leslie's hobbies were inclined to the artistic—perhaps after his grandmother. He served on the Town Council for seven years as a Councillor and then a Bailie. In connection with the Quater-Centenary of the granting to the Burgh of the Royal Charter by Mary, Queen of Scots, in June, 1558, he, like his grandfather before him, was made on 15th June, 1958, an Honorary Burgess of the Royal Burgh of Inverurie. This involved the hilarious ceremony of being "doupit" on one particular stone in a wall at Brandsbutt Farm.

Like his father, Edward was a good shot and owned a small moor on which to indulge his hobby of shooting. During the 1939-45 war he was in the Army Catering Corps in Europe. On its formation he became a member of the local Rotary Club and later a President.

Perhaps the greatest changes of all took place in the business after the end of the last war. The most up-to-date machinery was installed, including an automatic dough divider and moulder, which produced buns and soft biscuits at the rate of 4,200 per hour. In the 1950's the Scotch oven which had given excellent service for more than a century was demolished to make way for the latest rotary-type oven, heated by gas and with automatic temperature control. Shortbread, which was made throughout the history of the firm, was in ever-increasing demand and large quantities were posted to all parts of the world, for Christmas and the New Year especially. In 1954 the firm was formed into a private company, A. W. Gray Ltd., which in 1958 employed a staff of forty, several of whom had worked there most of their lives. Seven motor vans supplied a country area and villages within a radius of ten to twelve miles.

It is well known that behind every successful man there is a woman, his wife, and this is true of the Gray family down the generations. Perhaps special mention should be made of Alexander William's wife who was most active and interested in all spheres of the business.

In 1960, on the retirement of his brother, Alexander, full control of the business was assumed by Edward and his immediate family. The branch at Monymusk was closed a year or two later because it was found that the van round supplied all demands in the area. The firm continued in good fettle until Edward's untimely death in 1969. Thereafter his widow and son, with the aid of a manager, carried it on until October 1974, when it was decided to wind it up. And so came to an end what had been almost a way of life in Inverurie and the district.

Throughout the years the firm was most faithfully and competently supported by the staff, and more especially latterly by those of long service who knew three generations of Grays. And of course no business can survive without customers. As the firm existed for 159 years it is obvious that there were many and that "Baker Gray's" was handed on from generation to generation. Such loyalty should not be lightly passed over and has indeed not gone unnoticed or unappreciated by the present-day descendants of the founder.

MEMORIES OF THE GARIOCH
By Mrs Mary J. S. Harris, M.A.

I stood on a little bridge here in Somerset spanning the Bratton Brook hastening on its way to the Severn Sea. The music of the clear water playing on the stones in its course carried my thoughts to a scene far away where "the Gadie rins at the back o' Bennachie" playing an identical melody, for I was listening to the very same sound that had grown familiar to me in early days on my father's farm in Premnay, where the merry little Gadie with its brown-mottled yellow mimulus and blue forget-me-not skirted our fields and sped on past the miller's croft to turn the big meal-mill wheel not far from the village school where I first met Julius Caesar and Thucydides each in his own language, and carried home each afternoon a strapped edifice of textbooks based on the broad brown Euclid and roofed with the little red French reader. "Ower mony beuks, Mary," said the sturdy little blacksmith to me as I passed his smiddy one day. I see him now as he stood therein blackened leather apron, tools of his trade in his hands, the anvil behind him. His own children were at school. We were a' bairns thegither. "Ower mony beuks," and some had to be patiently worked through in the summer holidays, in solitariness for concentration, but with an open door for sweet air from summer fields, the shimmering Gadie below, and steadfast Bennachie above.

But my first acquaintance with the Gadie was in earlier childhood on visits to my paternal grandparents' home at the foot of the Correen Hills with a view to Tap o' Noth. The little farm of Smallburn reputed to hold the second-highest cultivated ground in Aberdeenshire, took its name from the infant stream rising in the heathery hillside above, the Gadie itself. It flowed by the farmstead in a tiny channel which I delighted to jump over. Life here was austere, but to a child in summer delightful as I accompanied my grandfather driving four cows along a little open space among clumps of invading heather and broom to a fair fenced pasture, where cultivation had held its own. Behind us obediently at heel came the wise collie, remembered as remarkably knowing Sunday and retiring into a dim recess under the stairs where firewood and peaty turf were kept, there to sleep—or perhaps to listen in silence? The old mare was idle, the people were moving about in a leisurely, detached kind of way. Those able would presently be off to church. There was nothing for a dog to do. I used myself to imagine in those early childhood days that the sparrows' chirpings sounded differently on Sunday mornings. Did a subtle something emanate from the grown-ups to pervade mind and senses? And it was to this little home under the hill that my grandmother's nephew, James Adam, came in his student holidays with a load of books from Kinmuck near Inverurie. My grandfather built him a little turf hut up on the hill, and there he would spend whole days alone absorbed in his Latin and Greek, among the grouse and the curlews. He was a favourite pupil of Professor Geddes, and he himself later became Fellow and Senior Tutor, Emmanuel College, Cambridge, and Gifford Lecturer at Aberdeen in 1904-6 on "The religious teachers of Greece."

Our own childhood home was down-country at Kirkton of Culsalmond, home-farm of the estate of Williamston near Insch. There also we had our water-music from the stream that flowed by the ends of the lowest of those pleasantly sloping fields. We called it the Urie, proud to have it for our neighbour, but to the Ordnance Survey it is the Glen water, tributary to the Urie, and given its name presumably from its upper course through the Glen of Foudland, where the old coach road used to pass from Aberdeen to Huntly and Elgin. This road was near to Kirkton and well known to us especially where it curved through the little village of Colpy, which I chiefly remember as visited on errands in the morning before school, its quiet air filled with the soft cooings of many pigeons wheeling and lighting and wheeling again over the craftsmen's homes and places of work. There was the vricht's (carpenter) with stacks of fresh wood, the smiddy with farm implements about, waiting to be repaired, the souter's where strong tackety boots were made for farm folk, and the merchant's shop with grocery, drapery, hardware, and other commodities including red herrings to be grilled on a wire brander over a clear fire. And unforgettable is the little cottage where Kethrin Home had a clean-scrubbed white wooden kist, replenished on certain days by Mennie, baker, of Premnay and Insch with white loaves that would be sparsely retailed, being almost a luxury in those days of huge weekly farm-kitchen bakings of girdle oat-cakes, with a few white-flour scones and bannocks. Unforgettable too is the Mennie farthing biscuit with blackcurrant jam I was regaled with at another cottage when I was sent in a morning in the heid hurry o' hairst to request the extra field-work help of a strong young woman resident there. Never has any blackcurrant jam since then tasted so superb.

Near to the smiddy at Colpy a little side-road diverged, trodden by us children once a year on the day of St. Sair's Fair (commemorating St. Servus), when we were permitted to go with the maid in the afternoon to see whatever ferlies might be on view, Aunt Sally and the coconuts, a Cheap-Jack lauding his wares (pocket-knives and the like), stalls for the sale of plunky (a special kind of toffee), gingerbread mannies and horsies, and toys and bric-a-brac. The more serious business of the Fair was done in the forenoon, the sale of cattle and horses, and the feeing of men and women for the coming harvest on the farms. But our greatest enjoyment was the excitement of anticipation, for the night before we had gone to bed knowing that in the morning we would look across at that little hill-top dotted with white tents never seen but there and only then. And uncles and others would come from up-country for the Fair, and their gigs would stand empty in our farm-close all day till time to yoke again for the homeward journey.

There was another annual Fair that we children only heard about, being too distant for us to visit. This was Lowrin Fair, commemorating Saint Lawrence, and held in Old Rayne. We liked to listen to a sad old song about it sung for us by our happy-hearted rosy-cheeked golden-haired kitchen-maid:

A nivver hid bit twa richt lads,
bit twa richt lads, bit twa richt
lads, 'it ivver likit me.
An' the t'ene wis kill't in
Lowrin Fair, in Lowrin Fair, in
Lowrin Fair, an' the t'ither
wis droont in Dee.

And we knew that near the site of Lowrin Fair there lived our revered family doctor, father of sons destined to be distinguished, Dr Mitchell, and he was always at home on that day for the farmers of a wide area to call and pay their bills.

There are many Kirktons in Aberdeenshire and several even in the Garioch, the name meaning church-farm, and the kirk with its high belfry stood in the kirkyard across the road from our home. The bell was tolled twice every Sunday morning, at ten o'clock to warn the country folk to be ready, and at eleven to ring them in for the service. The old bell-ringer was our friend, and spent the hour between in our farm-kitchen with a glass of home-made ale, a memorable figure with his pipe and his paralysis agitans and an artificial left hand. Memorable too was the annual Gooseberry Treat at the Manse, when all the children of the parish were gathered for tea and games and then ushered into the big walled garden where tubs of ripe gooseberries were standing ready, and the handkerchiefs we had brought were filled brimming and carried home by the four corners pinched together.

Kirton was a cheerfully busy place for children to find themselves in, with its large herd of prize-winning black Aberdeen-Angus cattle (though we were sternly warned to keep well away from them, especially when the cows had their calves with them in the fields;, its three pairs of heavy working Clydesdales with their horsemen much respected by us for their prowess, sheep sometimes, and always a collie. Big black-and-tan Yarrow had such a sense of law and order I once saw him snap at the tail of a hen that had dared to get on the high rim of the large drinking-trough for the horses at the stable door. My special care was the tribe of cats ruled by big yellow Tom. They had porridge and milk every morning and were left to earn their own living the rest of the time tracking down destructive rodents. The large garden gave us fun and flowers and food. It had two laburnum trees that could be climbed, and a tall scented poplar. How subtle and potent a scent can be in reviving memories! A tree of that same kind stands in a little public garden by the Bratton Brook here, and on still moist spring mornings its perfume pervades the air right to my door, bringing the whole complex of Kirton with it.

The old laird of Williamston died, changes came, and my father chose to move. Assembled neighbours brought our parents tokens of appreciation and goodwill. Our next abode was at Druminnor home-farm near Rhynie, the birthplace of Mackay of Uganda, under the Tap o' Noth. Druminnor is now a sad centre of antiquarian interest, but then it was a lively family residence with coachman, footman, butler, maids and gardeners. A children's Christmas party at that time is still warmly remembered. Our great friend here was the gamekeeper, who let us help him feed the pheasant chicks he was rearing in the wood close to our home. He had gathered eggs and hatched them in a coop an run under a broody hen, and very charming they were. So were his lively pointers whom he called wicked puppies, and the lovable spaniels Don and Nellie, and the big solemn black retriever. He went to fight in the Boer War in South Africa, and before that was over we had moved again, down to Premnay, where these reminiscences began, and where we now entered the scholastic domain of that very forceful headmaster, G. A. Simpson, who later became rector of Fordyce Academy. He knew well how to get us working at our hardest, and before long I was on the path deemed by the practical-minded blacksmith to be that of "ower mony beuks."

By 1904 I was a bajanella at Aberdeen, but it is of the Garioch I am writing, and yet another little stream is calling for mention, the little Kearn burnie at Boghead of Clatt, our final family home, up-country again. It had its source not far from that of the Gadie, but its destiny was determined by the lie of the land on the watershed between the Gadie valley and Bogside. Whereas the Gadie reaches the sea eventually at Aberdeen in the volume of the Don, the Kearn burn joins the Bogie and so the Deveron for the Moray Firth. The farm of Boghead was romantically situated where three estates met, being the most westerly acres of the Leith-Hays of Leithhall, meeting the boundary of the land of the Grants of Druminnor, and in the same neuk the limit of the estate of the Gordons of Knockespock. And just there the Kearn burn emerged from the grounds and gardens of Druminnor Castle to pass under a bridge on the road that had come up from Kirkton of Oyne through Leslie and Clatt and now led on to Rhynie and the Cabrach. And Tap o' Noth looked down on our labours, "powdered white with April snow" as described by William Angus in his beautiful little poem "Garioch Spring-clad" in *The Countryman* of spring 1971, or dark with heather in the "muted tartan woven by Spring" in the same delightful poem. What an eloquent and evocative image is in that phrase "a muted tartan," eye calling on ear to listen to a quietly colourful landscape that speaks!

We were no longer children when we moved to Boghead, and never all together now except in holiday times. One brother prepared to enter the Church, another was on his way to becoming a schoolmaster, and two followed the plough, up and down those sloping fields, one composing poems in his head the while, and the other planning his own chosen leisure-time hobby of smithing. I graduated, trained for teaching, taught at Buckie, and then lectured to students for Professor, later Sir Herbert Grierson. The loom of Time wove on variedly. The "whin's gold threads" of William Angus's poem sometimes were below the surface of the fabric, but always reappeared. The Kaiser's war coming in 1914 threw darkness into our souls. I had no sister, and ere that time I was needed at home, or I thought I was. I became immersed in farmhouse labours and concerns, while always hoping to return to teaching sometime somewhere, and sitting up at nights to read. The wet harvest of 1916 comes greyly back to mind, as we struggled late in November to get in the last of the crop, my father, one brother, and myself coping as we could with horse and cart between the fields and the cornyard, where the rucks had gone up so slowly, while the rain had kept on coming down.

The war wore past. The absent brother was back to the fields and his loved evening-time home-made smiddy. I went back to teaching.

IN EXILE

By Jas. Pittendreigh McGillivray

Up by the back o' Bennachie,
Up North an' hyne awa
Och, that's far I would like to be,
For a'thing here's a thra'.

Up at the back o' Bennachie,
Far Gaudie rins sae sweet!
Gin I were there I'd be at hame,
An' off the hard steen street.

The street, the street, the weary street,
Be't day shift or at nicht—
A hell o' shops an' motor cars,
In bleezin' waste o' licht.

The thing roars by like Don in spate,
Bu God knows far it gings—
I'm on the bank an' needna speer
Foo't a'thegither hings.

I just pace on wi' steady beat,
An' files rak' up a stan'
At corner bits, to ease my feet
An' gie the tyauve a scan.

An' then I'm back 'tween Oyne an' Insch,
In blithesome caller air,
Wi' ae e'e on the Mither Tap,
The tither plooin' fair:—

Back far I ken it's fine to be
In hairst time or in snaw—
Roun by the fit o' Bennachie,
The ae kind bit o' a'.

A DAY IN SPRING ON BENNACHIE

By Andrew Galloway Fordyce

Ploughing a lonely furrow on the lands of his croft at "Hillfoot," on the north-western side, or "Back o' Bennachie," the tall broadbearded elder of the Kirk was a-thinking. And what did the tiller of the soil turn over in his mind as he gently coo'd to the straining beast in that fast fading horseman's vocabulary of "wish-min, hey-min" and chauved with the plough as he steered the unified trio on its shortest distance between two dykes. A regular acquaintance with the "auld buik" and reflection upon the Sabbath sermon provided material for silent deliberation, while hours apart in the open glen let soul searching thoughts develop unchecked and gain freedom in the realms of the imagination.

The monotony of the daily round was broken one day some eighty odd years ago when my grandfather had an experience which made such an impression that knowledge of it was passed to my father and on to this generation. He related how as he followed the plough, a questioning thought which came to his mind was, "What like place was Hell?" At once, and as if by persuasion he turned towards the hill, and what an amazing sight he saw. In his own description, "the hill wis a' in a bleeze." Surely an awe-inspiring experience and what a premonition!

The sequel to this event was to be provided many years later and to us in our day and generation.

Broadcasting the news one morning in January, forty-nine, the announcer stated that the greatest heath fire in Scotland for many years was now raging in Aberdeenshire and that the Hill of Bennachie was ablaze.

This news attracted more than the usual attention with us, for we in Kent realised that our hill, the mecca of the Fordyces of the South, had become a flaming beacon.

Some four months later, at Eastertime, with my younger son, Hector, I left behind the opening blossom in the Kentish orchards and journeyed by night in the northbound train. Soundly asleep, I missed the exile's thrill of crossing the Border, but awakened to a rumbling change of sound. Peering out into the night, I could see the huge slanting tubes and ladder-like girders of the Forth Bridge as they passed in slow procession. Gazing beyond, came the reward of my awakening. Placed geometrically and timed to the opportunity, I was presented with a striking picture of light and darkness in vivid contrast as the train passed over the bridge. On the meridian of the Firth and midway up in the eastern sky a brilliant crescent moon with pincers outstretched was chasing plumb downwards the one bright star through the gloom of night and lighting the rippling face of the waters below like the newly-ploughed wake of ship gone over the horizon.

Early though it was, we were met at Aberdeen Joint Station and escorted on the last lap of our journey, and what a salve to homesickness it is, to hear the porter in the broad mother tongue, calling the stations ahead. Chugging up the inland ascent, we passed by Kittybrewster, Kintore, the ancient Bass at Inverurie (still defying the aggressive Don), the Urie flowing peacefully by the foot of Harlaw field (where on that fateful day, and for days after, her waters ran red with the blood of battle); and the woods of Logie where the waters of Urie and Gadie meet (a trysting place so romantically set to song). We rumbled over the iron bridge and into the Shannoch Glen, whistled to the auld kirk (standing so proudly on Hart Hill), caught our first glimpse of Craigshannoch peak and pulled up gently by the station platform at Oyne.

Sitting by the fire in the evening, and as the pine logs glowed and sizzled, we listened intently to the story of the great hill fire. The fire broke out on the eastern side, down by Monymusk, and spread wider and higher, sending its red glow to the evening sky and watched in suspense by the people of Oyne.

Available forces of woodmen, firemen, and soldiers were rushed to the scene, but all their efforts were in vain. A seven-mile front of flame and smoke ascended the hill and came over the top with a consuming roar as though to devour the glen, but halfway down it stayed in its course and spared the lands below. My laddie's face was a study to watch as his grandfather told the story, but strange though it may seem, it never occurred to me to remind my father of his father's "vision of hell."

The winter of forty-nine had been unusually mild and now at Eastertime, except for the northern corries and high levels of the Cairngorms, not a vestige of snow was to be seen.

The mood of the weather-clerk, however, at this time of the year can quickly change, so if the hill was to be climbed during this short visit, we must not miss taking the advantage of ideal conditions presented to us on arrival. One dare not return south and admit that one had failed to climb Bennachie.

Next morning, with packs and flasks and walking sticks, we set out for a day on the hill, waved cheerio as we turned the corner of the Post Office, and planted our feet on the old road which has known the tramp of five generations.

The cart roadie with its nobbly surface on "muckle steens" prepares the eyes and ankles for the rocky steeps yet to be encountered, but offers no invitation to the horseless carriage of to-day. Due to the mildness of the winter and early warmth of the sun, nature had provided for us a rare spectacle of beauty by displaying under the trees and along the dyke sides a thick carpeting of sprouting beech nuts, each tender stalk bearing aloft its pair of "split-bean-like" primary leaves. The elderly shepherd, with whom we passed the time of day, commenting on the display, said he had "rarely seen the like o't."

As we passed the Berryhill, a knoll on our right, it was giving sweet graze to the good man's sheep, spread far out on its grass-green rounded top. A mile beyond was the rugged outline of a sprawling mound which bears the name of Tillymuich, and how lonely, forlorn and neglected it looked. In my father's schooldays there came from the clustered crofts on Tillymuich more children than attend the present school, and what hardy bairns they were. They arrived with peat in hand for the "Dominie's" fire and nothing more than "a puckle o' dry meal in their pooch" for dinner. The folks have gone and their home-steads too, but need we lament, for many of the hardships too have gone, while the sons and daughters have spread abroad and helped to make the Common-wealth what it is to-day.

Halfway along the road with great-grandfather's farm house of Hillford on our left, we crossed the old Aberdeen road where the burn also decides to cross diagonally. Here we gave a thought to the high-spirited clansmen of the "Lord of the Isles" who splashed through this ford on the last lap of the journey which led to their doom at "Bloody Harlaw." Tramping on, we hesitated at the point where a mineral spring oozes from the bankside to discolour the waters of the burn. I related to the laddie how people with faith in the curative properties of this rust-coloured water made their pilgrimages to partake of the medicine, or to fill their vessels and carry away the waters for those at home who were "nae neer weel." Rounding the bend by the fir trees, our eyes lit upon the solitary cottage which stands at the end of the road. Here at Hillfoot the cottage is all that remains of my grandfather's homestead. The mill has gone, the barn and henhouses too, but the sight of grey smoke rising from the lum, and on the heath by the gable-end, a pram with its hood set to the wind, spelt life in the old home yet.

Circling above, a curlew bade us welcome as he piped his entrancing note and, though foolishly wasting a film, the temptation to snap him could not be resisted as he floated to the field below.

Though not of necessity, but for old times' sake and in honour of the hands which laid the pipes, we stopped down and drank of the waters, still gushing and plunging into the washing pool in the burn. After a word with the young wife and a peep into the pram we headed up the hillside path, with the heather brushing us on either side, until the peaty slope of the "Berry Pot" steadied our pace and called a halt for a breather. Then up the rocky face, tier after tier, until the summit of Craigshannoch was reached.

Looking over the high plateau a changed scene met our gaze for the hill was "barket black." Acres of charcoal stubs presented a drab picture, with only the white bleached, scattered boulders to relieve the carpet pattern. Devoid of heather, walking was made easy as we struck north along the hill edge and made towards the Mither Tap. Passing through the foothigh charcoal stumps, my light grey flannel trousers, criss-crossed with streaks of black, soon resembled the legs of a Roman gladiator. We strode by "Long John's length," a hundred yard stretch between two rock outcrops and reputed to be the resting place of the giant, "Long John of Bennachie." Legend has it that when enmity prevailed between Bennachie John and "Long John of Tap o' Noth," they hurdled boulders across the twenty odd mile glen, and sure enough great chunks of rock lie embedded on the western side.

Sun and cloud took turn about in dominating the sky above, and as we approached the base of the Mither Tap cone the sun held mastery, adding more heat to our bodies already warm with exertion. "Macks" spread out on a grassy oasis provided a couch for a full length stretch and in the warmth of the sun it was a pleasure to lie and not be pestered with flies; truly this is one of the great advantages of climbing early in the year.

Then with hands as well as feet we mounted the Mither Tap and surely this is one of the vantage points of Scotland. Looking to the North and East the greater parts of the shires of Banff and Aberdeen are spread to view and framed with a silvery sheen of light reflected from the North Sea and Moray Firth as far as the eye can see. Over the Urie and beyond the valley of the Ythan, the Hill of Comisty, Foreman Hill and the Bin of Cullen could be clearly seen, marking a district of particular interest to me. Around them lie, ancient Rothiemay, peaceful Drumblade, and turbulent Forgue, parishes which make up the genealogical geography in which were cradled the earlier generations of my family line. To our left and jutting out from the hill is the rock with the dreadful sounding name of Craignathunder, while plumb down below us ran that mysterious road, the Maiden's Causeway, an object of much speculation. Was it laid as an approach (as the name suggests), to the Druids' Mod? Was it a Roman road leading to an obvious lookout post? Or did the "Deil" really pave it for a wager with the kitchen lass? If the latter be correct, the poor lass has stood with the bight in her shoulder at the foot of the hill for a long, long time, paying the penalty of her broken contract. Ringing the rock on which we stood were the stones of the walls of the old hill fort which, could they but speak, would tell of raids and plundering, of kidnapping and retribution, but all these secrets and mysteries are to be withheld until that day when, as legend foretells, "the widow's son wi' ae ee sal find the key o' Bennachie."

A new feature added to this peak is the Ordnance Survey's triangulation station in the form of a three-feet-high concrete block, inset with bronze grooves as seating for the surveying instruments. Taking advantage of this as a photographer's stool, the laddie was set thereon, and snapped, looking like a miniature highland chief, with staff in hand and tall feather springing from the clan badge in his "Balmoral." Knowing a little more of the hill than the casual visitor, I was not decoyed by the distraction of some new feature for deep down in me lies the knowledge of the acquiring of the common lands of Bennachie by the covetous local lairds. There, on the bare rock face, on the top most point cut deeply for all to see, is what is, or was known locally as, the "thieves' mark," a square inset with the letters B, P, & L.E., representing Balquhain, Pitcaple and Logie Elphinstone, and the date A.D. 1858, being the boundary mark from which the lairds defined the additions to their property, and they got away with it, but that was a hundred years ago. With so much to see and upon which to reminisce, hours could be spent on this mountain top, but with a long day ahead and a temperamental sky above we left the Mither Tap, took to the eastern edge and made for the Garbit Tap. Halfway there and we had to run for it. Down came a shower of hail which hastened us to take what protection this rock afforded.

The next objective was the Bruntwood Tap, an eminence with its rock layer edges rounded by weathering and made to resemble a pile of long forgotten sodden pancakes. Maybe these had to do with the "Deil and the Maid," but I wouldn't know. Looking east from here, a hill below bears the name of the Millstone. Rising adjacent, Cairn William with his high-domed top was, within living memory, thickly covered with fir trees. One wonders will the Forestry Commission ever have the courage to attempt the planting of this hill again and repeat the success of an earlier landowner. Eastwards, on the coastline and clear in the midday sun, could be seen the Girdleness Lighthouse, standing sentinel at the seaward gate to the Granite City; also the radar masts at Portlethen with Clockendighter couchant at their feet. With backs to the rock on the leeward side we squatted and ate our "piece." Is there anything more appetising to a "teem wime" than buttered oatcakes with cheese between when eaten in the open air?

As we arose, with the inner man well satisfied, a shaft of sunlight broke through a gap in the grey-black folds of the southern sky and struck at the white pointed tip of Dark Lochnagar. This momentary and well-aimed shot, when all else was dull, lit up the icy peak which, even at forty miles distant, sparkled like a jewel and was caught in the aperture of my "five-bob Brownie."

Making a bee-line for the Oxencraig, we picked our footway across the wide expanse of peaty moss with its tiny rivulets, which under normal heather-covered conditions it would have been wiser to circumvent. Here the old folks cast the peats, stacked them to dry and sled them down the hillside to the "biggins" in the "how" below.

This great high level peaty reservoir gathers the cloud spilt rain and mountain dew and absorbs them like an enormous sponge, then passes the water down the gills, ensuring a flow for the trout to breed, and moisture, the "meal" to provide. What a classic example of nature's ingenious goodwill toward man and beast. It seems a pity that so much of this crystal clear liquid, charged with nature's elements of the firmament and flavoured with the sweetness of the hills, should go hurtling down to the sea and be lost. What would one not give at times for a draught of this live liquor in place of the sterilized chalk pumped water of Kent. Strewn over this level part of the hilltop are red-and-white stones composed of both quartz and hemetite ore and, in some cases, resembling fatty pork or bacon rashers. The souvenir piece of our selection would have served as the Sunday joint for a family of eight, though heavier than the butcher would wish to deliver. With this stone, shoulder-slung like Dick Whittington's pack, we reached the small knoll called the Avron Knapp, so named because of the propensity of the Avron, a rare mountain berry, growing on and around this mound. Black was the knoll and so was the great central peak we were about to ascend. From this position and devoid of colour variation, the Oxencraig presented the appearance of a mighty pyramid. On gaining the summit of this, the highest of the peaks, we searched around but without success, for the place where the Deeson memorial had stood. The durance of this public memorial must make a record for brevity. Due to the ill-advised wording inscribed upon the memorial stone, to which the unfortunate boy's mother took exception, with hammer in hand as darkness fell, she climbed alone those eerie heights and smashed the stone to smithereens. Sitting on the topmost rock, we surveyed the Western landscape and what a panorama of highland peaks, ranging from south-east to north-west and bearing names familiar to those who have knowledge of north-east Scotland. Clochmaben, Ben A'an, Lochnagar, Ben Macdui, and nearer, Tap o' Noth, The Buck, the Braemar Hills and the Hills of Foudland. Sweeping the view of the lower lands from the Vale of Alford through Shannoch Glen and away to Oldmeldrum, one feels that the great valley under its present pastoral garb reeks with legendary, ancient history, sentimental songs and family associations. Dunnideer, looking so diminutive from this high angle, could tell from its vitrified castle walls of attack, repulse and prolonged siege, of aquatic engineering and of the mare being used as a water diviner. Greeninches farm where once, trying my hand with horse and shem, I shemmed the neeps instead of the weeds, and the horse was not to blame. After a Christmas visit to this same farm, a happy recollection is of being taken back to the station by horse and sledge. Sitting surrounded by straw, we went bumping over the roadside drifts to the clup clup of the horse's feet in the snow.

Johnny Gibb's famous "Gushet Neuk," Oyne School, Parnassis Hill, West Hall, Torres Castle (gutted and roofless like many another, and a shameful blight on Scottish landscapes), and the forsaken auld kirk on Hart Hill with Oyne kirkyard nearby, where dear ones lie at rest, all claimed our attention.

This reverie may have continued by Auld Rayne, Colpy, and Culsalmond, but the bright sun of early afternoon bade us be up and moving so we descended the southern slopes of Oxencraig and started both grouse and mountain hares. The grouse protested with mocking laughter as they whirred up from the blackened ground, then with effortless flight planed away over the hillside. Whether the laugh was at us or at the hares who looked naked and ridiculous in their pure white winter coats, scampering through the burnt heather stalks, I do not know. Reaching the Watch Craig on the eastern side, we looked down "My Lord's Throat" across the winding ribbon of Don and into peaceful "Paradise," with its giant larches guarding the approach and the river like a moat, protecting the rear. With the view we take in couthy Monymusk lying comfortably in the valley of the Don below, the Loch of Skene glinting to the East, and round the edge of the hill to the South the home of my own "Clan Chief" at Castle Forbes. Still treading the black dust and startling the white-robed hares, we crossed the hill to the Hermit's Seat and then turned right on the western edge and made for the Hummel Craig. Standing on this mushroom rock with Oyne to North and Insch to South, we had a bird's eye view of what the old folks termed "the shortest distance between two railway stations," i.e. "een-inch." Following the edge of the hill in gradual descent on our way to the Lower Oxencraig, we came to the line of demarcation between the burnt and unburnt which, in long zigs and zags, stretched along the western side. Here we found a wire mesh beater with seven-foot shank, no doubt abandoned hastily, being less effective with the oncoming flames than even "Mrs Partington's brush" was with the sea. A hard pink shoulder of granite juts out from the hillside at the "Lower Oxencraig" which, in days gone by, made an ideal quarry for builders who were prepared to climb the thousand feet and work it. As the last of these builders was my own father, the visit was something of a pilgrimage. Lying there, row upon row, were sills and lintels up to twelve feet long, beautifully squared and dressed, and so they have lain for sixty years since the hill road was washed away in a storm. (The method of transporting these large stones down the hillside was to half-load the cart, chain together two or three of the largest stones and drag them behind to steady the horse and act as a brake on the cart).

Evening was now drawing in and my father and stepmother down in Oyne would be wondering about us, so choosing a seven-inch cube from the quarry rubble and hanging it on to the beater shank along with the other stone, we bade goodbye to the quarry and father's recumbent stones and set off "coolie-porter-wise" for the Westhall Gill. Reaching the edge of the gill near to where the water spout of 1891 struck it, we marvelled again at the effect the avalanche of water had on solid rock. A channel, several hundred feet long, thirty feet wide and fifteen feet deep, was within seconds, gouged out of solid granite, powdered to sand and swept down the hillside to cover for ever acres of land in the glen below.

Many scientific investigators who came to see this geological phenomenon called on my grandmother at Hillfoot for direction on the way up and for a cup of tea on their return. Farther along, but still on the high edge of the gill, we stopped at the "walley" and relieved our shoulders of their burdens. Here is the perfect picnic place of Bennachie, with table, chairs and refreshment all laid on, and with a commanding view from the Dee to the Deveron, all for the price of reaching it. A square trench has been cut on a level patch of heath, leaving a moss-covered table in the centre, while nearby, in the bankside, the tottle, tottle, tottle of dripping water betrays the "birth of a burn." Parting the herbage, we held our thermos cups to be filled and, with legs dangling in the trench, sat at the picnic table and took our "waught" of cool, sweet water. In the peace of the hills, as the sun sinks down, is there any sound so delightfully companionable as the gargling gurgle of a mountain burn? Reluctantly we rose to leave this spot and shouldered our burdens for the last and most painstaking lap of journey. Steeply descending through thigh-high heather, the foothold had of necessity to be secure, but the burn in the cleft of the gill was reached and crossed without incident. Along the reedy swamp and by the pine trees the going was easy, but on reaching the roadie the stones were deposited behind the dyke to await collection another day.

Our return to Oyne and "Bogie Bank" allayed the thought for our safety and round the table at the evening meal we recounted the events of the day.

Two days later, Bennachie was white-over with snow, but those stones had been recovered and sent off to the South by rail. Cemented in, and surmounting the steps in my garden at Orpington, are two small chunks of Bennachie, and what better reminder could one have of the day when we "tramped through the embers of hell."

Reproduced by the courtesy of *The Banffshire Journal Limited.*

THE ORDNANCE SURVEY FROM SOUTHAMPTON

By Alex. Beattie Campbell

There was five jolly fellows cam' till Benachie
Tae tak up the levels 'tween it an' the sea.
As merry a corem as e'er I met wi'
    Was this Ordnance Survey fae Southampton.

There was Gibson an' Wheeler, an' Sly, Dick an' Harry;
They a' cam' per rail tae Oyne fae the Barry;
They pitched baith their tents in Pittodrie's san' quarry,
    Did this Ordnance Survey fae Southampton.

They had sticks, they had canvas an' bagfu's o' ropes,
They had lanterns an' boxes an' big telescopes;
An' I hauled them a' tae the head o' the rocks
    For this Ordnance Survey fae Southampton.

They treated me weel, me an' the grey mare;
I got broth, beef, an' tatties, an suppies o' beer;
For they are the boys that believe in gude cheer,
    This Ordnance Survey fae Southampton.

Poor Dickie an' Harry wis cook week aboot,
Boiled the beef an' the tatties an' worked the dish-cloot,
An' baith the braw tents they sweepit them oot
   For this Ordnance Survey fae Southampton.

Gibson took a' oor photos, as sure as I'm here—
Me an' my sled, forbyes the grey mare.
On that cabinet card we are bound to appear
   Wi' this Ordnance Survey fae Southampton.

The Ordnance Survey Camp it's left Benachie;
On Mormon' noo they camp, and there they will see
The braw toon o' Strichen, although it be wee;
   An' for it poor Dick will be trampin'.

But noo they're awa'. an' may a' gude gang wi' them.
It's nae very likely that I'll ever see them;
But if they come back, my assistance I'll gie them,
   Yon Ordnance Survey fae Southampton.

BENNACHIE—THE HERITAGE O' MAIST WIRTH

By James Milne

A cam intae this warl on March 22nd, 1908 at 25 Aul Station Road, Inverurie—within sicht o' Bennachie, gi'en a hurl in the pram a puckle yairds up the Aul Kirk Lane.

That bonnie, kindly hill his been like een o' the femly tae mi a' ma life. Finiver A 'd scraipit aneuch sillar thegither tae get engaged tae the Inverurie lassie A hid the luck an' gweed sense tae coort, A het-fittet hame fae London. Sic wis ma love o' Bennachie that it jist seemt nateral that the ring hid tae be slippit on tae ma lass's fing-er somewye far there wis a gweed wide stretch o' the hill tae be seen. Fut better than the sicht o't A 'd seen fae the train that verra mornin? So it wis in a bonnie howe aside Fintr'y that we plighted wir troth. Fut's mair, A 've lived happily iver aifter, so dinna ye dar tell mi that there's nae fairies on Bennachie.

Fem'ly history records that A first set fit on Bennachie fin A wis jist a bairn nae lang past the 'aye haein tae be cairryt' stage. The soopler members o' the pairty hid clim't the Mither Tap afore wi hid wir picnic at the wallie. A 'm tellt that on the wye doon fae that ristin place A foonert an' besocht ma gran'father "Gin YOU cairry mi, A 'll PECH."

Later on, fin A wis able tae 'go the bike' (they war wechty breets at that time), trips tae Bennachie cam af'ener. It wis a gie sair chav up Skraichie's Brae an' past the Maiden Steen tae the startin-aff p'int for the lang wa'k tae the Mither Tap, bit ye 'd aye the view up there tae look forrit till an' the promise o' bickerin hey-ma-nannie doon the braes a' the wye hame.

An' sic a winnerfu sicht fae the Mither Tap! Stannin up there, the win' fuslin roon ma lugs, glowerin a' roon aboot tae see ither hills, miles an' miles o' countryside wi patches o' skyrie breem, the bonnie heather an' trees jist aneth mi, an' great dollops o' blue skye atween the hich cloods, a' livin things jist wee dots in the distance, an' toylike hooses an' trains. Wis 't ony winner that (a loon nae yet intae lang breeks), A fair thocht A wis Erchie?

(Och, A ken fine foo tirin' Bennachie can be on young legs, for ma gran'father wis a gamie an' mony a time A've geen up aneth Geordie Esson's hoose in Dey's brake wi ither Inverurie loons, tae beat fin the gentry war sheetin on the hill).

Bit "Erchie" got aul'er, an' eence he hid a bittle mair sense, wi ar least some o' the conceit knockit oot o' 'm, his thochts fin stannin on the Mither Tap war cheenged for the better. A 'm nae ower releegious, bit as A stood there A hid the same feelin as A 've gotten fin in a great cathedral—a feelin o' awe; o' bein' in the very Presence o' God; in fac', o' bein' een o' Jock Tamson's bairns.

Gin Jasper Petulengro hid seen Bennachie, he wid hae addit it tae his list o' the sweet things o' life, thus ".... there's likewise Bennachie and a wind on the heath. Life is very sweet, brother; who would wish to die?"

Nooadays fin A come hame tae the earldom A aye look the wye o' Bennachie first thing o' a mornin tae see fether it's gyan tae be a fine day or a weety een. It 's an afa lat-doon fin, gie near the en' o' 565 miles drive fae London, A come binnerin ower Tyrebagger an' canna get a wint o' the Mither Tap for mist or cloods. Muckle tho A deserve sic serin for usin 't as a barometer, A'll sweer it's nae Bennachie's wite fin sic a begeck—nay, calamity—befa's mi. Bit it *mith* be the wark o' Jock o' Bennachie. A winner gin he's broken lowse fae the fairies that speeritet 'm awa fae the hill langsyne? Yon wis a richt coorse deevil, an' A 'm thinkin that he man hae gotten hud o' yon ill-faard deem wi the fancy name that flaunts hersel jist up a wee bittie an' ower the road fae the Maiden Steen. Ae 'ear fin A cam him the limmer wisna there; the next 'ear she wis, an' fint a wird hid A heard aboot it. A some doot Jock hid a han in 't.

A' kines o' clever chiels, speecialists in their ain subjec's, hiv dug, prodit an' powkit a' ower Bennachie. They ca' their wark "resairchin." Gin that Scotch dictionary wir a' wytin for hid been tae han', A mitha been able tae spell the names o' the subjecs richt, bit ye'll jist hae tae pit up wi' the Inglish spellin, an that 'll be nae drawback to thon fowk up the Garioch wye that spik "panned loaf." Here it is:—archaeology, botany, ecology (it deals wi a lot o' things sic as fowk that throw their bottles an' their rubbish on tae the hill instead o' stappin them intae their pyocks, an' wifies atween Clatt an' Logie that poor soap suds intae the Gadie tae mak it rinse instead o' rin), etymology, forestry, geology, history, mineralogy, mythology, zoology—och, there's nae en' tae them. Mine ye, they've a' heen their eese, tellin's things aboot the hill that peer ignorant craiturs like wersels wid never hae fun oot. An' awyte it hisna deen the hill ony hairm that A ken o'. Gin ye can jaloose fut they write or spik aboot (it's hine awa abeen ma heid maistly), it adds tae yer respec o' Bennachie jist that bittie mair.

For ma ain pairt, A widna be ma father's son gin a didna hae great interest, respec an' love o' the hill. Tho A some doot A winna be able tae clim up tae the Mither Tap on ma 70th birthday, lat aleen ma 90th een as he did, A 'll rist content gin A get a sicht o't noo an' than.

A ken some fowk that winna pit fork tae moo fin they hiv a mince denner till they've made a mixter-maxter o't an' shape-et a Bennachie oot o't. Gweed sakes, architecture an' mair speecialists! Gin ony o' ye hiv iver deen that, dinna lat dab, or else yet anither speecialist (in psychiatry) 'll be wytin tae plunk ye doon on a heather cooch next time ye ging up the hill. Ye wid ken him easy aneuch, for he winna spik Scotch—in fact he winna spik ava. Instead, he'll "have dialogue" or "communicate" wi ye, an' if he says "at this moment of time," ye'll ken he jist means "noo." Pheugh! Gin the gowk hid ony gumption he'd ken fine fut's at the reet o' yer "behaviour pattern." Bennachie's in the vera marra o' yer beens!

Exiles think o' Bennachie ilky time they hear "Gadie Rins" an' in fac' ony Scotch sang or ony weelkent psalm (the 23rd, Aul Hunner an' 121st are gweed examples). Hunners o' things bring back memories o' the hill an' mak a muckle lump in their thrapples.

Bennachie is HAME, an' tho' a' Scotch fowk hiv a winnerfu heritage, we o' the North-East hae Bennachie, wir heritage o' maist wirth.

THE BANKS OF DON

By Archie Smith

Anyone who can look back fifty years or more will confirm that the banks of Don were once quiet, secret places exclusive to their rightful inhabitants, least of which was man himself. There is still much to be said in defence of the ancient feudal system and the creatures most likely to endorse that view are those whose destiny is shaped by the collective sanity or otherwise of the human race.

Fish life on the Don has suffered—and may continue to suffer to the point of near extinction—under mounting pressure from the masses in search of "lebensraum" and motivated by self interest regardless of all else. If the present trend proceeds apace, we may not have long to wait for that angling "big match" with a draw for pegs along the boundaries of some hallowed stretch, together with the betting and the booze and other infamies "which even to name would be unlawfu'." On a great many fishing beats there is much unproductive water relieved by a relatively small complement of "kittly bits" which provide most of the sport and dictate the rod capacity overall. Alas, on many open or public waters, admission tickets are "on tap" in many cases for benefit of a so-called "Common Good" which is a misnomer if ever there was one.

Fifty passing years have wrought some startling changes in the life-style on the banks of the Don. Myxomatosis has all but wiped out the dense rabbit colonies that used to dominate the riverside. Gone, too, are the enormous flocks of wintering wigeon of bygone days and with them the melodious accompaniment of their whistling drakes. Mallard are noticeably more dispersed away from the river banks where harassment by the growing shooting fraternity ensures this foreseeable result. The former upsurge of whooper swans at their adopted winter quarters on middle and lower Don has swung into reverse with all the indications that a return to the former status of passage winter migrant is under way. By contrast, there is now a solid winter presence on Donside of several thousand greylag geese. Sadly, these poor unfortunates are being chivvied unmercifully in the lower Don valley by batteries of syndicate "persons," armed in some cases with pump guns with which they evince considerable malice, not only to the wild geese, but also to itinerant curlews, oystercatchers and the like. Strangely enough, herons seem to have as good a prospect of survival now as hitherto despite destruction of traditional nesting sites by tree felling attendant on two world wars. Keepers and heronries are incompatible and the diminution of both has struck a satisfactory balance. Moorhens are still prolific and their ability to disperse among ditches, burns and swamps will ensure the future of the species. Nowadays, in early summer, the imminence of a hatch of river flies is seldom heralded by the uncanny appearance of a swarm of breeding sand martins. They seem to have gone elsewhere. Why? Otters are still in evidence on all suitable areas in Donside but the outlook for them should be no cause for concern so long as they are allowed to remain unobtrusive as is their wont. Their main requirement is peace and quiet far from the madding crowd. Finally, a dreaded incomer, the mink, is regrettably established as a permanent resident on the banks of Don and that bodes ill for all who dwell therein.

*　*　*　*

SECOND GUARDIAN OF BENNACHIE

Following the lamented death of Lord Aberdeen, our First Guardian of Bennachie, Dr Maitland Mackie, Lord Lieutentant of Aberdeenshire, has kindly consented to be our Second Guardian.

*　*　*　*

The Bailies' Council wish to express their gratitude to the Editor for the long hours spent in his painstaking task. This labour of love is only one of the many services which Archie W. M. Whiteley, M.B.E., M.A., J.P. has rendered to the community. Mr Whiteley was parochial schoolmaster of Monymusk for over 30 years and later of Kemnay Secondary School. He was author of "Parish of Monymusk" in the Third Statistical Account of the County of Aberdeen.

INFORMATION PLEASE . . . .

Any information about the hill not already published
would be greatly appreciated for any future edition.

. . . . THE EDITOR

PERSONALIA

Maitland Mackie, C.B.E., LL.D., the last convener of Aberdeen County Council. His unique service in the development of the north-east has been recently rewarded by his appointment as the Queen's Lord-Lieutenant for Aberdeenshire. His raciness of speech is reflected in his writing—witty and warm.

Alexander Keith, LL.D., author and editor. His Classic Thousand Years of Aberdeen will remain a book of reference for many generations. A close friend of Charles Murray and Chairman of the Hamewith Memorial Trust, he was born in Kintore. His affection for Bennachie is very deep.

Professor John Craig, LL.D., emeritus Professor of Child Health at Aberdeen University. In a lifetime as a visiting physician in the north-east he knew Bennachie from every angle, and on the high tops he frequently assisted his brother-in-law, the late Dr Douglas Simpson, in his researches on Bennachie and Dunnideer.

Jim Buchan, M.A., Ed.B., rector of Peterhead Academy, whose "School History of Aberdeenshire" was published in 1961. His work on local history as scholar and lecturer brings him to-day into a line of great men like J. M. Bulloch, James F. Tocher, G. M. Fraser, Douglas Simpson and Fenton Wyness, now at rest. Their common bond is that like the living writer, Cuthbert Graham, they can join the poet Sir Alexander Gray in saying "this is my country, the land that begat me."

Dr A. A. Woodham, F.S.A., lecturer in biochemistry at the Rowett. Although Sassenach by birth, he has become our leading local archaeologist. When the bulldozer unbares a short-cist grave as at Ellon, or sculptural stones as at Cairnie, he is called in. He organises "digs." In this exciting period of archaeology when scientific dating is now possible, his chief concern is that we clodhoppers do not destroy our heritage of the arts and crafts of our forefathers.

Rev. James Wood, M.B.E., D.D., retired minister of the South Church, Aberdeen. Sometime chaplain in the 52nd Division, where mountain training improved his ski-ing, he was at that time minister of Insch. He found for us the German translation of "Whaur Gadie Rins." His lucid prose flows smoothly as Gadie itself.

Alexander L. Young, C.B.E., M.A., B.Sc., M.Ed., retired director of education for Aberdeenshire. His period of office saw a massive expansion in education particularly in school building, to make up for the twenty lean years before the wars. His quiet unassuming efficiency remained unruffled.

Daisy Bruce of Heatherwick. Descended from the long line of farmers whose graves lie generation by generation in the shadow of the Bass, she is well known for her wide-reaching service to the Inverurie folks. Her verse and plays continue to give pleasure.

William Cook, F.S.A., now ninety-one not out. At Little Meldrum of Tarves, this great character has over the years amassed the most amazing collection of the furniture and implements of the farming folk of the last two centuries. A beautiful speaker, his grand strong voice has delighted audiences from far and near, who flock to Little Meldrum. Like a lot of country-folk, he can also play you a spring on his fiddle.

Mrs Mary Harris (nee Cook), M.A., second bursar at the age of fifteen at Aberdeen University in 1904, born at the Back o' Bennachie, has spent most of her life in England. Written in her beautiful English, her "Memories of the Garioch" warm the heart.

Flora Garry whose publication in 1974 of "Bennygoak and Other Poems" has got such an enthusiastic welcome. She made a memorable visit to Bennachie in October, 1975, to hear Louise Donald, May Thomson and Will Maitland read her poems far up the hillside. Cuthbert Graham acclaims her as our greatest living doric poet.

Helen Fraser. Mrs Fraser is Chairman of the "Keep Aberdeenshire Tidy" campaign, which has now got the new name of "Keep Grampian Beautiful." One of the most hard-working bailies, she is tireless in the fight against litter.

A. A. Cuthbert, B.Sc. (Forestry) District Officer of the Forestry Commission. As Bennachie is one of the forests under his care, the Bailies have had many contacts with him and are grateful for his continuing courtesy and co-operation.

Archie Smith, retired banker, with the countryside in the marrow of his bones. He says "wha wid weary in a wood?" While his knowledge of the local wildlife is very deep, perhaps he is most at home on the river bank where the otter enthralls him.

Andrew Fordyce, born at Nursery Cottage at the foot of Craigshannoch. His exile for most of his life in Kent, the garden of England, has not diminished his love for Bennachie.

Alexander L. Gray tells with rare feeling the story of his family business, which for many generations baked the bread for the Garioch folk. He is a bibliophile and antiquarian. Generous to the Bailies' cause, he provided the 1807 Bennachie Club badge, off which the 1973 Bailies' badge was modelled.

James Milne, the Inverurie tinsmith, climbed the Mither Tap on his ninetieth birthday. One of the finest chapters of Bennachie is to be found in "Twixt Ury and Don and Round About" published in 1947. His book of verse "The Gangrel Flute" was produced in 1935.

James Milne, son of "Tinny" Milne started life as a banker but later studied and took his degree in engineering at Aberdeen University and now lives in London. His chapter in our native doric tongue is superb.

Thomas R. Angus, dental surgeon, has just retired after a lifetime "fighting the devil in other men's mouths." Few appreciate the hard grind of a dentist's life. Laying down his dental drill, this moustachioed extrovert has picked up his flowing pen and turned to journalism.

Dr James Gordon Anderson, a Peterhead loon, is a geologist on the staff of Aberdeen University. He took the geology of Bennachie as the subject for his degree thesis and spent six weeks on the mountain one recent summer.

The Master of Forbes, son of Lord Forbes, premier Baron of Scotland, head of the House of Forbes, twenty-third of his line. Both take a keen interest in the Bailies' cause and are Honorary Bailies. The Master of Forbes is laird of the south-west slopes of Bennachie with its finely managed woodlands.

Dr Douglas Stewart of Insch. Hermit Seat, the north-west Tap looks down on his daily round. As warden of the western marches, he gives faithful service and he is an invaluable member of council.

William Leslie Gavin carries the Leslie name in virtue of his birth at the Meal Mill of Leslie about the time of Queen Victoria's Diamond Jubilee. Spending his life as the Culter Miller, he has found time for many years' service as a county councillor. Rob Roy's famous statue at Culter is his care and pride.

James R. MacKay, B.Sc., M.I.Biol., biology teacher and Deputy Senior Bailie. Meticulous in all he touches from the planning of the indicator to the leading of botanical expeditions, he has found time to capture with his camera many exciting glimpses of plant and animal life on the mountain. Seldom a week has passed in the past two winters but he or Algy Watson and sometimes both, have delighted town and country audiences with talks on Bennachie illustrated by their marvellous colour slides.

Algy Watson, M.A., B.A., the lynch-pin of the bailies, their tireless clerk and organiser. Kipling would have been proud of him as one who "can fill the unforgiving minute with sixty seconds worth of distance run." He originated the idea of a book on Bennachie. His model of the massif in relief from Don to Gadie, adds a new dimension of knowledge to his geography pupils at Inverurie Academy, and also to the Bailies and their friends.

Dr Daniel G. Gordon, our Senior Bailie. There would be no Bailies of Bennachie without Danny's tremendous enthusiasm, drive, and wise counsel. His beautifully-written booklet, "Welcome to Bennachie," published in 1974, was an instantaneous success and deservedly received wide acclaim. For many years he was the well-loved physician at Ellon before he retired to Coldwells, Inverurie.

The late **Rev. N. L. A. Campbell, M.A.**—the devoted Minister of Chapel os Garioch. He is remembered by all his parishioners with much affection. He was a very keen historian and he made a special study of the History of the Squatters on Bennachie. His widow, now residing in Helensburgh, gave the Editor special permission to reproduce his article on "The Colony" which was first given at an Open Air Church-yard Service at Chapel of Garioch on Sunday, 23rd July, 1939.

The late **James Smith** resided at Essie Cottage, Kemnay. Born 1905, died 1962. Attended Kemnay School, trained as a gardener with Baroness Bentick at Banchory and for many years was gardener at Crathes Castle.

He was beadle and senior elder of Kemnay Parish Church and was an authority on antiquities.

Alan Mackie, Burnside of Fetternear—a farm which he has occupied for many years. For some time he was District Councillor and he has taken a lively interest in local affairs. He recently purchased the farm of Woodend of Braco just below Esson's Croft on the slopes of Bennachie. He has a great interest in the hill and in a way of life which has largely disappeared.

Mrs M. Erica Smith of Pittodrie has set her face against the neglect of the ancient monuments which have survived, when so many were broken up centuries ago in the land hunger of the time.

Alexander McGregor, M.A. was Dominie of Woodside School, Aberdeen. He was born at Rayne in 1880, the son of John McGregor, merchant. He graduated Master of Arts in 1904.

Norman Dixon, M.A., Ph.D., F.E.I.S., J.P., retired at Easter, 1976. If we think of the influence of an individual in a community, surely the work of Dr Dixon—28 years rector of Inverurie Academy—will live on. It is said he knew almost every pupil by his first name—a no mean achievement in a school of 1,500 pupils!

Frank Davidson, Advocate in Aberdeen, has many country interests. He is a bonnet laird at Banchory where he plies his bill-hook in his woodlands.

Frank Benzies, M.B.E., author of 'The White Family' and 'A Benzies Quest,' who has made a meticulous research into the origins of the Benzie Clan and the Benzie Howe back to Harlaw.

W. Hutcheon, a noted journalist and poet of the North-East. He lived at Northfield House, Inverurie, when he was young.

Michael Kidd, M.A., sometime a Senior Master at Blairmore School. When he resided at Old Rayne, his love for Bennachie grew with the years.

Of the poetry and verse included from authors now gone from our midst, it would be presumptuous to write. Their fame is sure. Arthur Johnstone, the great Latinist, born at Keith-hall, was a contemporary of King James VI and his private physician and also rector of King's College in Old Aberdeen. His poem in Latin on Bennachie must be the first. The folk-singers of Gadie and Harlaw are unknown. John Imlah put polish on "Whaur Gadie Rins" in his version. William Thom the Inverurie weaver-poet of the first half of last century was the sweetest of singers. While the name of Charles Murray is a household word, David Rorie, the Cults doctor, will be best remembered for "The Lum Hat Wintin' the Croon." Pittendreigh McGillivray, born in the Garioch, achieved fame as Sculptor Royal of Scotland. Known as the Bennachie poet, Alexander Beattie Campbell, a tenant farmer on Pittodrie, in "The Heather Bells of Bennachie," published just before the 1914-18 War, celebrated in verse many local occasions.

For the beautifully detailed illustrations of the sculptured stones and their Pictish symbols and the sketches of Dunnideer and the Mither Tap, we are most grateful to Henry J. L. Mantell, A.R.I.B.A., who vies with his father-in-law, Dr Douglas Stewart, in enthusiasm for Bennachie.

BIBLIOGRAPHY

1. *Bennachie* by Alexander Inkson McConnachie, 1890.
2. *Twixt Ury and Don and Round About* by James Milne, 1947.
3. *The Province of Mar* by Dr Douglas Simpson, 1943.
4. *The Earldom of Mar* by Dr Douglas Simpson, 1949.
5. *Inverurie and the Earldom of the Garioch* by Rev. John Davidson, 1878.
6. *Aberdeenshire Castles*—James Giles, R.S.A., with *Memoir of Giles* by Dr William Kelly, edited by Dr Douglas Simpson, 1936.
7. *Place Names of Aberdeenshire* by Dr William M. Alexander, Third Spalding Club, 1952.
8. *The House of Forbes*, edited by Alistair and Henrietta Taylor, Third Spalding Club, 1937.
9. *The Leiths of Harthill* by Francis Bucklay, 1937.
10. *Rhymes and Recollections of a Handloom Weaver* by William Thom, 1844.
11. *Bog Myrtle and Peat Rick* by Pittendreigh McGillivray, 1922.
12. *At the Back o' Bennachie* by Helen Beaton, 1915.
13. *Glimpses o' Auld Lang Syne* by William Watson, 1905, Aberdeen University Press.
14. *A New History of Aberdeenshire* by Alexander Smith (two volumes), 1885.
15. *Hamewith and Other Poems* by Charles Murray.
16. *The County of Aberdeen*—Third Statistical Account, 1960.
17. *Dunnideer and its Three Fortresses* by G. M. Fraser, 1927.
18. *Donside* by Alexander Inkson McConnachie, 1901.
19. *Second Book of Legends* by Fenton Wyness, 1943.
20. *A Century of Aberdeenshire Agriculture* by Isabella M. Bruce, 1908.
21. *Education in Aberdeenshire before 1972* by Ian T. Simpson, M.A., ED.B., PH.D., 1947.
22. *A School History of Aberdeenshire* by Jim Buchan, M.A., ED.B., 1961.
23. *The Inscriptions of Pictland* by Francis C. Diack, 1944, Third Spalding Club.
24. *Murmurings Frae Ury* by T. L. Morrison, 1921.
25. *Johnie Gibb of Gushetneuk* by William Alexander, 1880.
26. *Let's Look Round the Garioch* by Fenton Wyness.
27. *From the Tone to the Don* by Alfred James Monday.
28. *The Cairngorms* by Sir Henry Alexander.
29. *Songs of the North-East* edited by Dr Alexander Keith.
30. *Last Leaves of Aberdeen Ballads*—Gavin Greig, edited by Dr Alexander Keith.
31. *The Book of Buchan*, edited by Dr J. F. Tocher.

32. *The Heather Bells o' Bennachie* by Alexander Beattie Campbell.
33. *The Statistical Account of Scotland*—Aberdeenshire, 1843.
34. *Balquhain Castle* by Dr Douglas Simpson—Aberdeen University Review, 1936.
35. *The Castellated Architecture of Aberdeenshire* by Sir Andrew Leith-Hay, 1870.
36. *Braes o' Bennachie* by Dr James Stark.
37. *A Benzies Quest* by Frank Benzies.
38. *Materials for a History of the Church and Priory of Monymusk* by Dr William M. MacPherson.
39. *The Cairngorms* by Dr Adam Watson.

This list is by no means complete, but it contains the bulk of what has been written about Bennachie and round about. In many other local publications, casual reference to Bennachie will be found.

The following titles may be of additional interest:—

The Gavin Greig Collection of Folk Songs of the North-East—a series of 600 articles contributed to the *Buchan Observer*, 1907 to 1911. The original manuscripts in King's College Library. These were edited and a selection published with notes by Dr Alexander Keith.

Old and New Bridges over the River Don at Inverurie (Tawse & Allan).

Historic Earls and Earldoms of Scotland—John Mackintosh.

A Thousand Years of Aberdeen—Dr Alexander Keith.

Aberdeen and Deeside—Cuthbert Graham.

The North-East Lowlands of Scotland—John R. Allan.

William Thom, the Inverurie Poet: A New Look—Robert Bruce.

The North-East of Scotland, prepared for the visit of the British Association to Aberdeen in 1963.

From a Scottish Study: weekly articles in *Aberdeen Press & Journal* by Alexander Keith while Assistant Editor.

Lord Cullen by Rev. Dr. James Stark.

Met By The Way by Rev. Dr. James Stark.

Rev. John Skinner of Linshart by Rev. Dr. William Walker.

The White Rose of Drumminor by Lilianne Grant Rich.

Agriculture in Aberdeenshire in the 1860's by James Allan. Deeside Field 1927.

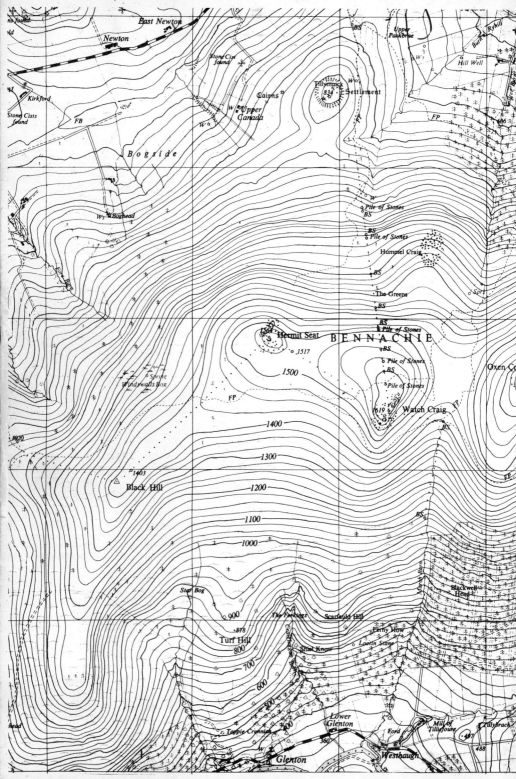